BERNARD CRICK

POLITICAL THEORY AND PRACTICE

ALLEN LANE THE PENGUIN PRESS

Allen Lane The Penguin Press
74 Grosvenor Street, London W1

ISBN 0 7139 0297 3

Printed in Great Britain by
The Bowering Press, Plymouth

Set in Monotype Baskerville

320·01

19878

IN MEMORY OF A. H. HANSON

Contents

Preface   ix
1 On Theory and Practice   1
2 Freedom as Politics   35
3 Toleration and Tolerance in Theory and
     Practice   63
4 The Elementary Types of Government   97
5 The World of Michael Oakeshott   120
6 'Them and Us': Public Impotence and
     Government Power   135
7 The Proper Limits of Student Influence   161
8 The Introducing of Politics in Schools   183
9 A Failure of Liberal Perception   203
10 The Peaceable Kingdom   216
11 A Reflection on Tyrannicide   228
12 Powell and Patriotism   236

Preface

LIKE many academics nowadays, I tend to do too much and spread myself thin. There is teaching (formal and informal), research, administration, university politics (in which the student of politics has more to learn than to give), committees of learned bodies, editing a series, some good causes, reviewing, too much casual journalism (one's own silly fault to fall to temptation, even when the temptation is notoriety more than money, although the rationalization is always communication), being joint editor of *Political Quarterly* (which I enjoy more than anything, as trying to bridge academic and public life in a plain style), and, of course, the good and ordinary life of friends and family – all of whom may suffer from, as much as share in, all the rest.

So I realize with some dismay that in the last ten years, since my *In Defence of Politics* (Weidenfeld & Nicolson, 1962; revised and expanded Pelican edition, 1964) I have not written any worthwhile book in political theory, except the semi-polemical, semi-theoretical diversion of *The Reform of Parliament* (Weidenfeld & Nicolson, 1964; revised second edition, 1970). When one is over-busy, perhaps too much energy goes into essays and journalism. But I do enjoy essays as essays, however unfashionable this is, as attempts to work out the consequences and associations of an idea or a problem suggestively and digressively, rather than definitively in monographs. I dislike particularly that kind of book which is really one good essay needlessly expanded by reworking familiar material in some new and technical vocabulary, either because it is difficult to publish a long essay or because it is felt to be less prestigious.

So this volume is a collection of essays written in the last ten years all of which somehow involve the application of ideas to political practice. Some of them represent positions I no longer hold, or now see as inadequate, certainly in need of revision; but I have left them all alone apart from tidying up some infelicities of style. Whether I have done so out of honesty or laziness, I am not quite sure; only sure that once one begins to try to rewrite essays to make them more consistent with each other and to avoid repetition, something of the character of a genuine essay is lost. They all seek to bridge academic and educated concerns. I am sad that so much academic political theory, like so much academic political science, has become too technical (or sometimes just plain boring) for the general educated reader. Sometimes that is necessary, but not as often as some of my fellow academics suppose. Only the title essay may be purely for colleagues and students, and the 'Elementary Types of Government', if simple, yet may well be boring to any others.

These essays reflect my preoccupations in the last ten years, except that I include none of my essays on the role of Parliament because they have all ended up in successive editions of the book (although if the reader wants the essence of the argument without the institutional detail, he could find it in my 'Parliament and the Matter of Britain', in *Essays on Reform 1967: a centenary tribute* (Oxford University Press, 1967)). Neither have I included any of my essays of the late 1950s and early 1960s on American political thought. These latter I exclude partly for reasons of space; partly because they now represent what was said to be Mr Herbert Spencer's only idea of tragedy, 'a theory killed by a fact'; and partly because I still hope sometime to rework and rethink them into a book on American political thought. I think the two best of them were 'The Strange Quest for an American Conservatism', *Review of Politics*, July 1955, and 'The Character of American Political Thought', *Massachusetts Review*, Summer 1961; and the rethinking begins in my 'The Strange Death of the American Theory of Consensus', *Political Quarterly*, January 1972. I have also excluded all my *Political*

Quarterly articles or long editorials, three alone of which might stand rereading: 'Socialist Literature in the 1950s', July 1960; a satire, 'The 1970s in Retrospect', January 1970, and even that piece on 'The Labour Leadership', October 1971 – perhaps also 'A Time to Reason', but that was revised and reprinted in the Pelican symposium, *Protest and Discontent* (1970) edited by myself and William Robson. And I have excluded all my journalism, which anyway either repeats or anticipates the themes in these essays, except one of my old *Observer* articles, 'Powell and Patriotism', since I think we are all very muddled on this issue, and also one broadcast talk, 'A Reflection on Tyrannicide', since it strives to strike that balance which citizenship needs between romantic glorification of all violence and liberal indiscriminate detestation (a balance that I don't think I struck in my 'The Peaceable Kingdom' written before the troubles of the late 1960s).

I thank Iris Walkland for going through this manuscript to protest as a general reader and correct as a good stylist should; my wife, Joyce, who has also attacked many of the articles with a zeal and a care that I hope her own students can withstand; and most of all my former Sheffield students who put up with me thinking aloud and arguing with myself instead of lecturing.

I thank all those who have given me permission to reprint these essays: where each first appeared is stated at the head of each essay.

I dedicate this book to the memory of a much older friend from whom I learned much, and whom I ventured to praise in an obituary letter to *The Times* for his 'determination to keep his subject relevant to policy while avoiding gross ideological bias'. In a review of Harry Hanson's collected essays, published not long before his death, I described him as a leader of a 'British school' of political science who

. . . are not entirely unsympathetic to 'model building' and 'systems analysis' in the American manner, but are basically aware of the inextricable relationship of theory to practice and

PREFACE

hence the need for political relevance. The world may not need political science – that is a hard and difficult speculation, but political science needs to be relevant to the world to be profound as a discipline. This is the character of a 'British school', far removed from the mathematical models of the Americans and the metaphysical hair-splitting or else ruthless 'objectivity' of so many of the Germans.

I would like to be regarded as of such a company.

BERNARD CRICK

Birkbeck College (University of London)
16 December 1971

I

On Theory and Practice[1]

BRITISH students of politics have rarely had any complicated doubts about having authority to say how institutions should be reformed – usually in the best Burkean manner, of course, of 'reform in order to preserve'. Long before debates about a 'value-free' or a 'committed' study engulfed us, most of us in Britain simply assumed that either one was studying the history of political ideas – which gave one some sort of loose authority to talk about morals; or else one was studying modern or contemporary institutions – which gave one some sort of loose authority to talk about what politicians should be doing or how they should be doing it. And these two branches of the study rarely showed any signs of being related to each other.

As a student of Laski, I never had any doubt that one should go beyond all this insular empiricism and be *committed*, but somehow after his death, when the magic of his manner and the intoxication of his matter ceased, many of us read his books, the morning after the night before, and were left, if not high and dry, at least a little sobered to find how arbitrary, or even absent, was the philosophical connection between his theory and the particular practice advocated. I count myself lucky to have then encountered the stimulating teaching of Carl Friedrich at Harvard before returning to the very changed, high and dry atmosphere of LSE under Oakeshott. The connections between ideas and institutions and

1. This essay first appeared in the *Festschrift* for Carl Joachim Friedrich edited by Klaus von Beyme, *Theory and Politics* (Martinus Nijhoff, Haag, 1971).

I

between theory and practice became more difficult to state with precision and certainty; but if intoxication vanished, Friedrich's teaching certainly did not induce total abstinence. Like the Athenians rather than the Spartans in Plato's dialogue 'The Laws', wine was to be mixed with water according to the occasion, not forsaken or fled. After working with Friedrich and the remarkable gathering of talent that was at Harvard in the 1950s, the blood has remained warm with the sensation that in some proper sense our academic subject has a valid prescriptive voice towards the world. It seems to me in the nature of politics that the academic study of politics is unlikely to preserve and to enhance objectivity and independence of judgement simply by isolating itself. Objectivity is not to be confused with neutrality. The world may not feel that it has a special need for political scientists (although influence may be indirect as well as direct), but political scientists may have a special need for the world. Like many others, I am in what appears to be a peculiar position, for the literature flies to extremes: I dislike equally those who clamour for the 'total commitment' of the subject (a position they often and oddly call 'social responsibility') and those who would create and defend a position of complete irrelevance from practice. The centre is not always a residue, particularly if it contains all those who believe in theory *and* practice. But of late moderation has neither been truculent nor precise enough, has ignored or tolerated extreme positions but has not answered back with the patience and stamina demanded by this whole problem.

So this essay is an attempt to define the main usages of 'theory and practice' and to suggest which are the most useful. It will fall into three parts. Firstly I want to suggest that 'political thought' or 'political theory', as the most generalized category is commonly expressed (and expressed using the two terms quite synonymously), can best be handled by adopting three consistent usages: *political opinion, political theory* (in a strict sense) and *political philosophy*; and by differentiating *political doctrine* from political theory. Secondly, I want to identify and to analyse critically the six most common usages of 'political practice'. For all of these usages, both of thought-and-theory and practice are commonly confused. By doing this I will not claim that certain perennial philosophical difficulties and differences are resolved or removed, but only that their range can be much lessened and the real issues made to stand out more clearly from the usual swamp of verbal differences. And thirdly, I want to indicate from the above what seem to be the residual and valid possible relationships of 'theory and practice'. Only two views I reject as a matter of basic prejudice: 1) that there are no inferences from any valid sense of theory to any possible sense of practice, or that all such inferences are somehow a part of the destruction of any possible 'true theory'; and 2) that there is or could be a body of true theory such that a unique and general programme of immediate social action can be deduced from it.

Valid Usages of 'Political Thought'

I would distinguish in this essay[1] more sharply than we often do between three levels of writing about political activity, initially simply to sharpen some ordinary usages without resort to the invention of yet another arcane or pseudo-technical vocabulary: political opinion, political theory and political philosophy – often confusingly lumped together as

1. This is only an essay, very literally, for any full account of the relationship of political theory to political practice would have to be a treatise on the dominance of all modern politics by the vocabulary and concepts of the Graeco-Romano-European tradition. (For I admit to finding no evidence that, even if there are distinctive forms of politics in the contemporary 'Third World', they are or even can be sensibly expressed in an alternative vocabulary. 'Western' political thought, like 'Western' science – a term less often used – is a product with particular cultural roots but with a universal human relevance.) So in an essay and not a treatise, I ask pardon for reasons of space and time for not giving footnotes to authorities, even those who obviously influence what I will now argue. The first section is based on a short review article, 'Philosophy, Theory and Thought', which appeared in *Political Studies*, February 1967, pp. 49–55. And some of my distinctions on 'practice' I took from a thoughtful, unpublished paper to a seminar-discussion on this same theme of Sheffield students given by my then colleague Jitendra Mohan, but I am sure he would have great reservations about the use I make of them.

3

'thought' or 'theory'. By *political opinion*[1] I mean the ordinary opinions that people hold, their immediate demands, assumptions and conditioned reflections about day-to-day public affairs – often called 'public opinion', or what Walter Bagehot called 'the political conversation of mankind', that is, attitudes and actions which can be studied as given data within an accepted or settled social context. I mean by *political theory* attempts to explain the attitudes and actions arising from ordinary political life and to generalize about them in a particular context; thus political theory is basically concerned with the relationships between concepts and circumstances. And I mean by *political philosophy* attempts to resolve or to understand conflicts between political theories which might appear equally acceptable in given circumstances; it can take two forms (not necessarily incompatible): a philosophical analysis of the terms and concepts of political theory; or (though many cannot come this far) an attempt to establish ethical criteria to judge between the desirability of different theories (so it arises when disputes need to be 'clarified' – some say – or 'resolved' – say others, when the 'can be' of disputants is broadly agreed and only the residual and ultimate 'ought to be' remains).

I intend these three distinctions therefore to refer to levels of discourse, not to logically distinct statements; or if one could define them precisely enough to be logically distinct categories, then their application to understanding or explaining events would always be imperfect. But they are, I think, genuinely distinct levels of abstraction (though each arises from the other). Political opinion is the immediate and the concrete; political theories are concepts as to how social and political order adheres, develops and decays; political philosophy is the most abstract expression and the most general – political philosophy must, indeed, be philosophy. (But this is not a hierarchy of political importance. If, for instance, Marx is not, in this light, strictly a political philo-

1. In my 'Philosophy, Theory and Thought', ibid., I in fact called this first category of *political opinion*, 'political thought'; but I now think that this usage is confusing.

sopher, indeed he is anti-political, then he is, in part at least, a political theorist; and this is no reason for not studying him – as at Oakeshott's LSE he was not recognized under the conventional rubric 'The History of Political Thought.')

Let me put the matter too crudely to be fully defensible except as a ladder to be kicked away once up on the wall: fact and opinion, generalization and explanation, and the ethical and/or analytical – these correspond to my three levels. In terms of syllabus there are ideally three distinct types of discourse: political opinion as a history and sociology of viewpoints, outlooks and events; the study of political theories, again both historical and sociological; and political philosophy as philosophy. This classification I hold to be more useful than the common distinction, in a multitude of forms, between *political science* (seen as description and/or explanation) and *political ideas* (seen as 'normative') or sometimes a tripartite distinction between science, description (i.e. 'institutional stuff') and prescription. For each of the levels I would distinguish can be (and are) the objects either of objective reporting or of prescriptive involvement: there can be either a philosophic or a pragmatic conceptualization of any of the three levels, but there is no firm boundary between these two conceptualizations and in practice one is impressed by how commonly they are combined, however naively. Certainly to talk of a study of 'political ideas' is to risk an unnoticed confusion between ideas as concepts and ideas as value-judgements, rather than a deliberate, explicit and critical fusion.

What, however, of the descriptive study of political institutions – the bread-and-butter of our trade, the stable product of so many of our more learned colleagues who patronize our odd interests, and vice versa: all those thick books on how institutions work or on politics seen through the eyes of Public Law?

I incline to regard them all as bad political theory. This may sound too sweeping. But they are likely to be imperfect forms of knowledge so long as their theoretical preconceptions are not made explicit, or even if suppressed or assumed,

5

are not rendered coherent by an unusually intense intuitive knowledge of the whole of the system of which they form a part. I am just making the old familiar point: pure description is impossible. Has not the novel taught us that? The world of relevant facts is infinite: some criteria of selectivity are always at work. And these presuppositions will commonly be, unless the study is based on premeditated, explicit and closely defined criteria, themselves political often in the most flagrantly partisan sense. (The most interesting and neglected task of political theory is, surely, discovering the presuppositions of actors in political events and of the authors of famous descriptive books who claim to be purely practical or purely empirical: the theories of the untheoretical, the ideas or concepts of those who claim to have 'no time' for ideas, and these are often the most interesting and the most dangerous ideas.)

The belief that there is a separate study of institutions has been unfortunate in several ways. It leads authors and even actors in events to take too narrow a view of the context in which they move. This narrowness in England has usually taken a quite specific form, an inversion which is truly *un vice anglais*: to write about a government department or some aspect of Parliament as if these things are self-sufficient and can be kept apart from politics. (Often such authors hold a specific political doctrine implicitly: they believe that the more decisions are made by a bureaucracy and the less by parties and politicians, the better for stability – a view known for short as 'Public Administration'.) And people can come to think of institutions as 'bricks and mortar' cemented by legal definitions, rather than as the institutionalization of concepts about how certain aspects of government work best in particular circumstances. Institutions, social anthropologists would suggest, are to be seen as 'behaviour-patterns' – but behaviour in specifically political cultures has then to be understood (following Malinowski in his great and neglected *Freedom and Civilization*) as the adaptation of human groups to changing circumstances: a compound of new ideas and habitual adjustments, of free actions and conditioned reactions.

6

Hence it solves nothing at this point – to digress slightly – to leap from the 'institutional approach' (because too narrow and uncritical) to the *behavioural approach*. For the behavioral approach (perhaps best put in its American spelling) is, at best, either truism or tautology. Yes, everything is related to everything else; but neither to equal effect nor to equal importance. And, at worst, it is a democratic doctrine whose nativist fervour is only matched by its disdain for history and ignorance of foreign scholarship. Behaviourism (in so far as it is not simply an intellectual mistake, a belated analogy from long discredited biological theories) arises from the inadequacy of the old, uncritical institutional school. Suddenly everything becomes horizontal flows of related process and activity, 'affect and effect', 'in-put and out-put', etc. rather than the vertical pillars of prescription, checks and balances, rational career structure and clear legal distinctions etc. of the old school. But may I be very simple-minded-Schweik-Parsifal in the Laputa of the computers? Obviously politics must be looked at in both ways at once: that is why it is so very difficult.

Neither account alone is adequate. Everything is related to everything else (as the Hegelians, the Marxists and the modern American social scientists agree), but some significant patterns or semi-permanent diversions of behaviour are created by the arbitrary (when looked at unhistorically) blockages of institutions. The behavioural approach has cut itself off, by concentrating too much on 'how' questions and too little on 'why' questions, from the most obvious range of explanations of how these patternings, blockages or – to use another language – 'arrests of experience' occur: history. The most ordinary explanation, after all, of why something works the way it does is that something analogous occurred in the past as part of a series of preconditions, not as the statistical correlations that can be established between the something and however long a list of 'social indicators' in the present (which correlations, in any case, only establish new relationships: they explain nothing).

Put it another way. We need to remind ourselves that to

7

talk about a 'social system' is logically either a *hypothesis* – which then needs either to be empirically verified or at least, following Karl Popper, to be open to empirical refutation, if it is not a closed web of definitions; or else it is a *tautology* – as in Talcott Parsons's general theory and his specific reduction of all politics to the social (involving as it does the destruction of any area for freedom of choice determined by reason: the deepest heritage of European political culture and one of the greatest cultural inventions of Man). Is it true that everything interacts and conditions everything else – a system? Perhaps, but then a truism: no inferences can be drawn from it until not merely are the different effects measured but also their relative importance evaluated morally or in terms of pre-conceived purposes; otherwise the trivial and the important are indistinguishable. Some political situations are, of course, more systematic than others; but only if one assumes or defines a context, virtually a closed system: so no inferences can be drawn from it, or more strictly, they can only be drawn in the most speculative and hypothetical way. But talk of social and political systems usually turns out to be tautologous: we simply assume by definition that there is such a system and then provide a strait-jacket of subsidiary definitions – as in economic theory. But as in economic theory, we are then wrong to complain that political factors spoil economic rationality. We should then either correct the model or, more often, simply remember that it is a model: its very perfection renders it imperfect, though often of a limited use, as a predictive tool. Political theories seen purely as models of political behaviour are thus always subject to 'arbitrary' correction (in terms of the model, if not in terms of history or practice) by changes in political thought or opinion, and they always assume or beg questions of political philosophy.

Each of my levels – to return to the main theme – can be studied historically, and to some extent must be if explanations are to be offered. The failure of the social sciences in the United States and Britain to use historical evidence sufficiently has actually led to a strange neglect of what was once (in the tradition that ran from Aristotle through Machiavelli to Montesquieu) the central problem of the study of politics: the conditions under which types of government rise and fall. A whole tradition of political theory (in Aristotle's sense) and of republican theory (in Machiavelli and Montesquieu's sense) has been lost, and with it a wealth of experience about the conditions for freedom long antedating anything that can usefully be called democratic government – with which it is now so often and grossly confused. So there is now much speculation (much construction of conceptual-frameworks, I mean) about the conditions for democracy, indeed about 'the emerging democracies' (the African or Asian autocracies); but very little real work is done on the general problem of the conditions for types of regime and their political stability which draws on the evidences of the past with the methods of a comparative and historical sociology. The most obvious explanation for this is, of course, the sheer ignorance of history (in the most ordinary sense) shown by some of the prophets and practitioners of the behavioural approach. (But if this is getting *ad hominem*, one must add in fairness, that it is matched by an unwillingness of most historians and institutionalists to generalize and to explain rather than simply, they believe, to describe).

What do we commonly find? We find courses in the 'History of Political Thought', meaning political philosophy, which are then so abstract and analytical that one becomes doubtful whether there really is a history, rather than just a few masters scattered here and there at odd points of time. And they are also so diffuse that they have to be anchored to the 'texts' of these few masters: they cannot attempt to follow the modulations of politicians' thinking from opinion, through the theoretical to – on rare but discernible occasions, as in the English Civil War, the American War of Independence and the Napoleonic Wars – the philosophical. So we rarely find books or lectures on, strictly speaking, the history of political theory, what obviously is a historical subject and now to be sharpened by modern sociological concepts: an account of the growth of a body of knowledge about the conditions in which various types of regime prove stable or not. On the contrary, we more often find an ill-focused enterprise giving us a rather blurred vision of the purely philosophical aspects of certain writers. (To stress theories about stability in Aristotle is not to ignore or supplant the philosophical problems of ethics and justice: it is simply a different level of problem, and is at the moment the one more likely to be neglected by those who call themselves 'political theorists'.) Some elementary classificatory work is attempted in 'comparative government', but then all classifications are really theories anyway, if they have any explanatory value – which they all too rarely do. But seldom is due weight given to the most obvious preoccupation of even the great texts – Aristotle, Machiavelli, Hobbes and Hegel – with the basic problem of (in my strict sense) political theory: political stability, or if that sounds too static, the conditions of the rise and fall of regimes. Political philosophers, quite properly, neglect this – they are concerned either with the analysis of concepts and/or with 'political justice'. The theories remain neglected so that every year some wise fool rediscovers, for example, that Machiavelli had 'very modern' ideas about the positive role of social conflict as a factor in the strength of republics (an argument well known to Harrington and to most republican theorists of 'mixed government' in the seventeenth century).

Thus our books and syllabuses continue to ignore the central Western tradition of theory about politics and republics in favour of ridiculously anachronistic concepts of democracy. Although I have doubts that 'constitutionalism' (as Charles MacIlwain and C. J. Friedrich have used the concept) is a general, as some think, rather than a perhaps too specific halfway house between legal and political explanations, yet its pedagogic use did avoid this fracturing of ideas and institutions. And we may now smile at the confidence with which Henry Sidgwick used his secondary authorities and the simplicity of his method, but such a book as his *The Development of European Policy*[1] did ask the right questions

1. Published posthumously in London, 1903. The first two notes in the analytic table of contents state: 'The purpose of this book is to treat the History of Political Societies or States from the point of view of Inductive

and did carry the ideas and institutions together; indeed, more profoundly, he saw them as the same thing. Certainly, it is an intellectualist fallacy to think that we can understand a society simply by understanding the concepts it uses (as a few anthropologists and a few intellectual historians seem to claim); but we do understand it if we follow, as Professor Ernest Gellner well argues, the *working of these concepts* (what looking backwards with historical knowledge, but not forward teleologically, we may then properly call their 'function').

One further explanation, since I am claiming that my proposed classification would make it easier to handle the largely meaningless dispute between 'science' and 'evaluation'. Each category can exist in either mode and the comingling of them in practice is unavoidable. I find it an odd way to kill time, which is so terribly short, for so many English philosophers to approach politics simply through 'the texts' – which they then rummage either in order to expose triumphantly (if not surprisingly) implicit 'value judgements' or else in order to find verbal contradictions in the assumed system. Such enterprises should, at the best, be the beginning of something more interesting and important, not the end. But rarely if ever does such a philosopher, wandering in politics without history, discuss the positive theories of order asserted by Hobbes, Locke, Rousseau, J. S. Mill (the usual hunting grounds) and whether they are, in principle even, verifiable or refutable. And, equally oddly, rarely do 'histories of political ideas' tell us anything about the dominant concepts of the rulers and politicians of an age, only about those of certified 'political philosophers', or they occasionally add a bit of contextual top dressing to this barren or far too personal soil. Anthropologists attempt to study the dominant concepts or the total value-system of a whole culture, but only a very few historians of political ideas go beyond the certified texts.

Now plainly a political theory states that something is the case. But equally plainly there are *political doctrines* which

Political Science' and 'It is concerned with the development as well as the classification of forms of polity.'

state that something ought to be the case. But these are not antithetical things; they are modulations of each other. One *can* hold a political theory without espousing it as a doctrine, but only if one maintains that it fits uniquely and exclusively some particular society or circumstance. Often a little sociology of politics seems to suggest that for each society there is a unique form of regime and pattern of conduct in public life; but a little more political sociology will probably suggest that such circumstances are extremely rare. In practice it is likely that the theorist will get drawn, both intellectually and personally, into asserting why one theory is *better* than another in a situation in which both or (why be Platonic or Marxist?) several may work – work in the simple but important sense of appearing to assure the survival of the society.[1] Political theories consider the relationships between concepts and circumstances; political doctrines assert a connection between thought and policy.

So the difference between theories and doctrines is important but is not absolute. This makes it foolish to try to regulate the study of doctrines (which are then loosely and pejoratively called 'ideologies') to some inferior status. One cannot live with a theory without hoping that it will not merely work, but work for the best; and no doctrine, which has any relevance to government at all, will not claim, however crudely and vaguely, to be capable of implementation. Take various formulations of old friends like Conservatism, Socialism and Liberalism. Each of these is, in quite ordinary terms, a social theory before ever it can be taken seriously as a political doctrine. They could not be asserted as doctrines if they could not be plausibly argued as theories: as true (or partly true) theories of how particular societies or society in general works. Each may assert that it is the only possible way in which a society may work (paradoxically Liberals often say this). But we know that the evidence is almost always against them. Since I, personally, hold Socialist doctrines, the saddest thing for me to see is that plainly Conservatism

1. And this possibility of alternatives is the ground on which a vindication of the compatibility of freedom and planning would begin.

can work, after a fashion; and that as a theory it can explain more about *some* social phenomena than Socialism (though the contrary, is also true). However, as a holder of Socialist doctrines I then argue (in the appropriate place) reasons both for thinking that society would work better if . . . (if ever tried etc.) and for believing that the theory implicit in my doctrine leads me to consult a wider range of relevant factors. An argument between a holder of Conservative and of Socialist doctrines will be mutually inconclusive and may descend to the level of political opinion, simply swapping opinions in the form of political rhetoric; but it may also, though with more difficulty, ascend to philosophy. Granted that both may work well enough (theory) in some manner compatible with order and a reasonably predictable stability, yet which should we rationally wish to work best? The discussion may not move the particular advocates, but someone might be listening. (Otherwise it is just a case of 'I am a philosopher, you are a theorist and he is a doctrinaire'.)[1] Now it is not, I agree with Oakeshott, the special business of a political philosopher to offer advice to politicians or to presume to make people's minds up for them. For one thing, the minds are almost always made up already. But it is part of our business to follow truths and their implications, whether we see them as theories or doctrines, and to debate (if we care to be understood or if we notice criticism at all) on a level above both political opinion and political theory (as contingency and relativity). After all, we may be overheard; and politics in the Western tradition has been essentially a public activity, however limited at times have been both the public and the sense of what is public. We will not change opinions, but we may refine and civilize the manner in which they are held and thus provide an essential part of the conditions for intellectual and practical synthesis.

Now one final point on the terminology of 'theory'. I see *ideology* as a particular type of doctrine: nominally a theory

1. A doctrinaire, as distinct from any holder of a doctrine, is someone who cannot see the genuine theoretical element in other doctrines. This is why, quite simply, he is likely to be insensitive and to make big mistakes.

which claims universal validity, because of a belief that all ideas derive from circumstance, but which then also holds that this truth is deliberately obscured by ruling elites, so that the only theory has to be asserted in the form of propaganda to the masses. This is a very special and peculiar modern sense, but an actual one whose lineage can be traced from Marx's attack on the autonomy of philosophy in the *German Ideology*. Such claims for universal validity (that race explains everything, or that control of the factors of production explains everything) mark it off from the *study* of ideology, of how *far* ideas can be understood as a product of circumstances: an interesting matter. But otherwise 'doctrine' is the far more accurate word than 'ideology' in all those dreary contexts where people speak of 'the decline of ideology' or of the (silly or harsh) 'ideology' of this or that party or group. Few of these groups have got, in fact, ideologies; most neo-Marxism or 'student Marxism' is, in fact, if our nerves are strong enough to see, anti-ideological;[1] and as for the alleged 'end of ideology', we are in the midst of a vivid revival of political theory – good, bad and indifferent.[2]

1. Their writings exhibit a much more concrete sense of being oppressed by a total system (a very undiscriminating, crude and misleading flattery, incidentally) than of any clear, comprehensive ideological alternative. And their positive assertions (if one looks at what they say about the nature of the world, rather than their narcissistic preoccupation with Marxism) tend to be highly particular, peculiar, individual, romantic (in good and bad senses) but concerned with freedom and undeniably free. They furnish an odd testimony to the apparent discontinuity of things, that the world is, after all, full of contradictions, and necessarily so, rather than to 'the system' or to imminent and total better ones.

[2] If by the 'end of ideology' is meant the declining plausibility of comprehensive accounts of world history, yes indeed. But those like Daniel Bell and his friends who popularized the phrase plainly meant also the decline of doctrinal conflict. This now appears to be ludicrously untrue. Indeed precisely as people lose faith in total descriptions, they also lose faith in 'mere practicality' or 'empiricism' as the modest-grand alternative; and they have to turn, almost perforce, to defining middle-term objectives in broad contexts, which can be justified in some universal terms: theory and doctrine. Or else, more subtly, they become more self-aware of the implicit moral assumptions on which all accounts of 'practice' and 'pure practicality' build.

Thus I have argued that *political theory* should form the hard centre of our study. A study, on the one hand, of relatively low-level theories that seek to explain how particular institutions work (having in mind the impossibility or the deception of any 'purely descriptive' approach); but, on the other hand, of theories of a higher degree of generality and abstraction that seek to explain the rise and fall of political systems and the conditions associated with them. *Political philosophy* is a rather precious activity attempted too often, in the form of books and treatises, even though we are necessarily involved in philosophic discussion at some level, however well or badly, technically or ordinarily, whenever doctrines and theories conflict. (In political argument a positive answer to 'could it work?', however tentative, must lead on to 'should it work?'; but it is pointless to continue if the answer is negative.) Political opinions are all common, uncritical and unreflective activities (but even the study of these will involve some simple theories about what is important). None of these can exist without the others, but – the practical point to be made – most theoretical enterprises do not begin with philosophical issues of values: those who assert this are usually philosophers whose knowledge of politics is limited entirely to a peculiar way of reading certain traditional texts, so as to exaggerate their ethical content and to play down their empirical content. The academic philosopher is the judge if a case arises, but he is ill-equipped either to begin an action or to marshal the evidence and act as examining magistrate. He should be honoured for claiming an ultimate jurisdiction, irrespective of the fact that he cannot enforce it; but he should not attempt to claim an original jurisdiction.

Common Usages of 'Political Practice'

To assert that theory and doctrine necessarily involve each other, although they may and should properly be stressed separately for the different purposes of generalization and explanation and of recommendation and persuasion, may seem to some to have begged the question. But the very nature of political activity must beg the question. For the very concept of politics, whether in its broadest sense of the study and carrying on of any type of government or in its more specific sense of carrying on government in a specifically political manner, assumes that there are different interests, whether material, ideal or commonly both, which have to be commanded (governmentally) or conciliated (politically). Hence justifications are always demanded and are always given, even if in the thinly disguised and empirically dubious form that, objectively, there are no real alternatives (which means that, in fact, there are conceivable alternatives – the argument then becomes whether these are, in the short, middle or long term, practicable).

As I have argued elsewhere:

Politics thus rests upon a sociological generalization and an ethical commitment. The sociological generalization is that territory organized under a government is normally 'an aggregate of many members' (Aristotle), that established, advanced or civilized societies contain a diversity of interests – whether moral, social or economic. The ethical commitment is that there are limits beyond which a government should not go in maintaining or creating order. No fixed limits can, of course, be demonstrated. They are all relative to time and place, but the *principle* of limitations is general and the empirical distinction is usually clear between systems which strive to limit power and those which strive after total power.[1]

1. See my *In Defence of Politics*, revised Pelican edition, 1964, p. 170. Before the modern era, power may sensibly be viewed as total (as by Wittfogel), but only in the restricted sense of power as something immune from challenge. But only in the modern era have people attempted to use power in a total manner to achieve, in the other vital sense of power (often confused with the first), some premeditated effect, in this case a total or fully comprehensive effect or change. I do not think that in fact this is possible, but I would defend both Friedrich and Arendt strongly against the critics of their 'totalitarian hypothesis' by arguing that it has been *attempted*, may be still in China, and could be again. But before modern technology and technological ways of thought, power which sought to be unchallengeable had to limit its sphere of alleged competence severely. (See my 'The Elementary Types of Government', *Government and Opposition*, Winter 1968, pp. 3–20).

The limitations are always partly human, material or physical, but they also always arise out of the need to justify power: the impossibility of pure coercion sustaining order through time. Thus also:

> Political theory is itself political. If a political system is fundamentally a descriptive recognition of diversity plus an ethical recognition that this should be normal, then a political doctrine will display the same characteristics (a political doctrine is simply a more partial and specific, hence less general, theory).[1]

Theory-and-doctrine plainly involve practice: they both arise from practice, provide the concepts by which alone we can define and delimit a particular practice, and any specific theory-and-doctrine has inferences for practice. To be any more precise depends on what one means by practice. I can identify six main usages with relevance to government and politics. (I am aware that the English word 'practice' is not used so widely in either German or French, for instance – other words are used; but the same distinctions are still made.)

I HOW THINGS ARE DONE, OR CUSTOM

'It is the practice in America to address people by their first name, irrespective of length or depth of acquaintance'. 'Whatsoever is believed or practised' (Preface to the translation of the English Bible, 1611). 'Some things are of faith, but some practices are of time and circumstance' (Hooker). All these senses describe some rule or rules that must be accepted *if* a particular activity is to be pursued at all. But no further justification is offered or is relevant. If you don't want to travel on that road, then you must go somewhere else. Such practices may be necessary to a particular activity, or it may just be necessary that there are some established practices whatever they are – as in playing a game; but none of them have or need intrinsic justification. Plainly it is as fallacious and self-defeating to denounce all such practices in general

1. *In Defence of Politics*, p. 118.

('down with custom, convention and all institutions') as it is to argue that there is nothing in politics and the good life but learning and accepting social practices ('Manners Maketh Man', as is the motto of an English Public School).

2 A TRADITION OF BEHAVIOUR

'Whatever you intend to change, you will discover that in practice things work out differently – and much the same.' The sense of practice in (1) above, *custom*, calls for no justification, but these second senses do; and the justification is the basic one that it is impossible, or extraordinarily difficult, to do things otherwise when considered in the whole social context; it is more humane to go along with what has worked, after a fashion, than to risk changing, still less to want to change, the whole social fabric – Edmund Burke's 'the present good' rather than 'the speculative better'.

Proust's Swann is the perfect man of practice as 'how things are done', but he never seeks to justify; indeed he is both pained and lost, all that he stands for is defeated already, when he is asked to formulate anything as serious and pompous as a tradition of behaviour. And in this second sense there is an important subsidiary and prescriptive sense: the superiority of someone who repeatedly and continuously does something (particularly governing) – the practitioner – over the student, the commentator and the moralist. This is the conservative version of the alleged superiority of practice over theory, as in Burke's forthright cry: 'Give me the farmer rather than the metaphysician', and in his advocacy of prescription, sentiment and feeling before reason. And thus tradition is held to be more concrete than reason: those dreadful things in France were done in the name of 'A Constitution, that at the time of writing had not so much as a practical existence' (Burke, *The Regicide Peace*). But the converse is equally clear: Rousseau's identification of all practice with moral corruption, and the cry for the judgements of innocence unsullied by long experience (a cry which has recently been revived). Tradition can be thus invoked both as self-justifying and as self-evidently oppressive and immoral. Certainly it is fallacious to believe that a particular practice can be determined by rational first principles (what Oakeshott well calls 'rationalism'); but it is equally fallacious to believe that theory is determined by practice (to turn rationalism upside-down is also a poor way to study the complex interplay of theory and tradition).

3 ACTION

'We must act before the vision fails.' 'Blessed are the men that keep their word and practise thy commands' (Psalms, 69 I ii). But if these still maintain some kind of balance between thought or action, they can lead easily to the proverbial, 'actions speak louder than words', or to Dr Faust's wilful translation of the first verse of the Gospel of St John the Divine. Here is, I suspect, one of the most frequent forms of the common theory and practice debate and the one that leads to the famous formulation, 'I agree with you in theory but not in practice' (which may be simply an objection about practicality, see below, but is more often the philistine acceptance of a radical disjunction between theory and practice). But it is doubtful, I will argue later, whether *specific* actions necessarily follow even from doctrines – and certainly not from theories – as distinct from *some* actions (that is, there will always be alternative means to achieve any doctrine). Thus some of these senses of practice as action are a little empty, as in philosophical pragmatism. (Sure, 'truth is what works', but many different things can work; or, more subtly, 'all thoughts involve consequences', all ideas involve action, but some of these consequences and actions are intended, some unintended, some trivial, some important: higher criteria must be invoked.) However, specific actions, like specific events, can refute theories, but they can neither prove a specific theory nor replace theorizing in general. Actions are thus specific, ultimately random, whereas a tradition of behaviour is general. A specific subsidiary sense is politically important: quite apart from full-blooded anarchist demands that *any* action (violence even, or particularly) will clarify or expose a situation bemused by rationalizations,[1] there is the gentler: 'You may do this on occasion, but you must not make a practice of it.' Action may thus, it is held, occasionally fall outside a tradition of behaviour without destroying it – indeed particular and exceptional acts 'pour raison d'état' can be invoked by the traditionalist.

4 POLICY

'QUEEN: Banish us both and send the King with me. NORTHUMBERLAND : That were some love but little policy' (Shakespeare, *Richard II*). 'Luther understood that the Emperor, and diverse Princes, would practise the decree of Worms' (Dau's translation of Sleidane's *Commentaries*). 'If the Liberal Party has come to hold an agreed policy on many issues of the day, it will long resist the Radical demand to have a programme' (*anon.*, 1885). Policy is what has to be done deliberately and consistently in order to preserve some State or interest within it. Thus practice as *action* (3 above) can be specific and *contingent*, but policy is either a known general rule or the attempt to achieve, by a variety of different means perhaps, some public benefit or result. Policy can stop far short of *planning*, being both less comprehensive and explicit, but it has a rational and deliberate intent to it, an almost explicitly secular flavour of man the maker and shaper of society;[2] and this can make those who see practice as a tradition of behaviour suspect both the concept of policy as overreaching and the practices of politicians as something occasionally necessary, but base – again specific actions, but neither a rule nor a code of conduct. Traditions of behaviour are, however, always relevant to policy; but policy claims to be able either to effect them, or to discover diversities amid the alleged unified tradition that need

1. Or the flabby liberal desire to be active and busy however vague the intentions or uncertain the result.
2. 'Oh what a world of profit and delight, of power, of honour and omnipotence is promised to the studious artisan' (Marlowe's *Dr Faustus*).

managing politically. Thus 'policy' and 'politics' were words both of great threat and promise in the sixteenth century when the idea of a self-contained realm of political activity arose or was revived. Strictly speaking, theory can lead to *policy*, but political *action* is either simply any implementation of policy or else it is a specific rejection of theory in specific circumstances ('If it were done when 'tis done, then 'twere well it were done quickly' – Lady Macbeth). Otherwise action appears as a general refutation of both theory and established practices ('When the rifle knocks man dead Something drops from eyes long blind', as the poet Yeats said, or as could have been said by any Fascist or Anarchist about the primacy of action over theory). Violence can flow from policy (and policy used to have a bad name for justifying exceptional acts of violence), but no amount of action *per se* can constitute policy.

A modern subsidiary sense, established by Lasswell, is that of 'the policy sciences'. But this is, one suspects, a derivative of *ideology* more than theory. For if theory cannot be separated from doctrine, then it is never sensible to say 'Politicians determine the ends and we social scientists simply determine the means'. This separation is so crazy, both logically and morally, so much less even plausible in the social sciences than in the natural sciences, that one must assume that those who say things like this are more deeply involved in the ends than they either care to admit or have the critical insight to recognize. Are they knaves or fools? Perhaps there are a few who are simply naively happy that their knowledge is being put to use for their country.[1] We may choose to help implement policy, but we choose when: this is not the only role of political science nor yet a peculiar obligation to the State. I may choose to be an amateur prostitute, I may be forced into prostitution, but that is no reason to think like a prostitute. But scepticism about 'the policy sciences' formulation does not involve scepticism that theory leads to policy but, on the

1. Neither of these 'policy science' views would be those, I am sure, of Dr Henry Kissinger, for instance. He is an authentic theorist, but a wrong one.

contrary, only denials that that is its only role (for also to explain as well as to prescribe). But one must deny that theory can be derived from policy, or is the servant of policy of State.

5 PRAXIS

'His great achievement was always to assert the unity of theory and practice' (Engels on Marx). Perhaps it is an odd surprise to Germans that the German usage *'Praxis'* is always used by American, English and French Marxists (in preference to the English and French 'practice' – which has been surrendered to conservatives); and is used simply to beg the whole question: each body of theory or doctrine ('ideology' in the Marxist sense) is defined as the reflection of a practical present or a specific set of systematic and exploitative social relationships etc. *'Praxis'* is intoned, like some mysterious element, to explain any possible relationship between ideas and institutions, between theory and policy.[1] Such pseudo-technicalities do not, of course, explain anything: they only restate the problem: the solution is purely verbal. And it can become comically close to the English and German conservative usage of a 'tradition of behaviour' as a description masquerading as both an explanation and a justification. The only difference is that tradition demands that nothing important shall be changed, because everything hangs together; and *praxis* demands that everything important must be changed, because everything hangs together.

It is in contrast to this pseudo-meaning of *praxis* that we can modestly be sure that political theory is always concerned with limited and tentative explanations – but our 'limited' always means more. We eliminate more errors, we can narrow the field of acceptable and possible alternatives, so in

1. There was once upon a time an English Professor of Politics who used to use the word 'subtle' with an equally grim frequency to explain relationships between things which he could not understand, but was apparently impressed by (e.g. compare and contrast 'the subtle relationship between liberalism and capitalism' with 'liberalism and capitalism find their essential relationship in *praxis*' – which I overheard in a discussion with some of Lukacs's disciples).

these negative senses are still left with possible truths. And we
can be modestly sure, also, that political doctrines are always
concerned with limited changes – and that limited changes
are possible, all things do not affect each other equally. This
may sound a very conservative utterance to an ideologist, but
political conservatives are always having to rediscover that
the limits of possible and deliberate change are greater than
they had thought – there is no particular reason why we
should wait for them, but they catch up if we do. So there is a
sixth sense of practice, quite simply:

6 WHAT IS POSSIBLE OR PRACTICABLE

Here is the famous 'good in theory, but will it work in practice?' 'In the present temper of popular opinion, Sir, your
policy is impractical.' Or what leads one to say 'in practice
one can go far beyond policy and statecraft, even beyond
programmes, into planning without coming near to totalitarianism'. A distinction is drawn between the possible and
the actual, or between the ideal (or the ideal type) and the
possible. Doctrine, perhaps even based on philosophy through
theory, may define some objectives or criteria for conduct,
but analogies based on other theories may make one want to
say that the doctrine is not yet fully practicable, but potentially so. Thus *practice* is here a kind of mediation between the
ideal and the actual (now I am almost tempted to call this
'*praxis*', or simply the Aristotelian 'best possible' or '*political*
ethics', if one assumes, as I do, that there is always a clash
between different kinds of equally plausible justice).

The proverbial 'practice what you preach' is here often
used as the basis for the most worrying and effective accusa-
tions of 'hypocrisy'. 'Why don't you put it into practice,
rather than invoking practice as an excuse?' Well, often
people are hypocritical – doctrines are only given lip-service.
But sometimes it is the fault of the doctrine to couch itself in
terms either impossible to realize, or intolerant of realization
by any other than single given set of means which are treated
as part of the doctrine itself (a foolish way to deal with the

future and with changing events). And sometimes, also, it has to be seen, by the very factors of practice in (2), (3) and (4) above, tradition, action and policy, that while not to try to practice what you preach is, indeed, hypocrisy, yet to succeed fully is simply very unlikely, to fall short is human. To use this as a general excuse, is a form of super-hypocrisy; but to fail to accept its descriptive truth is obtuse and is usually cruel in consequence – cruel not merely to the backsliders, if the anti-hypocrites are in power, but cruel to the anti-hypocritical reformer who must then, for fear of being accused of compromise (practice as the mediation between the ideal and the actual), set himself goals quite impossible of realization so that in failure his sincerity shines forth (failure now, for so many, supplants success as 'the bitch goddess'). Thus the practical is the whole range of what is politically possible (whether desirable or not), whether or not arising from or seen in terms of political theory; whereas policy purports both to be immediately probable and to be consistent (either in means or ends), and thus rests heavily, if often unconsciously, on theory through doctrine.[1]

Possible Relationships

So now we can narrow the field. The first sense above, *custom*, is simply the level of policital opinion. By itself it raises no theoretical problems at all, it is simply the datum on which both theory and doctrine build: it cannot itself explain, generalize or prescribe generally – unless we are naive majoritarian democrats who consider that public opinion polling can discover what ought to be done. But the

1. There are, of course, things which are technically possible but politically impractical in any time span worth considering: these I would call 'scientistic' or 'scientism' – a kind of utopianism; but there is another kind of utopianism or visionary thinking which is moral and does not claim to be either technically or politically practical, and so is not to be criticized or despised on those grounds, but which is simply and sometimes grandly – like Sir Thomas More's *Utopia* or William Morris's *News from No-where* – a reminder of the perpetual gap between the 'is' and the 'ought', thus valuable for this.

moment we start generalizing about political opinion and
seek to explain a specific set of attitudes, customs or practices
and how changes take place in them, then we are involved in
theory. Such data need to be established, however; they cannot be assumed. The political philosopher can often be
tendentious as well as tiresome when he assumes so many
'hypothetical examples' instead of using real instances; and
certainly the political theorist is useless without the historian
and the sociologist. But methodologies of research are themselves either forms of theory, or else so theoretically naive and
unconscious that they are often simply political doctrines in
fancy dress or ideology in disguise.[1] The second, *a tradition of
behaviour*, cannot replace theory, its concepts themselves need
explicating in terms of a theory at least logically independent
of, even if culturally linked to, the tradition in question. And
even as regards doctrine, it is usually simply not true that a
single tradition expresses or monopolizes anything we may
call a society – certainly not advanced societies (different
traditions commonly pertain, for instance, to different
classes). But tradition is always the major limiting factor in
relation to 'putting ideas into practice' in either of the main
relevant senses of practice as policy or simply as practicability.
Most of the work of political theorists, in fact, consists in explicating traditions of behaviour and this cannot be by-passed
without being unconsciously trapped by traditions, usually
the very traditions we may seek to turn our backs upon or
even erase. All I seek to show is that tradition cannot replace, subsume or determine theory. While it is true that
theories usually arise from a modification of the established
ideas of a tradition, it is perfectly possible and does happen,
infrequently but influentially, for relevant theories to arise
outside tradition: innovation, invention and even importation *can* occur. Certainly the doctrines arising from the
theories then become severely limited or changed in practice,
they are not as they were elsewhere or in the original plan,
proposal or pamphlet; but the original tradition is also

1. See further the section called 'Method as Doctrine' of my *In Defence of
Politics* (Pelican edition, 1964), pp. 190–98.

modified in a way that otherwise would not have happened.[1]
(Similarly it is unnecessary to believe as a general rule that
political theory only arises from political problems or crises,
or that, *per contra*, if theory only arises independently from
pure contemplation, then problems are actually created if
doctrine is deduced from theory. Either can happen and
does happen. 'Ideas influence action', but every case is
unique.)

The third sense above, *action*, has a distinct meaning either
as an irrational rebuttal of all reason and theory, or as an
unreflective and uncoordinated involvement in things ('better
to do something than nothing'). Otherwise it is simply the
specific means, on the level of political opinion, by which we
may validly seek to put theoretically plausible doctrines into
practice – and thus better called 'policy'. But it is a rash kind
of doctrine that is doctrinaire about the means – except in the
most immediate and limited contexts: theory should have
taught it that the achieving of premeditated effects, or the
putting of principles into 'practice', cannot be limited to one
set of predetermined means.[2]

1. Thus the denial of the importance of theory in a revolutionary
situation, as compared to tradition or circumstance (thinking of the
debates on Marxism and Russia and of Nazism and Germany) is more
sensibly and temperately put as the denial both that specific doctrines
are necessarily entailed in specific theories (although in practice they are
modified by them) and that the new practices follow directly from the
doctrines (although in practice they are modified by them). The situation
is always complex, many factors are involved, but the theoretical framework can still be of vital, if never of exclusive, importance, a necessary if
never a sufficient condition for what in fact happened (and if not, perhaps,
as direct causes at all, then at least indirect causes as the explanation of
the concepts that the new rulers use to interpret changing conditions).

Similarly much of the debate about the importation or transference of
institutions to the 'Third World' is confused in the same way. The claim
that institutions can be transferred entirely with the same doctrines and
practical consequences is as absurd and false as the belief that all such
transfer is imposed and then utterly transformed by indigenous factors,
unless massive external coercion is present. Such extreme cases are not
likely to be found, and every actual case will vary in the manner and
proportion to which the importation is changed as it changes.

2. For example, English and German Socialists used to regard the state

26

The fourth sense above, the Marxist sense of *praxis*, simply states the problem – useful to insist upon, perhaps, but is merely an insistence, not a solution: particularly for people who believe that there are unique solutions. It makes great play with 'action', hence the 'unity of thought and action', but thoroughly confuses action with *all* the possible senses of practice above (for even humble or indifferent *custom* is grimly seen as always instrumental of some particular class ideology). So we are left with the fourth and sixth senses, *policy* and *what is possible* as the most meaningful areas in which it can be sensibly asserted that theory relates to practice. Theory helps us to understand what is possible. This is the minimal but most important relevance. But different things may be *possible*; and theory is certainly not limited to what is politically probable at any given time: theory is free to explain the whole range of possibilities. For instance, I would assert categorically, though some sociologists may shudder, that there is no advanced society that cannot be governed effectively (in the simple sense of maintaining stability and a reasonably predictable order) in some manner radically different from the way it is. Everything is not possible, social limitations are severe, but the very complexity and diversity of societies and the very power and skill of governments create some range of

---

ownership of major industries as part of the doctrine. They are now usually wiser to see such a policy as a means, among other possible means, according to circumstances, and not as an end in itself. Other means to the ends of equality and social justice (or 'liberty, equality and fraternity') may be less radical, such as fiscal planning of 'state-capitalism', but they may also be more radical, such as 'workers' control' or the *'commune-ization'* of society.

Similarly much liberal theory has been notoriously over-committed to a whole host of procedural devices and an ever-lengthening list of natural rights, as if these contingent means and formulations were necessary ends. I would even argue, in another place, that both 'constitutionalism' and 'the multi-party system' are simply means to freedom and responsible individualism: such ends could be pursued with a minimum of formal constitutional law and even within a one-party state (or a state in which party counts for relatively less, among other kinds or pressure groups, than in many past or present accounts).

diverse possibilities. Which *should* we adopt? However we decide such questions, or decide how to decide them, an interaction between theory and *philosophy*, at however simple a level, is necessarily involved. Justifications have to be given explicitly. Doctrine, however crudely, does just this (though the kind of justifications it gives need philosophical analysis and criticism). Theory, if it claims to be purely empirical, is then either irrelevant at this stage or, more often, has to be critically examined and rephrased to make its own moral assumptions explicit. (There will be assumptions about the nature of man, of rights and of freedom, at least.) Once again, changes in theory are not necessarily a response simply to practical political problems; they can have their effect on these problems through philosophical changes of a purely logical or, at times even, theological character.

All policies, of course, purport to be practical (which is not always true), but they sometimes claim (as a consistent set of actions concerned with the preservation of the State, for instance) to be amoral and are frequently denounced as immoral. The early modern usage of 'policy' had an almost built-in amoral or immoral connotation. But closer examination will show (as the whole weight of modern scholarship about Machiavelli now shows) that such apparent immorality is always, in fact, if the presuppositions are made explicit, itself some alternative or counter-morality to the established tradition of behaviour. Sometimes the advocate of policy will argue the necessity of an immoral act: he is wrong to urge 'necessity', but he may on occasion be right to show that in terms of political justice things can be justified which could not be justified according to the common ideas of justice in the established tradition of behaviour. One justification may, indeed, be superior 'in practice' but the other 'in theory'; neither, however, refutes or abolishes the other: they both exist in very tension and coexistence of 'theory and practice'. Here we are at the point at which, as political theorists and political philosophers, we cannot help ourselves; we can only help others by sharpening the clarity of such dilemmas, not by pretending that we have the means to remove them.

I would thus deny that there is any valid sense of political theory such that to study it in any meaningful way does not have some implications, intended or unintended, positive or negative, either for policy or for more specific discussions about whether a particular thing is practicable or likely to stay practicable. A theory may seek simply to explain, to generalize or to understand; but the explanation or the understanding is itself incomplete if some values are not attached to it. For some effect involving values will inevitably be created, whether we like it or not, intend it or not: so we should simply be responsible for our own actions – as utterances – by constantly considering the values and assumptions involved in what we are doing and trying all the time (rarely, if ever, with complete success) to make them more explicit. For ultimately it is my knowledge and I will not have you misuse it, even if you are the rational State or even the regenerated People; but I must then make sensible steps both to limit my claims and to make explicit publicly what I consider use and misuse to be.

In politics we are necessarily concerned with a diversity of relationships which represent both interests and doctrines (even, or especially, if we wish to reduce, if never to abolish, this diversity). Any account we give of such relationships can never be final. If we give accounts at all, we must presume either that in some sense the relationships are stable and should be stable, or are changing in a reasonably predictable direction and should be changing in that direction; or else we say that the relationship is stable, but unjust, or is changing, but in an unjust direction. What we cannot do is to avoid some value-judgement upon them, especially if we see things as likely to happen that we do not want to happen. But there could be no possible sense of 'not wanting things to happen that are likely to happen' which could be meaningfully understood unless put in some terms, however sketchy or relatively unlikely, of a possible alternative. Ordinarily, however, precisely because politics is about an ordering of priorities in diverse society, we always seek to rationalize moral possibilities as empirical probabilities. Even so, we do so as probabilities not certainties: *political* theories can only deal in possibilities and probabilities. But uncertainty is no excuse for silence, nor for saying that everything is either arbitrary, or a matter of will or subjective taste both for the politician and the student of politics; nor yet for saying that things are determined by causes we cannot ever fully understand (as the traditionalist says), or cannot understand until the social basis of bourgeois 'false-consciousness' is removed (as the neo-Marxist says).

Politics is then unavoidably 'the art of the possible', a lame, trite and vague conclusion indeed, if I did not add from what has gone before that 'the possible' is not simply defined by a tradition of behaviour, but by the interplay between a tradition of behaviour and theories and doctrines (which may arise from quite outside that tradition). The interplay is between things as they are, as they could be and as they should be: an interplay which constantly extends the range of what is possible, and is thus of fundamental importance in the adaptability of human societies to social, technological and moral change.

Thus we are always concerned in political thought with three dimensions: what is the case, what is thought to be the case, and what ought to be the case. Political theory, drawing from all other relevant disciplines, describes what is the case and offers tentative explanations of the different relationships involved. It also explains, describing and summarizing political opinion, why what is thought to be the case may diverge from what is, in fact, the case. And these divergences can only be lessened, sometimes resolved, by considering what ought to be the case in terms of political philosophy.

'Should political studies be practical?' Yes, they cannot help at least be relevant. Political theorists must use the same concepts and values as politicians, but at different levels of abstraction and immediacy. There is not a vertical division between 'facts' and 'values', but a horizontal division of different degrees of abstraction and concreteness in relation to policies and possibilities. There is no fact so concrete, unless utterly trivial, that is not gathered and conceptualized for

30

some political purpose; and there is no theory so abstract that some inferences for policy do not follow from it.

Political theory and political doctrine are different activities, prudentially they should be kept apart as much as possible, but logically they arise from each other and cannot be completely separated. Theory is relevant to practice, but does not lead directly to particular practices. Doctrines can lead directly to practice, but they are likely to be very short-lived and over-specific things, or simply dogmatic and doctrinaire, if they have no sound theoretical foundations. A doctrine is doctrinaire and likely to prove impractical less by the character of its intentions, than by whether or not it claims that its set of principles or its set of intended results must entail a unique and specific set of actions-as-means. For political theory would lead us to believe, both on empirical and moral grounds, that the means must vary according to circumstances. Ends no more determine means than means determine ends: they limit them; but both logically and in practice, there are always alternative means, except perhaps in the very simplest and least adaptable kinds of society. If I stand at a fixed point, I must either take this road or not reach Rome without great difficulty; but there are many roads to Rome and I may, for all kinds of other reasons, choose to take a more difficult or simply a longer road. It may not be very efficient, but it may be quite practicable. And the longer road may be morally preferable. Many more things can be done than should be done, but also many more things that should be done can be done, but can be done by a greater variety of means than is often supposed. In politics, there are always alternative ways of realizing the same purpose.[1] And it is at least as important both to keep different doors open *and* to make use of them in societies which believe that they have a common and general purpose or 'consensus' as in societies which believe that they can contain a diversity of purposes. When policies cannot be changed without under-

1. 'Policy' has often had a bad name for being flexible; but it is more sensible to suspect, but not to reject *a priori*, doctrines for commonly being inflexible.

mining the authority of the doctrine, then the doctrine must have been formulated in terms over-specific and insufficiently generalized. This can be shown from political theory, but it would not be the task of political theory as such to show that, perhaps as well, the principles and intentions of the doctrine are thoroughly bad as well as unnecessarily rigid in the means – that could only be, if anything relative to a discipline, the task of political philosophy.

To put the final question which 'theory and practice' raises, 'should the theorist be committed?' To relevance, always: he cannot avoid it, but not to specific solutions especially by specific means. It is unlikely that he will have any special competence in matters of practice, although there is no real reason why the converse should be true. Such is an unprofitable debate: the impractical theorist in power wreaking havoc on normal politics is a pretty rare bird, balanced at least by the stubborn, blinkered empiricist who may comprehend practice by the most incredibly abstruse, but wholly implicit, almost metaphysical assumptions (for instance, 'the gold standard', 'a balanced budget', 'sovereignty', 'nationalism', 'territorial integrity', 'the rule of law', 'racial character' and 'class-consciousness'). It is more immediately clear that the political thinker, in terms of his vocation, needs the world than that the world needs the political thinker. He should beware of overrating his own influence, either for good or evil. But I think, in fact, the world does need him, although in a more indirect way than is often supposed (especially by those former believers in a 'pure science of politics' who now stumble straight from a rediscovery of the relevance of political theory into the advocacy of its being wholly a 'policy science'). The world needs him for the effect he has on the way others formulate their doctrines, policies, opinions and perceptions of what they choose to call political practicality, but neither as a formulator of policies himself nor for his own actions.

He has both to satisfy himself in terms of his craft and to prove himself publicly as explainer, generalizer, specific critic of other theories and as continual critic of the concepts used in doctrines, but not to set himself up as a direct assertor of doctrines or censor of political opinions.

Privately, personally, publicly, he may, of course, do so, moved by the same motives as everyone else (or not, as the case may be); but then pragmatically he should take care to be clear that he is being polemical lest he discredit his profession and contaminate his own craft. He might even happen to be a particularly useful advocate, planner or practical moralist, but he should always make clear that his authority as a scholar relates to a different function (as all authority, except that of God, is relevant only to specific and definable functions). For a teacher of politics to put on a great public show of commitment may be useful if he wishes, for instance, to vindicate a particular doctrine about the role of intellectuals in society or to be applauded by some of his students rather than to try to teach them all to think critically, but it is irrelevant to the true relationship between political theory and practice. For here there is a necessary and unavoidable *critical* involvement, not a policy-making involvement: the continuous interplay between what is, the many things that are possible and what ought to be. Once the playing ceases and we *all* become committed to one truth and one way of reaching it, thus to one level of talking about it, then we had better have no doubts, for we will have burned our boats preparatory to walking on the water. Theory is philosophically relevant to policy, but there is a wide and arbitrary gulf between theory and action.

'Intellect is action that takes place for humanity; and so let the man of politics be intellect', wrote Heinrich Mann in his *Zola*, 'and let the man of intellect act.' Thomas Mann made some notes in answer to this assertion of his brother's, as part of the preparation for his *Betrachtungen eines Unpolitischen*, 'No, let *not* the intellectual act. . . . The gulf between thought and deed, fiction and reality will always be wide and open . . . the intellectual's task is to have an effect, not to act.'[1] In this

1. Both these passages are quoted by Heinrich Wysling, ed., in his Introduction to Thomas Mann, Heinrich Mann, *Briefwechsel 1900-1949* (Oldenburg, S. Fischer), pp. l-li.

essay I have simply tried, firstly, to clarify the kind of effects that theory and practice can and should have on each other; and secondly, to defend true theory both against its reduction to or from action and its useless elevation into practical irrelevance.

2

Freedom as Politics[1]

Need a student of politics apologize for a tedious obsession
with the matter of freedom, particularly when so many
people, both philosophers and the man at the back of the bus,
appear to believe that freedom is keeping politics at arm's
length?

My point will be that there is a reciprocity between freedom and politics, properly understood, not an animosity.
Certainly freedom and government or freedom and order
live always in tension and often in animosity; but in so far as
any government responds to some political factors, this is then
a sign of some freedom; and those comparatively few governments who govern in a manner systematically political are
then properly called 'free governments' – which otherwise
might seem empty rhetoric and a contradiction in terms.

Indeed, I am persuaded of the value, both moral and
scientific, of an old and unfashionable way of looking at things
which would link politics and freedom together, not merely
in civil wedlock, but in permanent progenitive embrace.
Politics is the collective need to bargain, to compromise and
to conciliate between differing interests, whether conceived
as material or ideal, whose existence is accepted, at least for
a time, as natural. Freedom is the act of an individual making
choices among all such relationships and activities; it cannot

1. This was originally published by Sheffield University as delivered as
an inaugural lecture in 1966, but follows here the slightly chastened
version as it appeared in P. Laslett and W. G. Runciman, eds., *Philosophy,
Politics and Society*, Third Series (Blackwell, 1969), except that I have
restored the 'Popular Summary' which appeared as an Appendix.

35

simply be regarded, as even some liberal philosophers and many artists have thought, as freedom from politics and publicity. Put in its most abstract way, the very possibility of privacy depends upon some public action; and conversely public life is indeed all just 'telegrams and anger' if it does not accommodate private happinesses.

This is not a very fashionable point I want to make. It may sound more like rhetoric than analysis. Certainly I am more inclined to stand on my chair than to sit on it. So I must insert some argument that freedom is *both* a value and an institutional precondition for any scientific study of society. Freedom, indeed, I will seek to show, need not be either just rhetoric or analysis; for being both a concept and an institution, it has a history. If it has no end, it has a fairly clear beginning; that is why students of politics have to go back to the *polis* of Athens. If the Greeks were not the first to experience it, they were the first to give lectures about it. To say that history is the unfolding of freedom, as would Hegel and Marx, may be meaningless or at times simply false; but it is far from meaningless to say that the most important task for history and political studies, both intellectually and morally, is to write an account of the origins and conditions of freedom. The task is difficult but conceivable: Lord Acton was to be pitied for failing to complete his history of liberty, not blamed for the brave attempt.

That we in the West, where freedom grew, are sometimes simply too embarrassed to state the obvious can be seen by the clarity with which a masterly Japanese contemporary, Professor Masao Maruyama, has argued that freedom is both a fact and a value for political science (and is indeed in its origins as distinctively Western as science). 'It is unreasonable to expect any genuine social science to thrive', he says, 'where there is no undergirding of civil liberty.' He suggests that all forms of autocracy depend on the truth not being known about how they are actually governed. But equally, the other side of the coin, he says: 'The extent to which politics can become the object of free scientific inquiry is a most accurate barometer by which to measure the degree of academic freedom in a country.'[1] It is interesting that much the same answer to the same problem has recently been reached independently by someone else who has also lived under both autocracy and freedom. Professor Giovanni Sartori, in discussing Max Weber's famous demand that the social sciences should be *wertfrei*, value free,[2] points out that this is a very fine ideal which could only possibly be applied in a free society: modern totalitarianism persecutes both neutrality and objectivity and old-fashioned autocracy allows it only subject to censorship. And I think our instinct to go further is not wrong. The laboriousness of marshalling the evidence should inhibit us more than any embarrassment about the claim: that scientific advance itself is closely related to the political history of liberty (though we then need to distinguish between science and technology).

So the matter is still important. So important indeed is the concept of liberty that we are all reluctant to define it too closely, wanting to apply it to everything we value. Other people's states of freedom, after all, commonly appear as either wilful self-deception or as anarchy – however gentle. Thomas Hobbes had quite a lot to say about liberty and anarchy; even 'conscience' to him was but 'a worm within the entrails of the body Commonwealth'. And then there are some who while they do appreciate what freedom is, better than some of its democratic champions, yet reject it either as an intolerable burden, too capricious, demanding and uncertain a companion, or else despise it as an unwanted brake, hindrance or obstacle to economic betterment and intensified nationalism. Erich Fromm wrote a psychoanalytic account of the origins of Nazism entitled *The Fear of Freedom*; and numerous authors have added wine to old hash by quoting Dostoyevsky's sardonic words on those whose supreme need

1. M. Maruyama, *Thought and Behaviour in Modern Japanese Politics* (Oxford University Press, 1963), pp. 227–8 and 229.

2. G. Sartori, *Democratic Theory* (Praeger, 1965), chapter 3. See also W. G. Runciman's brilliant discussion of this problem in his *Social Science and Political Theory* (Cambridge University Press, 1963).

it is 'to surrender as quickly as possible the gift of freedom ... with which they, unfortunate creatures, were born'. Thus freedom may always be rescued from platitude by observing the refugees from it and by mixing with its opponents. Acton once wrote to Mary Gladstone *à propos* the Jesuits:

> It is this combination of an eager sense of duty, zeal for sacrifice and love of virtue, with the deadly taint of a conscience perverted by authority, that makes them so odious to touch and so curious to study.[1]

In not claiming too much, we must beware of not claiming too little. This, I think, Isaiah Berlin has done in his other-wise admirable, influential, bewitching and powerful *Two Concepts of Liberty*.[2] I want to argue with deep and genuine respect that, while he has shown a great skill in defending the nymph of Liberty from abuse, he has been unnecessarily modest in denying her exercise and is at fault in letting her languish with so little to do.

Berlin has argued, using 'liberty' and 'freedom' virtually as synonyms, that there are two fairly clear and distinct tradi-tions of the use of the word and concept: 'negative liberty', which is freedom *from* constraint; and 'positive liberty', which is freedom *to* achieve some one good thing. 'Positive liberty' men thus commonly say of 'negative liberty' men that they are being 'just negative': liberty to them must consist in fulfilling the proper object of the good life. Berlin shows that 'negative liberty' is what is often called 'the liberal view'; and he argues that attempts to go beyond that, to assign a positive object to free actions, prove philosophically paradoxical and politically autocratic.

He makes no bones about 'negative liberty' being just 'negative liberty': that it is inadequate as an account of political activity, certainly of the alleged 'ends of political activity' or of 'justice'. He quotes Bentham: 'Every law is an

---

1. *Letters to Mary Gladstone* (1st edn), p. 251, quoted by Gertrude Himmelfarb in her edition of Acton, *Essays on Freedom and Power* (Free Press of Glencoe, 1948), p. 1.
2. Berlin, *Two Concepts of Liberty* (Clarendon Press, 1958).

infraction of liberty.' Laws are plainly needed; but to be under the constraint of laws is not to be – as some positive liberty men would say – free or more free. He even quotes Bentham again, with evident approval, as saying: 'Is not liberty to do evil, liberty? Do we not say that it is necessary to take liberty from idiots and bad men, because they abuse it?'

'Positive liberty' is characterized as the valuing of freedom only as a means towards some end, identifying it with some good extrinsic object, even if just 'freedom from error'. Berlin quotes a dictum of the Jacobin Club: 'No man is free in doing evil. To prevent him is to set him free.' Here one agrees with Berlin wholeheartedly: agrees that there is such a theory of freedom and that its consequences are both linguistically self-contradictory and often morally obnoxious. Indeed, I would make so free as to slightly extend Berlin's analysis here to identify three common sub-groups of theories of positive liberty: there is a *moral* theory of positive liberty – as in the degrading confusion of either 'Oh God . . . whose service is perfect freedom' or 'the truth shall set you free'. There is a *material* or *economic* theory of positive liberty – as in Harold Laski's 'liberty is the existence of those conditions in society which enable me to become myself at my best'[1] (to which the answer is quite simply that not being unemployed etc., is not the same thing as being free). There is finally a *psychological* theory of positive liberty – as in Rousseau's argument that one must only will generally, that one must sink one's selfish self utterly in the general welfare and that he who does not see this 'must be forced to be free', for he is really denying his own chance of self-realization.

Plainly, whatever freedom is, it is not being forced. But even if not being forced, freedom surely also appears pragmatically paradoxical, at least, if of one's own free will one puts oneself in a situation in which one's freedom of choice is radically

1. But compare several such formulations in chapter 4 of his *Grammar of Politics*, Allen & Unwin (5th edn, 1948), with an explicitly negative formulation throughout his *Liberty in the Modern State* (Pelican, 1937), p. 49, for instance. Laski appeared to adopt whichever best suited his mood of the moment or 'the felt needs of the time'.

diminished. Does it really tell us anything to say that a man is free to put himself under a discipline of silence, continence and abstinence from all worldly things? Or that those Germans who mistakenly voted for Hitler were still free at the moment of voting? If freedom simply means absence of constraint, then actions that destroy the possibility of exercising freedom are free actions. In a logical sense so they are; but in the same sense, so is everything else. Here I begin to get slightly restive and to feel that the subject is unnaturally restrained by Berlin's too purely linguistic analysis (or too purely contemporary?). Isn't it, in fact, more *informative* and *explanatory* to say that such people are rejecting freedom – often very consciously – rather than exhibiting it?

Berlin argues that we should realize that we cannot always be free and that there are always some things we think so valuable that we gladly sacrifice some liberty in order to achieve them: full employment and a decent standard of living, for instance. But let us not call this sacrifice, he says, freedom. In times of emergency, let us admit, he suggests that we *are* being repressive, otherwise the distinction is lost for ever between free and necessary actions (or actions deemed to be necessary); and we then end up by saying that 'freedom consists in the recognition of necessity'[1] or some such blinding nonsense. One agrees. Basically all advocates of 'positive liberty' are, at the very best, confusing the conditions of freedom with the thing itself. 'There cannot be freedom until X and Y' is very different from 'X and Y, here they are. So you're free – damn you.'

But in avoiding one error, Berlin walks too cautiously. He virtually separates the word from any possible social or political context. Can one really just 'be careful', as distinct from being careful about and for something? Is liberty simply

1. Engels, *Anti-Dühring* (Martin Lawrence, 1934), p. 128. But there is, admittedly, a certain melodrama in his use of 'necessity' where the argument of the whole passage plainly implies 'circumstance', 'conditions' or 'limitations' – something not, as it were, 'necessarily necessary'. Some criticism is purely verbal. How rarely do people mean 'necessity' when taken contextually.

an absence of constraint? I don't find this very precise or convincing even just as a matter of verbal usage. I would call such a condition simply 'isolation' or more often 'loneliness' – put more sympathetically, 'splendid isolation' or 'the self-reliant individual' (who is not human, but an anatomical abstraction, and put sociologically, impossible). The strange gap in such defensive battles as Berlin's against the arrogance of 'positive liberty' is any systematic recognition that freedom is, firstly, a peculiar type of relationship between people and, secondly, an *activity* by people.

Berlin can only tell us in the end that we are free to do what we are not stopped from doing: freedom consists of the infinite range of opportunities to act, not in a limited range of actual actions. Things move until they are checked. This is an analogy from physics and mechanics under the influence, remote, refined but precise, of Thomas Hobbes. But why draw one's analogies from mechanics? If one presses linguistic analysis into philology, both 'freedom' and 'liberty', both the German and the Latin roots, indeed the Greek equivalents, had little to do with natural science but were primarily 'status' words – words that described certain legal and social rights. But back to this point later. What is missing in Berlin's analysis, odd though it may sound to say so, is any analysis of the link between freedom and political action – a typically liberal lack, if a socialist may say so (though a Tory could say so equally well). Freedom is being left alone from politics – is it?

He cannot indeed entirely avoid this impasse of triviality. He has to cover it, as we all do, by exhortation. And as readers of Hume will know, no one can exhort more forcefully than a prince of sceptics on a negative tack:

> The 'negative' liberty that they strive to realize seems to me a truer and more humane ideal than the goals of those who seek in the great, disciplined authoritarian structures the ideal of 'positive' self-mastery, by classes, by peoples or the whole of mankind.[1]

Now, as much as one agrees with much of this, it seems to me not very helpful to speak of 'negative liberty' as an 'ideal'

1. Berlin, *Two Concepts*, p. 56.

which people can 'strive to realize'. How can one strive to realize a state of affairs in which one is constrained as little as possible when everyone recognizes that social and moral constraints are always present and, in fact, these restraints more often form the object against which men strive in order to get them taken off themselves and put on others? Some content is needed somewhere. While it seems dangerous and paradoxical to attach freedom to particular objectives, yet it seems trivial and hopelessly incomplete to leave it purely negative.

I think certain positive things can be said. There is, for instance, fairly general agreement about the formal condition in which it is held to be justifiable to constrain people. Other things are sometimes tacked on, like 'public decency', 'good taste', libel and slander, but the essential condition is commonly held to be that even established and habitual liberties may be justifiably constrained if their exercise threatens public order – the fact of government at all. Governments govern and even in a well-nigh perfect liberal state, presumably, things will be stopped when they threaten the survival of the State. Abraham Lincoln put the matter nicely:

> It has long been a grave question whether any government not too strong for the liberties of its people, can be strong enough to maintain its liberties in great emergencies.

Disputes flourish, of course, about what constitutes an emergency: Élie Halévy once suggested that it was the distinctiveness of modern tyranny to preserve artificially a 'state of emergency' from wartime on into what could well have been peace.[1] But this formal recognition that liberty depends upon order is neither trivial nor unimpressive. When we wonder whether Weimar Germany and Republican Spain did not cut their own throats by appearing to apply a liberal American 'clear and present danger' test to restricting the liberties of enemies of republican government, rather than using the harsher (though admittedly more speculative) Roman '*princi-*

1. *L'Ere des Tyrannies* (Paris, 1938), pp. 213ff.

piis obstat', we are shifting the argument, quite properly, from 'what does one mean by liberty?' to 'what does one mean by public order?'

Friends of 'negative liberty' do in fact tend rather hopefully to say, as it were, 'Locke until Hobbes', even if they can no longer quite believe in 'Locke after Hobbes': they recognize the difficulty, but seem unwilling to stop and talk to it. If there is this positive limitation of 'public order' on even such 'negative liberty', may we not be able to put a little flesh of historical and sociological circumstance onto the otherwise rather dry linguistic bones of liberty? Berlin himself says that 'to demand more than this [negative liberty] is perhaps a deep and incurable metaphysical need'.[1]

Indeed it is. Some synthesis is needed which will avoid the extreme of tyranny latent in 'positive liberty' and the anarchy or quietism of 'negative liberty' – if we take them to be political concepts at all. I am not criticizing Berlin's distinction as far as it goes. Down with positive liberty and two cheers for negative liberty! But the distinction is a dangerously incomplete account of what freedom has been and is.

At one point he himself comes near to the view I am about to suggest. At the end of a passage in which he points out that all ideas of 'natural rights' imply absolute values – which are never, in fact, clear, enforceable or universally agreed upon, he says:

Perhaps the chief value for liberals of political – 'positive' – rights, of participating in the government, is as a means for protecting what they hold to be an ultimate value, namely individual – 'negative' – liberty.[2]

Berlin has to admit that 'negative liberty' at least needs positively asserting if it is to be political at all. He is at least close to the view that true freedom is something neither positive nor negative in his senses, but a relationship and an activity: an individual acting voluntarily in public or for a public – whether in art or politics.

Free actions, surely, are *actions* of individuals; but they

1. Berlin, *Two Concepts*, p. 57.   2. ibid., p. 50.

arise from and affect the actions of others. Free actions are unpredictable, otherwise we would say that they are determined and necessary; a free action is an action of which it cannot be said that it must have happened. All public communication and actions are subject in some degree to constraints, both necessary ones which arise from the other people and the materials involved, and contingent ones of social circumstance; but it can never be said that there are no alternative actions possible, unless the person simply chooses – in Berlin's pure negative sense – not to act and then, presumably, to hope for the best.

In Thomas Mann's short story, or parable of Fascism, *Mario and the Magician*, he portrays the 'gentleman from Rome' as initially resisting the hypnosis of the charlatan in the seaside village, but eventually he succumbs and is publically degraded. Mann's educated observer notes:

As I understood what happened, the gentleman was beaten because he took up a posture for the struggle which was too negative. It would seem that the mind cannot live by not wanting to do something. It is not sufficient in the long run not to want to do something. Indeed there is, perhaps, such an uncomfortable closeness between the ideas of not wanting to do something and of not wanting to be bothered to make any longer the effort of wanting not to do it, i.e. being prepared to do what one is told, that between the two the idea of freedom is gravely endangered.

Berlin really commits what logicians call a 'category mistake'. Freedom is not an attribute of all possible actions, it is one type of action; it is *political* action. Even Acton saw this in his famous definition – if I am correct in putting emphasis where I think it should be: 'By liberty I mean the assurance that every man shall be protected *in doing* what he believes his duty against the influence of authority and majorities, custom and opinion. . . .'[1] The Whig cart of consent is here put before the Tory horse of government, but at least they are together: participation and action are part of freedom, neither conditions nor consequences, but the thing itself.

1. Acton, *The History of Freedom and Other Essays* (London, 1907), p. 3.

Freedom, then, needs rescuing from the philosophers – or from a type of philosopher who construes usage too narrowly – and needs placing in its historical and sociological setting. The earliest words we have for freedom have little relation to words for 'absence of constraint' or 'unimpeded movement' of matter. They were social status words: one suspects that the mechanical words were in fact analogies from these – not *vice versa* as is usually supposed. After all it is a bold metaphor to say that the wheel is free, rather than the man who chooses to make it come unstuck.

The Greek *eleutheros* means free in the sense of not a slave. Someone was *eleutheros* if his status was such and if he displayed the qualities which the Greeks associated with this status: disinterestedness and generosity – also a certain outgoing forcefulness.[1] A freeman would possess *arete*, like Homer's Achilles,[2] would be 'a doer of deeds and a speaker of words' – what the Romans called *virtus*, or, in a debased and revived form, Tom Brown's 'manliness', or better what both Robespierre and Jefferson, liking it, or Dr Johnson, disliking it, meant by 'patriotism' – before that word became debased too: the active citizen moving freely from private to public in the common interest. The Latin *liber* and *liberalis* correspond almost exactly to the Greek. In time the social meanings of the Roman word grew less: from the constant contrast between the freeman and the slave and between the freeman and the barbarian (who did not know freedom), the ethical meanings came to dominate it: a man's character would become *liberalis* – as we still call people 'liberal-minded' and once called people 'liberal-handed'. The English word 'free', from the Anglo-Saxon *freora manna*, kept, in a feudal world, its social significance longer and its ethical significance appears more vague and empty, as in Chaucer's knight who had 'Trouthe and honour, freedom and courtesye'. Am I alone in fancying that the word 'freedom' even today carries a

1. See the section on 'Free' in C. S. Lewis, *Studies in Words* (Cambridge University Press, 1960).
2. See Werner Jaeger's discussion of *arete* in vol. 1 of his *Paideia* (Blackwell, 1947).

slightly more positive connotation, a status enjoyed or a status to be achieved, than does the gentler 'liberty'? At any rate, Berlin chose the word 'liberty' where I have chosen 'freedom'.

If we treat freedom, then, as a social-status word and thus susceptible to historical and sociological study, we can sensibly study the relationship between freedom and order – even though the result will be different in every circumstance. But I am naive enough to see no general philosophical difficulty. It is not enough, though it may be occasionally necessary, to polemicize against 'determinism' or 'historicism' as does Karl Popper. I take 'freedom of the will' for granted – what else can one do? The problem remains of relating freedom of the will to action and to order. Indeed I can see two types of order in which constraints are not merely justified, in the nature of the activities, but may be sensibly felt positively to enhance liberty: politics and love. I simply limit my remarks to politics.

Politics, like freedom, very like freedom, is ubiquitous in some minimal and thin sense, but in thicker and richer senses is something highly specific and by no means universal. Politics cannot exist without government any more than freedom can exist without order: freedom is always freedom within a context. Some governments harry freedom and others nurture it. Government is the general ability to make decisions between different groups which can collectively be regarded as society for most purposes. Politics as an institution is the conflict of differing interests (whether ideal or material) in an acknowledged mutual context. Politics as an activity is the conciliation of these differing interests in the public context created by a state or maintained by a government. Politics as a moral activity is the creative conciliation of these interests.

Now perhaps some politics exists everywhere – even in the court of the Grand Mogul, the Kremlin or the Brown House. And by the same token *some* freedom must then exist – though the barber, the court jester or the second gravedigger may appear far more free than even the Grand Vizier, the Chief of

Police or old Polonius. In a palace or a court they will dislike it, but will try to ignore it; but in the party headquarters of a modern one-party state they will commonly hunt it down: differences of opinion are a sign of insufficient dedication or of unpurged Jewish, bourgeois or colonialist decadence.

Politics as a *system*, however, only exists in relatively few states: those states which actually make their decisions in a political manner and encourage politics, which then becomes (the most vital distinction of all) public politics. These states, which I pedantically call 'political regimes', are commonly and misleadingly called democracies (which they all became during the First World War as casualties mounted); but *all* industrial and industrializing states are democracies, whether they allow free politics or not: they all depend on the consent of the majority, as peasant cultures never did, and most of them need the actual enthusiasm of the new class of skilled manual workers.[1] These states are perhaps better known by their more proud and ancient – and once more precise – name of 'republic'.

In such political regimes or republics, freedom varies in its scope and content, but always it exists as a positive activity.[2] As both Montesquieu and Rousseau said, quite correctly,

1. It seems to me quite unjustifiable (*vide* nearly all American political scientists) to deny the equal propriety and to miss the theoretical significance of the Napoleonic usage of 'democracy' rather than the Jeffersonian. Democracy can be an element in many different kinds of government, but no government can be democratic. See chapter 3 of my *In Defence of Politics*, and also C. B. Macpherson, *The Real World of Democracy* (Clarendon Press, 1966).

2. I do not see that this sense of 'positive' offends Berlin's logical objections to 'positive liberty'. He objects to identifying liberty with any one goal or good; my objection is to identifying it with one particular goal or good. Freedom as human activity must always be attached to some object; what is objectionable is when it is held that there is only one true object for everyone. Freedom is choice-amid-clash of alternatives, not the absence of conviction. And it is a different matter, even, for individuals to hold 'positive liberty' views in our shared objectionable sense, than for the state power. The threat they then represent will be relative both to their influence and to the character of the ideal. Some of Professor Sir Karl Popper's objections, for instance, to 'essentialism' (the great killer) are fairly silly when one considers the character of most such folk and the

47

the stability of republics depends on the virtue of their citizens.

This was once seen more plainly than now, before the rhetoric of 'democracy' obscured the precise and limited sense of the word 'politics' which I find so useful; and before there began a kind of liberal panic at modern power which, fortified by literary aestheticism, turned freedom from participation in communal affairs into a conscious attempt to be left alone – which one never is. Just one example: Chief Justice Fortescue could write sometime in the 1470s in his *De Laudibus Legum Angliae*:

A king of England cannot at his pleasure make any alterations in the laws of the land, for the nature of his government is not only regal, but political. Had it been merely regal, he would have a power to make what alterations and innovations he pleased in the laws of the kingdom, impose tallages and other hardships upon the people whether they would or no, without their consent, which sort of government the civil laws point out, when they declare 'Quod principii placuit legis habet vigorem'. But it is much otherwise with a king whose government is political, because he can neither make any alteration or change in the laws of the realm without the consent of the subjects, nor burden them against their wills with strange impositions, so that a people governed by such laws as are made by their own consent and approbation enjoy their properties securely, and without the hazard of being deprived of them, either by the king or any other.[1]

We may know that in such a passage the signification of 'a people' and 'subjects' who give their consent is narrower, very much narrower, than the words might suggest. But this does not alter the fact that, however small the aristocracy or elite concerned, the relationship was political, and that in so far as there was politics there was an experience of freedom – even

---

context in which they act and react. Both Berlin and Popper seem to me profoundly unhistorical and unsociological in their imagery of, as it were, 'what would happen if things were taken to their logical conclusion'. When things were, it was not because of a mistake in logic.

1. Quoted by T. F. T. Plucknett in his eleventh edition of *Taswell-Langmead's English Constitutional History* (Sweet & Maxwell, 1960), p. 218.

if only within a governing class. That by itself is something. In history we must talk, like Edmund Burke, of 'liberties' rather than of liberty. Historically, indeed, liberty as we know it arose within aristocracies or the merchant oligarchies of the medieval free cities. It was practised in Parliament long before it was widely sought after or tolerated in the country. When men came to talk of a proletariat they were talking of a community shaped by oppression and dedicated to achieving justice by means of intense discipline and solidarity; individual freedom has seldom been even a working-class value, let alone something consciously proletarian. But this need only embarrass that kind of conservative who confuses the value of things with their origins. As a socialist, I can quite happily say that freedom was in England – and in most other countries – an aristocratic invention, but that it can, should and must be made popular.

Hannah Arendt has written, with only slight exaggeration, that 'the *raison d'être* of politics is freedom and ... this freedom is primarily experienced in action'.[1] As she herself comments, any attempt to derive freedom from the political must sound strange and startling because of two peculiarly modern fallacies. The first derives from the complete separation in many people's minds between the concepts of private and public – so that the very point of freedom is often thought to be an escape from the public realm (as if even lyric poetry did not need to be heard); the second arises because from at least the time of Rousseau we have thought that freedom is an activity of the will and of thought rather than of action. Sartre is one of the few moderns, besides Hannah Arendt and Simone Weil, who has seen this distinction clearly. In a review of François Mauriac's *La Fin de la nuit* he wrote:

We must understand that for M. Mauriac, freedom cannot construct. A man, using his freedom, cannot create himself or forge his own history. Free will is merely a discontinuous force

1. In her essay 'What is Freedom?' in *Between Past and Future* (Faber, 1961), p. 151 – to which I am in debt. Exaggeration, for surely politics is the institutionalizing of freedom, possibly its justification, not literally a *raison d'être*.

which allows for brief escapes, but which produces nothing, except a few short-lived events.[1]

Or as he said in his essay on Descartes, the 'experience of autonomy does not coincide with that of productivity'. Put in plainer terms, to mark the end of my criticism of Berlin, freedom is doing something with it, not just sitting pretty on it. Put in more complex terms, to show the importance of insisting that freedom is an activity, I would quote Arendt again:

> Political institutions . . . depend for continued existence upon acting men; their conservation is achieved by the same means as brought them into being. Independent existence marks the work of art as a product of making [she means, once made it is always there]; utter dependence on further acts to keep it in existence marks the State as a product of action.[2]

Where there is politics there is freedom. There is some freedom, even if limited to contesting aristocratic clans, wherever government recognizes by institutional means the need to consult with conflicting interests – whether (as I have argued elsewhere) through prudence (being unable to predict the outcome of coercion) or through principle (when, in some sense, the moral equality of individuals is part of the culture – whether in the manner of Jesus Christ or of Immanuel Kant).

'Freedom' can hardly be treated as a condition for a political system because, in a minimal sense, it is almost a pleonasm for politics; and because, in more elaborate senses, it is a derivative of an already existing political system or culture. A political system is a free system – though the order is thus: freedom depends on politics as politics depends on government.

It is notorious that political regimes will often consciously run risks with their very stability rather than curtail particular freedoms. Only anti-political regimes are for ever preparing the individual to sacrifice his freedom of action for the collectivity, or try to persuade him that freedom is not choos-

1. J.-P. Sartre, *Literary and Philosophical Essays* (Rider, 1955), p. 17.
2. Arendt, *Between Past and Future*, p. 153.

ing between *and* making possible alternatives, but is the euphoria or transfiguration that comes from making the right choice in good company.

Some freedom in a negative sense may exist in the autocracies, between the gaps of the laws, the indifference of the ruler, and the inefficiency or corruption of the bureaucracy. But in totalitarian and ideological societies not merely are fields of free activity hunted down, even in spheres irrelevant to the mechanisms of control of traditional autocracies, like art and music, but free actions are, as part of the ideology, deemed to be impossible. Everything, in theory, is sociologically determined – whether by economic or by racial factors, the only real competitors in this league. But political societies neither enshrine such fabulous theories, nor do they even imagine the need to claim that all human actions should submit to the test of public policy.

Freedom depends on some distinction and *interplay* between private and public actions, for it is neither isolation from politics (as the liberal often wants to believe), nor is it loneliness (as following the concept of being an 'intellectual' has often involved). Freedom and privacy both thrive when government is conducted publicly in the manner called political. Freedom, then, is neither isolation nor loneliness: it is the activity of private men who help to maintain, even if not personally participating in, public politics. Privacy is itself a social relationship. Men who cease either to identify or to value politics usually lose and at the best weaken freedom. Politics is the public actions of free men; free men are those who do, not merely can, live both publicly and privately. Men who have lost the capacity for public action, who fear it or despise it, are not free, they are simply isolated and ineffectual. As Aristotle said, the man who seeks to dwell outside the *polis*, or the political relationship, is either a beast or a god.

'Political freedom' – as we may now call it, to distinguish it firmly from 'negative liberty' – is simply the habit and possibility of men as citizens acting freely. An absolutely unique and a reasonably private man says or does something unpredictable and uncommanded in public – or for a public – which has some effect, however slight, on others: that is a free action – whether in art or politics. Freedom depends upon people continuing to act freely in actual public affairs, and in being willing to run risks by speaking bluntly in public, not in constantly taking one's own temperature, according to some abstract standard laid down by god, don or judge, or according to the foundation myths of one's country, to see if one is still left free or not. Eventually the answer will then be – not. Freedom does not consist in being able to choose between pushpin and poetry, but in actually choosing. Although both choices are possible, neither is necessary or entailed.

By such purely negative conceptions of freedom, such people then discover, not surprisingly, that they are cut off utterly from society, are 'alienated', and then 'the whole system', nothing less will do, is blamed. This whole system must then be changed and freedom becomes the concrete service of some one single abstract idea. It is both sad and instructive to see how readily 'great individualists' fall victim to systems of thought and allegiance in which *nothing but* public values and social purposes are allowed. Such exciting extremes of unnecessary despair and unguarded hope come from a failure to accept freedom for what it is: a creative relationship between the private and the public, the assertion of both as complementary, not rival.

There is *fortuna* as well as *necessitá* in politics – as the greatest of all republican apologists, Machiavelli, reminds us. We have been simply fortunate in England that the habit of acting freely in public affairs came so early, so that tolerance of the free actions of others became accepted as a condition of one's own. Tolerance is always relative, of course, but so it must be; for there are always some things, quite simply, which we should not tolerate.[1] We should not tolerate, for instance, threats to toleration: we should not allow freedom to destroy freedom. And nor should we tolerate tyrants: tyrannicide is

1. As recently argued with great brilliance in Robert Paul Woolf, Barrington Moore and Herbert Marcuse, *A Critique of Pure Tolerance* (Beacon Press, 1969).

praiseworthy and is an essential part of the tradition of political thought.[1]

I find these questions easy in principle – not worth an examination question even; the difficulties are entirely practical. Yet toleration was far stronger when it was accepted as one of the facts of political life than when it was finally and pompously espoused by the Victorians as a matter of principle – so as to remove it from the low company of compromising politicians. For tolerance became important and secure in England not because most men just believed, out of indifference or out of the exhaustion of ecclesiastical animosities, that many different things were not worth the discomforts and risks of public life, but because many of them believed that many different things were worth the risk. Tolerance arose from the clash of moralities, not from their absence. The means of conflict became more civilized, literally politicized, but the causes did not vanish. We tolerate opinions because opinions do matter: if not, it would be simpler not to tolerate them (the manner in which most governments of most countries do, in fact, act). Tolerance comes not through caring for nothing, but through caring for many things – just as freedom comes from *acting* freely, not from just being left alone or having some narrow 'everything' done for one.

Freedom and toleration supplement each other in one very important respect: they make it easier both to find out and to tell truths about human behaviour. Freedom implies, as in the scientist's use of hypothesis, creative speculation on goals and an exploration of alternatives. Tolerance implies, as in Coleridge's 'willing suspension of disbelief' for the literary critic, greater understanding. Valéry's maxim seems to me as good for the practice of politics as for scholarship: 'The first task of anyone who would refute an opinion is to master it a little more surely than its ablest defenders.' Now it is an evident peculiarity of 'political regimes' or republics that they

1. See Irene Coltman, *Private Men and Public Causes* (Faber, 1962). And Hobbes warned against reading the 'books of policy' of the Greeks and the Romans: 'From the reading, I say, of such books men have undertaken to kill their kings.'

are the only type of government whose system of authority is not destroyed by allowing significant truths to be discovered and told about who actually rules and how. All governments try to hide things, both for lazy convenience and for *raison d'état*. But general censorship is only a necessary device in autocracies; political regimes can cheerfully admit that things are done as they are done, and for political reasons.

If consultation and compromise are to be effective, if it is possible at all to govern politically amid freedom, then it is necessary for a government to find out reasonably accurately what various interests want or are likely to put up with, and what is their relative strength. There must then be found people representative of these groups who are free to speak the truth. Representative institutions are fundamentally a matter of communication and not of rights. Aristotle remarked on how difficult it is for a tyrant to find people who will tell him the truth about what is going on. If this is to be done – and it surely contributes to the stability of any government – then the penalties of mistaken or unwelcome advice must not be too drastic. Particularly in complex matters of modern economic planning, it is helpful to any government for there to be some spheres of independent thought and action. The weakest of all justifications of autocracy in some developing countries, for instance, is that economic shortages (including those of manpower) do not allow the 'luxury of public debate' on economic policy. One wonders how they can afford not to, since the consequences of mistakes must be so much more drastic. Of course, they do get independent advice – but in the only possible way that does not extend internal liberties and knowledge: from outside experts. This is related to an ancient device of autocracy, the recruitment of key advisors from abroad who are given a life of isolated luxury in the palace compound or the Grand Hotel.

The plea of 'necessity' is, indeed, the great enemy of freedom and of knowledge. Professor Ernest Gellner has recently suggested that there are in fact only two conditions needed in our times for a social order to make valid and rightful claims on members of the society – that: '(1) It is bringing about, or successfully maintaining, an industrially affluent society. (2) Those in authority are co-cultural with the rest of the society' (he is referring to nationalism).[1] This is a commendably short way, at least, to treat the problems of political obligation and justice. 'The question of how to retain or acquire liberty', he says, is only meaningful after 'the hump' of wealth is passed.[2] One ventures to suggest that in societies which do have such a simple view of government, the recognition of 'over the hump' will always be delayed. It is a view of government which arises naturally from, but which then can fatten unnecessarily upon, emergency. As Machiavelli argued, this is a view appropriate to state-founding or state-saving (in an emergency), but one not likely to preserve a state through time. In order to create or save a state, he implies in *The Prince*, 'concentrate power'; in order to preserve a state through time, 'spread it' (*The Discourses*). If Gellner's categories of industrial affluence and nationalism were indeed crystal clear, then freedom and politics might in practice be willingly squeezed out. But the ambiguities of these categories will lead to dispute, over means if not of ends; and it may again be dramatically discovered that some degree of freedom is a functional necessity for economic and social advance. To my mind this has nothing to do with capitalism or free enterprise; state planning will inevitably arise in circumstances of war and emergency, of acute shortages or of acute aspirations. But effective planning must depend on the most public and honest gathering of information, discussions of how to evaluate it, criticism of plans and preparation of those likely to be affected by them. Planning is in no sense the necessary enemy of freedom; in many practical circumstances, it is a necessary precondition for its exercise.

That conscious control of an environment increases, not diminishes, the range of choices to be made was the theme of Malinowski's posthumous book, *Freedom and Civilization* (1947) – overshadowed by Popper's *Open Society and Its*

1. E. Gellner, *Thought and Change* (Weidenfeld & Nicolson, 1964), p. 33.
2. ibid., p. 38.

Enemies but, I think, a greater work. He argued that freedom was to be seen as a cultural phenomenon before ever philosophers tried to say that this or that was private or public. Certain cultures had been able to make deliberate choices of what purpose to achieve, or what policies to adopt. These had in fact been the successful cultures, both economically and intellectually. Freedom was the capacity for adaptation, and so a clue to survival as well as to increased knowledge. So Malinowski, in terms less ponderous than Arendt, argued that freedom was not to be identified with any particular object, but with a type of process or activity which was self-critical, self-perpetuating and inventive, concerned with both means and ends. Since it is seldom read – and embarrasses most anthropologists for having gone somewhat beyond the evidences of field-work – let me quote two passages at some length:

Those who attempt any definition of freedom in terms of negative categories are chasing an intellectual will-o'-the-wisp. Real freedom is neither absolute nor omnipresent and it certainly is not negative. It is always an increase in control, in efficiency, and in the power to dominate one's own organism and the environment, as well as artifacts and the supply of natural resources. Hence freedom as a quality of human action, freedom as increase of efficiency and control, means the breaking down of certain obstacles and a compensation for certain deficiencies; it also implies the acceptance of rules of nature, that is scientific laws of knowledge, and of those norms and laws of human behaviour which are indispensable to efficient cooperation.[1]

He concludes a chapter on 'The Semantics of Freedom'

. . . our conception of freedom is positive and objective; it is essentially pragmatic, and implies a social and technical context. It implies always the benefit from action and responsibility by individuals and groups alike. The instrumentalities of freedom we find in the political constitution of a community, its laws, its moral norms, the distribution of its wealth, and the access to such benefits as health, recreation, justice and religious or artistic gifts of culture. To scour the universe for possibilities of freedom other

1. B. Malinowski, *Freedom and Civilization* (Allen & Unwin, 1947), p. 59.

than those given by the organization of human groups for the carrying out of specific purposes, and the production of desirable results, is an idle philosophic pastime.[1]

All this has been very abstract. I have said little or nothing about the actual history of freedom, about its conditions in the modern world, nor about its relation to politics in Britain at the moment. All these things need to be done and, in bits and pieces of gold, silver and lead, are being done. But important and laborious enterprises usually go wrong at the beginning, not at the end. If one asks the wrong question, one will never get an answer. Thus 'negative liberty' is the wrong end of the right stick; it only defines what we seek to avoid harming in others while we act more positively ourselves. Without action, there is no liberty of any kind. Even Lincoln was too negative in saying that 'the price of liberty is eternal vigilance'. Better to have said that liberty is eternal vigilance – if by vigilance is implied 'observer-participation'.

I have really returned to a view of 'freedom as citizenship' which was current in the late seventeenth century and throughout the eighteenth, but which hardly survived the mid-nineteenth century. It was swallowed either by worship of the state – as in nationalism – or by alienation from the state and a belief, among many liberals, that all power is inherently evil.[2] This viewpoint did not centre so much on individual rights against the state, but on those conditions which were necessary to operate successfully the kind of state characterized as republican. The viewpoint was often called 'Roman', or writers spoke of 'the liberties of the ancients' (as in the title of Benjamin Constant's famous essay).[3] But its genius was Machiavelli in his *Discourses*, where republican power is shown to be stronger and more stable and lasting than that of a *Principate* – given citizens who have not lost their *virtu*: the qualities of endeavour, involvement and

1. ibid., p. 95.
2. See Preston King, *Fear of Power* (Frank Cass, 1967).
3. 'The Liberty of the Ancients Compared to that of the Moderns'; see the discussion of this in Bertrand de Jouvenel, ed., *Futuribles* (Droz, Geneva, 1963), pp. 99–102.

audacity which hold states together – 'the native hue of resolution'.[1]

A recent author writing on Tocqueville, while using Berlin's categories of 'positive' and 'negative' liberty, points out that Tocqueville is not easy to understand in these terms: for there is an element of both positive and negative liberty in him, of social responsibility and of personal freedom. 'Both require, in his eyes,' writes Mr Lively, 'the defence of politics against socially determined activity.' Tocqueville, he concludes, posed the 'essentially classical' idea of the free man as an active participant in communal affairs.[2]

Tocqueville was important not so much because he was the sayer of wise and quotable saws, but because he was among the first to appreciate the distinction between cause and condition in the writing of history. History does not determine the outcome of events, it narrows the range of alternatives. History presents us with alternatives: we are not just 'free to choose', we are not truly free unless we do choose. Freedom is thus moral freedom: it involves choosing and acting in such a way that the area of free choices for others is not impaired – which it always will be if we do not act at all.

1. Oddly Berlin comes close to this view, but then shies away. He refers (op. cit., p. 45) to: '. . . what Mill called "pagan self-assertion". . . . Indeed, much of what he says about his own reasons for desiring liberty – the value he puts on boldness and non-conformity, on the assertion of the individual's own values in the face of the prevailing opinion, on strong and self-reliant personalities free from the leading strings of the official law-givers and instructors of society – has little enough to do with his conception of freedom as non-interference, but a great deal with the desire of men not to have their personalities set at too low a value, assumed to be incapable of autonomous, original, "authentic" behaviour. . . .'

Now I am not saying that Mill was ever wholly consistent, but 'little enough to do with' indeed! Mill plainly meant what he said: such behaviour was freedom. 'Non-interference' is a necessary but not a sufficient condition for what Mill meant by freedom. 'Pagan self-assertion' was equally important. (Here is my whole difference with Berlin – perhaps in some circumstances a slight one: between being able to choose and actually choosing.)

2. J. Lively, *The Social and Political Thought of Alexis de Tocqueville* (Oxford University Press, 1962).

Men may not always act that way, but Tocqueville is saying that if they choose to recognize each other as men, then, very simply, they should.

There are no protective devices which can be minutely and precisely copied from one country to another; but to Tocqueville the American example (for him it was only an example) was sufficient to show that a conscious and rational allegiance to some laws and customs could restrain even the majority against itself. No laws work without the will; but good will is useless if it does not become an institution. So to Tocqueville it was plain that understanding and action must go hand in hand. The individual is only truly an individual when acting a part with other men. The central state is strong when its roots are local and when allegiance is conditional. American Federalism was not the antithesis of power; it was potentially among the strongest forms of power. Freedom is not the antithesis of authority; it is the only form of authority – except, again, love – which can be accepted without force or deception. All this was once embraced in the classical concept of 'republican liberties'.

I am happy to take such a classical – even pagan – stand on the matter of freedom. Progress is not always in the same direction in everything. We need to recover this lost relationship between common citizenship and freedom. More precisely, we need to extend it to the people before other forces in our society succeed in treating them entirely as masses. But to characterize the view as 'classical' is perhaps better to identify its origins than to characterize its present mode – which is, quite simply, social, or even socialist. It is socialist at least in the sense that it is both an inadequate account of freedom to think of it as being left alone, as the liberal implies, or as simply preserving the fruits of experience, as the conservative implies, for it does involve the constant need to do new things in a premeditated manner – the adaptation of man to circumstance and environment in such a way that his capacity for future adaptation is not impaired.

Schiller wrote in his *Aesthetic Letters*: '. . . a political administration will always be imperfect when it is able to bring about unity only by suppressing variety. The state ought to respect not only the objective and the generic, but also the subjective and specific in individuals.'

But, in the end, nothing can be done if people do not wish to help in doing it themselves; the conditions can be provided, but it takes individual human action, since man is free, to bring about a result. Beaumarchais, good bourgeois though he was, still saw the dark side of this when he wrote in his *Notes and Reflections*:

> Slaves are as guilty as tyrants. It is hard to say if freedom can more justly reproach those who attack her than those who do not defend her.

We live in a world in which so many not merely fail to defend freedom out of ignorance, indifference, laziness or cowardice, but can either scorn her, from the loftiest of mistaken motives, or else underestimate her by usage too narrow and pedantic.

Appendix

'FREEDOM AS POLITICS': POPULAR SUMMARY

Pick a big one when, with academic sagacity,
One attacks to hide one's own inadequacy;
So, like Peachum to Lockitt, I abuse another
Who is my craft-master and elder brother,
No less than Professor Sir Isaiah Berlin
Picked not for any irredeemable sin
But for being, like a Liberal in love,
Reluctant to go far enough,
Sensing an impropriety in every call
On freedom made by rough political.
I pick no quarrel, just a bone over tea
With one of the *Two Concepts of Liberty*.[1]
In his inaugural lecture, Sir Isaiah,
Oxford but modest, said that he'd require
Positive and negative liberty well kept apart;

1. Published at 5s. od. by the Oxford University Press, at their more fancy Clarendon address.

If we must choose: the virgin, not the tart.
Positive is wanting some one thing so bad
That it drives German and Russian sages mad;
This view of things has come to such a pass
That zealot sees his leader in the looking glass,
And if I look in and still see reflected stubborn me
Then I must be freed from error, forced to be free.
Freedom as choosing rightly opens the college door
To everybody else's nineteen-eighty-four.
Negative at least preserves me as myself
Sitting down Don-like to a well-stocked shelf,
Choosing wines, teas and coffees not quite at random
But knowing *de gustibus non est disputandum*.
Now this is all quite so and very very well,
It saves me thinking heaven hell
But leaves me with no clear end in view
When restless Liberty demands 'What's there to do?'
Makes walking *Frau Welt* and *Femme Libre* home
Almost an object on its own.
Berlin treads so judicious, nicely and precise
That he trips up, old lady-like on ice;
Liberty is surely not just taking care
But taking care at least to get somewhere.
Sartre and Hannah Arendt complexly say
That freedom is living through the day
And acting out in public view
Some play purporting to be new;
Is shaping, through some mutual pact,
Some hand-made thing which once we lacked.
Freedom is not just avoidance of the State,
Like some computorized blind date,
Nor just an angry affirmation of 'my will',
It's more like doing something meant to fill
The social gap between the loneliness of I
And groups of demonstrators in full cry;
Something between lying naked in my sheets
And donning uniform to dominate the streets.
Freedom is painting it, but not quite knowing what
Will follow from each original job-lot;
But it is painting it, not just thinking around
Projects which never quite get off the ground.

Freedom is how she always mistreats me,
But neither enduring masochistically
Nor is it just how I can kick her back,
But simply how we interact.
Berlin has little answer for the rude
Who call our freedom just 'a breakfast food' –
And so it is, but Dr Bircher-Benner's Swiss Müesli
Which can sustain most needs of life quite nicely.
But don't measure politics by the aesthete,
I've no complaint at politicians cooking good red meat,
Just let's protect ourselves from those who want it raw
And fed our heart's blood, clamour then for more.

*

Freedom was Cicero and Pericles,
Not T. D. Weldon on his knees
Picking hairs off Oxford fleas.

Freedom was Lincoln, Lilburne and William Tell,
Not Goethe's doubting gentleman from hell
With the Don-like negative soft sell.

The modern sceptic's version of the Fall
Does not involve a tempter's stirring call
But simply not doing anything at all.

So ends my anti-Berlin for this day
In which – ungrateful wretch – I roundly say
That half truths are just a kind of play.

Does cricket mean we always field?
And get the buttoned foil to wield
Till left like Peer Gynt's onion peeled?

Life is real and life is free
To choose and make creatively,
Is wakeful coffee and not sleeping tea.

Life is you and life is me
Conceiving the community
Interindependently.

3

Toleration and Tolerance in Theory and Practice[1]

I would define tolerance as the degree to which we accept things of which we disapprove. Such a definition is only to define roughly, for the moment, what we are talking about, it does not settle any argument and it will require elaboration before it can be shown, as I hope to, that it is an important subject for historical and social research, hitherto neglected or often treated most superficially, that is either shallowly or purely on the level of ideas. 'Tolerance' I will use as a specific term – we are tolerant of this and that. 'Toleration' I will use for explicit theories or doctrines which state that we should be tolerant (or as tolerant as possible) of wide classes of actions or types of belief and behaviour. All societies accept to some degree, however small, some things of which government, public opinion or tradition disapprove. Many of these latter are trivial, both in contemporary and subsequent perspectives; but there are plainly many cases of significant and important degrees of tolerance existing in societies long before theories or doctrines of toleration emerge – which fundamentally are no older than the sixteenth century and do not become commonplace until the eighteenth. Indeed, in many ways, as I will argue later, degrees of tolerance in autocracies are more interesting to study (and have been less studied) than intolerance in political-democracies, or whatever term one chooses to use for modern polity. To say that tolerance is the degree to which we accept things of which we disapprove

1. From a symposium on toleration in *Government and Opposition*, Spring 1971. Dr. Preston King and I both wrote independently long essays which were then criticized by others.

is not, either, to imply any simple relationship between degrees of disapproval and degrees of acceptance. The very strength of one's prejudice, for instance, may in some contexts strengthen one's tolerance, or in other contexts a mild disapproval can lead to drastic proscriptions.

Tolerance is a value as well as a condition. Like Isaiah Berlin's analysis of liberty, it is a value to be held among other values – such as justice, and liberty itself, but also order and truth; it can never always be right to be tolerant, there are occasions on which we should be intolerant; and the sense in which it might, on one view of politics and morality, be an overriding value is one that must be hedged by qualifications. I agree with Dr King that these qualifications are to be found in any possible definition of the concept itself that would prove fruitful in studying historical or contemporary social problems. It is easiest, once the mental effort is made, to see tolerance as one possible negation of intolerance, as he argues, rather than a positive thing in itself. But the difficulty must be faced. I prefer simply to stress that both toleration and tolerance are always limited, must always be seen contextually, both logically and historically, rather than to begin by examining 'intolerance' which is as wide as all human history.

To be tolerant is always to be tolerant within limits; and if we do *not* disagree with certain ideas or types of behaviour, the question of toleration does not arise; to be permissive is often to be indifferent, not tolerant, sometimes indeed to be irresponsible and unjust. One can easily be too tolerant. In many cases toleration need not imply the absence of prejudice, but only its containment and limitation. What are these limitations? This we can only say for some particular social and cultural context; but it is meaningful to say that in general toleration implies limitations: in being tolerant, we are not to be pushed too far, although how far is a matter of time and place not of logic.

I would identify four common usages of 'toleration' and 'tolerance', all of which will be involved in any studies of the origins and conditions of toleration in any of its forms.

Firstly, those negative meanings which derive from the Latin roots – *tolerabilis*, that which may be borne, what one can bear or endure; and from *tolerare*, capable of being borne or endured, sufferable, or allowable. Thus when we used to say that he, she or the body politic 'cannot tolerate much more of that' or was 'in tolerable good health'; or when we say that 'he is very tolerant with little children' (which certainly implies that they make him suffer), or when we say that it was 'a tolerable meal' (which plainly means that we could sensibly expect better), there is a clear sense of toleration which seeks to define how far short of some standard we are prepared to fall, or how much we will put up with a condition which we could, in principle (even if very unlikely in practice), remedy. 'How long', cried Milton, 'must we tolerate the persecution of the saints?' But this, of course, from another sort of saint's point of view, could readily become intolerance. And, in any case, I do not really think that Milton seriously expected the New Model Army to start marching to the relief of those beleaguered Swiss cantons.

I doubt if this sense will prove very fruitful for investigation. It is too general. We have to put up with so much. Certainly it appears meaningless either to tolerate or not to tolerate things that are completely beyond our control. Hamlet, after all, had enough practical difficulties on his hands without having to complain quite so neurotically about everything – life and the universe, etc. Except that, as I will show, so far as to tolerate is *not* to accept fully (if we accept, we accept), we are always putting up with something. But, even so, there are those who make a philosophy or a habit of trying to accept everything – some Christian, Hindu and Confucian mystics as well as the gentle Flower People (are they still with us?), just as others rage against the sorry scheme of things entire. The famous woman whom Carlyle so massively rebuked did, after all, have a perfectly clear alternative to accepting the universe – just as Cicero, as Hannah Arendt grimly reminds us in her *Eichmann in Jeru-*

salem, urged the *duty* of suicide or hopeless resistance upon free people irredeemably enslaved. This goes too far for most mere mortals to demand of others; in such cases I would be tolerant even of passivity. But then the argument shifts from the moral plane to the empirical and historical one of how far are things subject to control, how far were things hopeless? The hopeless gesture in one decade may help to fan the flames of liberty etc., in the next. Certainly there is a sense in which we should all be sensibly tolerant of the need to put up with so much that is either wrong or could be better; there is a kind of economy of effort involved in leading a good life, just as in logic and scientific method: one can neither accept everything nor reject everything. Those who reject everything cannot possibly be tolerant, so toleration is in this simple and abstract sense a fundamental value. But those who accept everything are denying that there is any evil, imperfection or even otherness to be tolerant about.

This sense is then primary, but more down-to-earth senses will be more fruitful.

What can be done within the limits of not overthrowing authority?

The OED gives as one meaning: 'to allow to exist or be done or practised without authoritative intervention or molestation'. This *second* cluster of meanings is not what the object of external actions can endure (as in the first sense above), but what authority will allow. 'England . . .', said Froude, 'was in no humour to tolerate treason.' Or Wordsworth's sententious: '. . . by discipline of time made wise we learn to tolerate the infirmities and faults of others' – which is jolly good of us too. There is an unmistakable note of self-possession, at the best, or condescension, quite as often involved in toleration. This we had better not hide: 'I am more tolerant than thou, brother' can easily become 'holier than thou', and tolerance always implies 'more powerful than thou'. Tolerance is forbearance, the deliberate withholding of power that could be used otherwise.

66

George Eliot gives a splendid example of the condescension sometimes involved in toleration in the dialogue between the two sisters, Dorothea and Celia, in *Middlemarch*. The one is very devout, the other equally proper, but would be a little bit worldly if only she could and knew how. Going through their dead Mama's jewel box the younger is surprised that the elder will let her have, seeing her evident eagerness for it, a wonderfully ornate crucifix.

'O Dodo, you must keep the cross yourself...it would suit you – in your black dress, now,' said Celia, insistingly. 'You *might* wear that.' 'Not for the world, not for the world. A cross is the last thing I would wear as a trinket.' Dorothea shuddered slightly. 'Then you will think it wicked of me to wear it', said Celia uneasily.

'No, dear, no,' said Dorothea, stroking her sister's cheek. 'Souls have complexions too: what will suit one will not suit another... they are all yours, dear. We need discuss them no longer. There – take away your property.' Celia felt a little hurt. There was a strong assumption of superiority in this Puritanic toleration, hardly less trying to the blond flesh of an unenthusiastic sister than a Puritanic persecution.

There is no need to deny that this sense is a valid sense, and perhaps in accepting it as a valid sense, we accept a kind of therapeutic warning against too readily trying to see toleration as a general principle of conduct. Beyond condescension, even, tolerance can carry a positive contempt: the shrewd tyrant's 'Let the mob howl – it will make them feel better', or Edmund Burke's milder 'Let little dogs bark'. Now these cases of the limits to which autocrats, particularly, can tolerate opposition or dissent are of particular interest in any historical or sociological appraisal of toleration. But while still at the moral and definitional end of the stick, there is need to appreciate that the mob or the little dogs will not accept this kind of toleration any longer than they have to; one had better be right in one's facts that they cannot do any real harm, however distasteful their opinions or behaviour. One thinks of Rudi Dutschke warning his followers in Berlin against 'the blanket of toleration', or of Marcuse's 'oppressive toleration' – much the same charge that Maurice Cowling, from a different political position than Marcuse, has hurled at John Stuart Mill himself. I can just about see how 'some of us' in the universities, for instance, tolerant and liberal reformers, appear to 'some of them', intolerant apostles of freedom: 'We will tolerate every type of opinion and behaviour so long as they have no effect on anyone.' 'Let's all have a good debate, that's what democracy is about, kids; but don't get too heated – we all really agree about fundamentals.' Again, it is not necessary to go this far. We do not give strong and strange ideas the respect they deserve if we let tolerance slide into indifference so that no disapproval, even, is expressed: then people are rightly angry at not being taken seriously. As W. G. Runciman has pointed out, it is imperative to respect all men equally, but not to praise them equally. There is always some 'condescension', some differences of authority.

Authorities that do not defend themselves in the proper exercise of their accepted functions are not acting with any special tolerance or liberality, only with a particular kind of folly or cowardice. States should be as tolerant as possible; but it is not possible to be universally tolerant. We say, for instance, that the state should not be tolerant of violence exercised by any other hands but its own. Certainly it is meaningless to argue that a state should ever be so tolerant or even law-abiding, for that matter, that it should step down to armed rebels or vast demonstrative threats; but it is a highly relative matter how much internal violence a state can in fact tolerate. Some of our extreme attitudes at the moment to demonstrators and student extremists may probably be conditioned by our very low attitudinal tolerance of public disorder compared, say, to that of any English or European government in any eighteenth-century capital city. But we have scarcely begun to ask the empirical and historical questions about how tolerant can governments be. In what circumstances do they come to believe that it is possible to be more tolerant than in some immediate precedent, and in relation to what kind of disorders, threats or strong disapprovals?

Ultimately objections to toleration as being an exercise of power involve one (as we will see) in objections against authority as such, not simply against the bad rather than the good exercise of power and authority: the path from Robert Paul Wolff, Barrington Moore and Herbert Marcuse's *A Critique of Pure Tolerance*, 1965, to Wolff's *In Defence of Anarchism*, 1970. Wise restraints of power, particularly in face of verbal or written threats, even a politic refusal to be provoked by minor disturbances, can often seem to the object of them an intolerable condescension. So it may be, but if he cannot like it (which is always asking too much), he had better lump it. Agreement is impossible, by definition, in divided societies: acceptance is all that is needed. Tom Paine saw the danger long before Marcuse and Wolff:

> The French constitution has abolished or renounced *Toleration*, and *Intolerance* also, and has established UNIVERSAL RIGHT OF CONSCIENCE.
>
> Toleration is not the *opposite* of intolerance, but is the counterfeit of it. Both are despotisms. The one assumes to itself the right of withholding Liberty or Conscience and the other of granting it. The one is the pope armed with fire and faggot, and the other is the pope selling or granting indulgences.[1]

Paine was, as often, brilliantly and originally half right. Toleration is not the opposite of intolerance. Indifference is the opposite of toleration and love or full acceptance is the opposite of intolerance. But he was also half wrong. Toleration goes wider than religion, and even with religion Paine would indeed be a rationalistic fool if he thought that the language of a constitution could remove strong social disapproval and related actions between one type of believer and another. The state might still have to *enforce* tolerance in society, in a sense in which it could not possibly hope to enforce, but only to encourage, 'universal right of conscience' and 'liberty'. The only alternative to recognizing the fact of toleration is then to attempt to enforce or indoctrinate one true and official view of 'conscience' and 'liberty'. While

1. T. Paine, *Rights of Man*, Penguin edition, p. 107. (I thank Anthony Arblaster for this reference).

men have differences, of a religious, ethnic or cultural kind, there will be toleration of some sort, if these differences neither lapse into indifference (or aspire to indifference?) nor get treated as being, by the mere fact of being differences, pathological. If variety results from liberty of conscience, mutual disapproval could actually increase, but so may powers and intentions of forbearance.[1]

So we can begin to build up a concept of toleration as a social relationship of a special kind, neither good nor bad in itself, whose component parts are always degrees of disapproval and degrees of acceptance. The most general sense then becomes:

What can be allowed that is strongly disapproved of?

In this *third* and most comprehensive cluster of meanings we only tolerate things of which we do not approve. We can, of course, be intolerant of things of which we normally approve, if our approval is limited by some other and overriding set of principles – either substantive (as when we wish to limit political activity in times of emergency, or suppress the truth about the late-lamented for the sake of the widow) or procedural (I approve of folk song, but not at Faculty meetings). It is meaningless to say that we tolerate things of which we approve, or to which we are indifferent – as people who pride themselves on their tolerance often say; we simply approve them or are indifferent. If one walks down Carnaby Street or the Kings Road, Chelsea, in a happy buzz of 'tolerant pleasure', all this can mean is that one is applying to *their* behaviour some standards which oneself once held, but which one is now happy to observe are crumbling. The converse of this would be 'that I force myself to be tolerant' (which is probably a much more meaningful, common, if

1. Where Paine and Marcuse go wrong is to identify all procedures with ideology. It is obviously reasonable to expect men positively to agree with some procedures, the occasionally unwelcome results of which they may only merely tolerate, even reject morally, but none the less accept peaceably.

sometimes misguided, occurrence). For instance, I tolerate smoking in lectures and seminars, and provocative styles of dress. More profoundly, I am very conscious of having to tolerate (indeed having, at times, to try very hard and consciously to tolerate) the opinions and public utterances of Mr Powell on immigrants, but I am not particularly conscious (unless I am being hypocritical) of having to be tolerant towards coloured immigrants. Thus, 'I tolerate Mr Powell, and I do not (have to) tolerate West Indians'. I simply accept them. Perhaps this is rather surprising, or perhaps I am blinded, Mr Powell would think, by ideology – an ideology that would lead me, when I think about the question at all, to welcome rather than regret an increased communal articulation in English life and to see his attitudes as themselves very un-English.

Why do I tolerate the Muslim attitude to women? I do not, for there is nothing I can do about it. Why do I tolerate the Government's attitude to Vietnam? I do not, but there is nothing I can do about it (although if you could convince me that there was something I could do about it, then I would find myself involved in tolerating it, or not). Why do educated, liberal, socialist even, Arabs tolerate the low status of the other half of mankind in their countries – women? They do not tolerate it, they are plainly in favour of it. Why do they tolerate homosexual behaviour so much more than we do? They plainly do not, they regard it as a matter of moral indifference. The Manchu emperors were not a shining example of religious toleration; they simply could not begin to understand what on earth the transcendental Christian religion of the Jesuit missionaries was all about, and nor could they perceive in it (mistakenly) a threat to their own Confucian system of authority and ethics based on conduct.

If I approve of something, then it seems meaningless to say that I tolerate it; or if so, only in respect of some secondary characteristics. I tolerate her smoking in bed, but I don't tolerate her, damn it, I love her. Or to give a less extreme example, I tolerate *queers*, but I simply accept the fact that this friend of mine is a homosexual – so long as this, to me, secondary aspect of his behaviour does not impinge upon me, toleration does not arise. But to take queers as a category, I emphatically do not approve of them, that is a fact for which I will produce rationalizations if necessary (nepotism, decadence, unfair to women, threats to youth, purveyors of rubbish about effeminacy and great art, etc.). And I do not think that I am being at all intolerant in expressing my dislike; but I was strongly in favour of changing the law, of extending toleration to them – that is a different matter. And if they feel that this is condescension, well so it is; I am not going to extend agreement and will only offer a limited acceptance, in their terms, behaviourally – as my friend well knows and knows the limits; so long as he observes these limits, the invidious issue of being tolerated does not arise. And likewise I assume that he tolerates me.

A distinction between tolerance as disapproval/acceptance and acceptance or indifference is extremely important to keep in mind if historical accounts of tolerance are to be written. The Jesuits in China are a salutary warning. What may appear extraordinarily tolerant to us, looking back or looking from the outside, may be a matter of indifference or positive approval to the people we profess to be studying. For the subject to be meaningful there has to be a clear disapproval and, I would suggest further, in order to avoid triviality, a clear shift or change in the circumstance: either that which was not tolerable at one period becomes tolerable in the next – the perceived threat is still there, but is either seen as now containable or as something that morally must now be borne; or that which was tolerable in one period becomes seen as intolerable in the next. And, of course, both the disapproval and the acceptance factors may vary quite independently of each other. Increasing religious tolerance does not imply lessening ecclesiastical animosity, perhaps only lessening foreign threat. And a diminishing racial prejudice through educational effort might not imply increasing toleration, still less acceptance, in hard times. All such cases need examining, but I would argue that they can be done so most meaningfully in terms of immediate generational contrasts rather than in terms of any absolute standards or web of philosophical definitions of what counts, or does not count, as tolerance. What counts as tolerance has to be discovered from the historical record of times of social change.

The OED gives as a 'special sense' of toleration: 'allowance with or without limitations by the ruling power of the exercise of religion otherwise than in the form officially prescribed'. The late J. W. Gooch wrote in an entry in *Chambers's Encyclopaedia* that religious toleration is 'liberty allowed by the government of a country where a particular form of religion is established or recognized, to practise some other form of religion or no religion at all'. And he added: 'Where a government does not specifically recognize any particular form of religion, and all citizens are equally free to organize churches, to worship or not as they please, and to profess and teach what doctrines and beliefs they choose (possibly within limits imposed for the sake of decency or public order), such a situation, while one of religious liberty, is wider than toleration.' To the distinctions between liberty and tolerance I will return later, but for the moment I would take for granted the distinction he draws and accept the OED's definition that religious toleration is something which takes place within a framework of official proscription. This is precisely what Paine complained about. But it is precisely the fact of the case. When the proscription vanishes, there is no need for tolerance: we have passed beyond mere toleration – if, indeed, the ending of the official proscription also miraculously ends social discrimination. But if we can find a sense or senses of toleration firm enough for it to have a history, I would suspect that religious tolerance, rather than racial or political, is the first and most important factor. But I think that the OED's 'special sense' can obviously be extended to other senses – particularly to sexual behaviour as well as religious and political. Part of the problem is to know how to keep a proper distance from groups of which we disapprove, or from practices we dislike; but to do this, we need to know something about them. To keep at a proper distance from someone, it is necessary to know their habits fairly well.[1] *Should* we teach children a true code of sexual morality? Perhaps – or perhaps not. But we must teach them to recognize the codes, cues and social indicators associated with the different patterns of sexual behaviour which they are likely to encounter – otherwise misunderstandings, shock and conflict attend them all their days. (In this sense I appreciate Professor Henri Tajfel's psychological conclusion in studying prejudice that cognitive factors are more open to influence than motivational factors – and does he not imply that we should not worry too much about motives anyway?)[2] Here empathy becomes relevant. If the Friendly 'to tolerate all things' has any meaning at all, it is to gain an understanding of 'the inwardness' of other codes as a clue to behaviour, but this understanding should not imply agreement. *Tout comprendre* by all means, but never *tout pardonner*. If we know how other people behave, we are less likely to tread on their toes, and they on ours, walking in this middle-earth of toleration in which we cannot ignore them and yet see no particular reason why we should embrace them utterly. I will suggest that an ethic of toleration in the field of race relations is, both in theory and practice, superior to that of assimilation – just as it is in religion. I want toleration, but I'll be damned, one might justifiably say, before I have ecumenicity thrust upon me, until all the Godly share some kind of Hindu-humanist-deist-unitarian-utilitarianism. So before one can tolerate what one disapproves of, one does need to know something about it. The tolerant personality is empathetic, curious but self-secure. To preach or teach (whether to counter religious or racial prejudice) 'what we have in

1. Michael Banton in a chapter on 'Social Distance' in his *Race Relations*, Tavistock Publications, 1967, quotes Robert E. Park: 'Everyone, it seems, is capable of getting on with everyone else provided he keeps his proper distance'; and he discusses 'social distance scales'. But while such scales can measure one type of acceptance–rejection factor they may have little or no relevance for our purposes to many types of *disapproval* factors present in tolerance.

2. See Henri Tajfel, 'Cognitive Aspects of Prejudice', published in *Journal of Bio-Social Sciences*, supplement no. 1, Bio-Social Aspects of Race, 1969.

common with them' may, in fact, very often have very little effect, even a counter-productive one (in that it may violate common sense), compared to 'see how differently and interestingly they live'. In other words, the Quaker 'let's get to know each other a bit better' does not necessarily, and nor should it, lead to a dawning recognition of sameness.

How much tolerance is possible within a society or system of government?

Our third sense was tolerance in a purely negative sense – like Burke's 'wise and salutary neglect' towards wayward and possibly illegal colonial assemblies. But now, fourthly, consider that toleration is positively advocated as a policy of state (the *Politiques* in the sixteenth century, the Whigs in the eighteenth), even if always conditionally. There must be some variation for the state to work and for society to thrive in a civil manner, but how much? The OED allows one more sense, which I think is the best general formulation of this fourth use, and the one most capable of rational discussion, control even and investigation: 'an allowable amount *of variation on the dimensions of a machine or part*' – as when we say that something can work to a broad or narrow tolerance, or when doctors or chemists can say that the tolerance of the body to arsenic poisoning is – such and such. The modern state is here to be seen, not literally as a machine, but as a powerful set of procedural conventions for making decisions in ways which increasingly need to be accepted by more and more people as legitimate. This obviously can and must be tied in with some discussions of general theories about political systems, the conditions for their stability and change. Here I think historians and social scientists have much to say to each other. Political systems may generally prove more stable to the degree that they can be tolerant, for toleration here implies adaptability to different materials or circumstances. Malinowski argued, in his *Freedom and Civilization*, the great survival value of freedom seen as adaptability. There are obviously some practical advantages for some toleration in all political systems in relation to the gathering up by the state of true information (toleration has to be extended to the messenger who brings ill news as well as good news, or else the jester, the court barber, the holy lunatic or the mistress from the common people have to be institutionalized as a way of finding out what is going on at all, etc.). But some systems attach a high and conscious degree of utility to this, others not. Max Weber saw objectivity as the great functional advantage of bureaucracy, and objectivity implies official tolerance of unwelcome discoveries or advice. And obviously the limits of toleration of regimes that can distinguish between threats to the government and threats to the state are different from those in which the government is identified with order itself. Some fairly conventional ground would need to be gone over again in any full account, but to be interpreted in terms of the function of toleration in different kinds of system of government.

The machine analogy is open to objection on the grounds that in social systems the precise limits of tolerance (without it breaking down) are themselves the subject of debate. But all I wish to point out is that the debate does then take place on this more or less empirical, historical or pragmatic level, not on the level of trying to define toleration and to say if it is, in general, a good or a bad thing. Yet some framework of identity will be assumed. One can find cases where states appear to miscalculate by being too tolerant to professed enemies of the whole regime (e.g. Weimar Germany), but no instances of where ruling groups feel that the regime has to go to the wall rather than abandon toleration for the time of emergency.

So it is sensible, indeed important, for historians and social scientists to ask, 'How much tolerance is possible within a society or system of government?' But does this appear too Hobbesean to put toleration as a policy of state so firmly in front? I fully grant that there are many philosophically interesting or even morally important questions of toleration between individuals and in group transactions which do not concern the state. All I say is that they are of less importance for the study of history or social sciences, and I find it hard to conceive how there can be much social tolerance, as distinct from mere indifference, until there is some official policy of toleration. If the issues that divide society matter, the state will not be able to ignore them: it will govern, persecute or even enforce toleration on reluctant subjects. In an age of faith, religious differences cannot (indeed would not, anyway) be ignored by the state. If toleration is a general policy, then some high degree of secularization is involved. There are plenty of examples of states being more tolerant than even most of their inhabitants, almost always more so than some. States grew not to tolerate the persecution of minorities, and now few states can tolerate mass unemployment. Daniel Boorstin's picture of frontier America is one of intolerant, one-Church small townships; but the society as a whole was tolerant because the federal power would have forbidden any extraordinary local punishments or proscriptions which would hinder (the essential condition to him of all toleration) freedom of movement (i.e. one can justify zealots wanting their own kingdom, so long as the unconvinced and the lapsed can move out and have somewhere to go). Similarly, I am deliberately a little Hobbesist (at least to create priorities about 'the word and the deed'). Only in a very secure and advanced liberal perspective can we think it obvious that toleration should be extended generally to words but perhaps more selectively to deeds. In a culture which believed that 'the Word was made Flesh' this was plainly inconceivable. It takes considerable experience before governments realize that words are not always subversive (although, of course, it is arguable that some kinds of words always are – a public political philosophy for instance: is it compatible with the whole political system that justifications for political obligation shall be examined critically, or the plain truth told about how decisions of government are made? For some systems, yes, but for autocratic or totalitarian systems, no). Certainly we will want to discuss what in our kind of state seem purely social types of tolerance or intolerance – the Devlin–Hart controversy over law and morality etc., and the real point at issue between them – how changing judicial rules of interpretation give more (or less) tolerance to old laws in new circumstances. But my only point is that we do not start at that point. Such controversies are only permissible and meaningful in certain types of state. In the age of faith or in the totalitarian state still, the distinction between 'public' and 'private' or between legal enforcement and social pressure appears not merely tendentious, but dangerous. (And, furthermore, I think it likely that many minority problems, which we commonly discuss in terms of tolerance and intolerance, are, in fact, better dealt with in terms of justice, equality and rights.) Tolerance and intolerance become significant when they become matters of public policy.

An extended definition of toleration

Now I can begin to pull threads together. Obviously the simple definition of tolerance as the degree to which we can accept things of which we disapprove needs extending. It needs extending both in the philosophical manner that Dr King sets out so well and to introduce some criteria which will place toleration and tolerance firmly in the broad context of political history and the comparative study of political institutions, that is to begin to show what types of tolerance are worth studying as matters not merely possible and interesting but also important in understanding – the claim is not too pretentious – human history.

Particular tolerances become generalized into toleration (that is the deliberate practice of as many particular tolerances as is possible) when (1) society as expressed in the state feels threatened by something – and when either the kind or degree of threat is new or the organization of the state or of society is changing; (2) when there is power to give or withhold; (3) when there is moral disapproval with whatever embodies the threat – idea, institutions or people (what Dr King calls ideational, organizational or identity tolerances or intolerances); (4) when there is some reasonably accurate knowledge or comprehension of the character of the threat (tolerance as empathy or under-standing);[1] and (5) when, notwithstanding these previous conditions, the idea, institution or type of person is accepted – to some significant degree when compared to practices in the immediate past.

Think of the first statute of William and Mary in 1689, 'The Act of Toleration . . . to Dissenting Protestants'. There was no doubt that the country still felt threatened to some significant degree by religious diversity. And there was no doubt that official policy still frowned on dissent, but it was no longer to be persecuted or proscribed generally (except for membership of the universities, commissions in the army, membership of Parliament and many of the professions). It was not tolerant enough, by our standards and by some at the time, but it was an act of toleration by someone or body of men having the effective power to give or withhold. And even the prohibitions were tempered, and were recognized to be so, by the doctrine and practice of 'occasional conformity': if people cared to affirm, that was up to them and their con-science, public order was satisfied, there was to be no search-ing into men's consciences – Cromwell and Hobbes had made their point, or had seen accurately what was bound to come in the context of the politics and society of England. Remember, of course, that the Act of Toleration, like Locke's *Essay on Toleration*, still left Roman Catholics beyond the pale. Why this was so should be obvious within the limits implied in any possible theory of toleration or practice of toleration at the time, as in my second and fourth general senses in the argument above. For to tolerate papists would be to risk the overthrow of the state which was being so tolerant; for they were deemed to be either a real threat to public order or a potential one in times of war. This was not a contradiction in the theory of toleration (and there was a

1. Some would argue that this comprehension must imply some respect for those who pose the threat. In some Kantian and minimal sense of recognizing that we are dealing with fellow men, yes; but I cannot agree that this is always conscious: much tolerance appears to be purely pragmatic.

theory of toleration then, as the Act itself showed), but simply a mistake in knowledge. The Roman Catholics did not, in fact, behave like this; and there was no real risk that they would alter the lesson of the Glorious (because bloodless) Revolution and the all too easy expulsion of the House of Stuart (in England, at least). They were not subsequently a threat, as their loyalty during the '45 rising showed, and in fact they were not treated as such, the laws were rarely enforced: the system could in fact tolerate them, once they ceased to be perceived as a great threat and once their actual behaviour became better understood – although popular prejudice and strong disapproval lingered on long, as shown in the Gordon Riots and in the controversy surrounding Catholic Emancipation in the 1820s.

Thus I would suggest that the significant problems of toleration which should be studied as a part of history and politics, in particular, are: (1) the explanation of the rise of toleration – and sometimes of its waning; (2) significant episodes where there is some sudden change in acceptance or rejection of the tolerance of ideas, institutions or types of person. I suspect that threat or changing perceptions of it is often a product of unexpected degrees of social mobility: groups may have been 'tolerated' when they lived in virtual isolation – indeed in segregated or ghetto societies acceptance can be so minimal as scarcely to raise the problem of social tolerance, only a bare and protected political tolerance; but when these groups begin to move or mingle, either geographically or socially, difficulties begin. And I further suspect that it is important always to try to ascertain the degree of knowledge that those feeling threatened had of these by whom they felt threatened.

Let me very briefly indicate the three broad and obvious areas of tolerance and some tentative perspectives for research.

Religious tolerance

Here we have more writing and received knowledge than in either political and civil tolerance or ethnic and racial

tolerance (always keeping in mind that studies of intolerance, if they are made in terms of contrast to some previous
relative tolerance – and are not done anachronistically
by some purported asbolute standard – are part of this
historical record). But much of the writing, like Jordan's
History of Toleration in England, concentrates too much on
state and church doctrine and documentation: we know
far less of practices. And, as a general reader, I risk the
judgement that we have a clearer picture in England of the
attitudes of the national church to dissent than we do of the
range of differences *within* the church at different periods.
What are the utmost limits of tolerance in different periods as
defined by still just remaining a member of the institution?
And the same question has to be asked in a systematic way
before the Reformation as well. Not merely the Christian
tolerance or intolerance towards the Jew and the heretic, but
also to the deviants within the church – or just within. There
may be no official desire to accept anything that is dis-
approved of; but, long before doctrines of toleration, how far
were radically divergent practices at least 'put up with', in
the primal and minimal sense of tolerance? Words of acceptance or toleration may be lacking, but what of the facts? Or,
vice versa, fair words may come, as with the Edict of Nantes,
but local justice and behaviour may – to what degree? –
negate them, prove intolerant in practice.

Civil and political toleration

Here we may seem to be walking a grimly over-trod path and
to be likely only to utter a faint and abstract cry for synthesis.
But, on the contrary, I suspect there is a great need to particu-
larize. It is most important to see that a history of toleration,
or studies of important episodes, is something different from
the great chimera, a history of freedom or liberty – something
both narrower and more subtle. It is narrower because there
can be toleration before there is any idea that freedom can be
general; and it is more subtle because it would concentrate
on the degree of acceptance where there is a prior and clear

disapproval, whereas it is notorious that most philosophical accounts of freedom as choice, in the tradition of Mill and Berlin, find it hard to anchor themselves in institutional history, to stipulate what are important *political* freedoms as distinct from the whole infinite class of actions which are not restrained, the important and the trivial alike.[1] Most histories of political ideas are concerned, directly or indirectly, with ideas about freedom and liberty, but few or none with its practices, with freedom as an activity and how this is closely related, in the classical more than the modern liberal sense, to man as citizen, so the whole thing tends to trail away into moralistic anachronisms. But in these very cultures particular tolerances may, none the less, be highly significant. There is a sense in which the study of the actual degrees of tolerance in autocracies is important and neglected. We have a hundred liberal denunciations of censorship, for instance, but very few books that throw any light on the strange limitations or tolerances of the Tsarist censorship. And quite apart from censorship of writing, how far did tolerance in fact extend to the discussion of matters outside the council and the court?

Consider tolerance towards political opponents. What forms of proscription are practised in different societies and why? Such punishments may be illiberal, but there are real and significant differences, perhaps capable of comparative treatment as well as treatment through time in particular countries, between, say, death (in various forms), imprisonment (in various forms and lengths), exile (again a varying condition), banishment from court, compulsory retirement from public life, a job in the provinces or colonies or a seat in the House of Lords – all forms of political punishment. Similarly there is need for some simple categorization of types of internal violence and to explain different attitudes towards them in different periods: rebellion, revolt, uprising, riot, tumult, demonstration, etc. cannot merely be given reason-

---

1. The emergence of toleration is a precondition for the emergence of free institutions – they are dependent upon it; but both logically and historically there can be significant tolerance without general freedom and liberalism.

ably distinct meanings but levels of toleration towards them vary. Civil war has been a legitimate way of settling the succession to high office, in Christian kingdoms as well as Muslim and African. We grow more and more to see that 'violence' as such is a meaningless abstraction: it always assumes highly conventional and limited forms – such 'limits' are often highly relative, but are relative to other forms, and can be compared. The social scientist is sometimes all too glib in providing 'conceptual frameworks' or 'typologies'; but without going so far, I sense that historians, certainly in England and America, are beginning to want to draw threads between 'periods' or 'episodes': there are similarities as well as differences: to disbelieve in universal or comparative history is not to be bogged down in a particularist nominalism that can then never explain but only exhaustively describe.

Freedom and liberty involve the *assertion* of rights. Toleration is a concept more grim and limited concerned with the granting of rights. The motives may stem from pragmatic considerations or from a gradually extended doctrine of respect and conscience (that men should not be forced against their beliefs); but the motives are irrelevant to understanding the phenomenon in general: the fact of toleration or of a relative tolerance (compared to some relevant point in the past) stands plain, and toleration or significant tolerances are plainly a precondition for anything we could call a free society; but it is a necessary condition without being a sufficient condition. It is possible to conceive of a tolerant autocracy in some meaningful sense. It is impossible to conceive either an intolerant 'free society' or, the true converse of toleration, an indifferent or wholly apathetic free society. We wish for both freedom and tolerance, but they can dwell apart. And while it is true that the concepts of tolerance and toleration can be meaningfully applied to relations between individuals, just as freedom can to relations between groups, it should be clear, none the less, that the most historically significant senses of toleration–tolerance apply to relationships between groups, most of all to the state and minorities, whereas freedom and liberty rapidly diminish in importance once groups are substituted for individuals as the vehicles of free actions. To be free, furthermore, to act freely, does not imply that I know what effects my actions will have on others – I may be acting irresponsibly (or as a great-aunt of mine was wont to say of the Kaiser, 'thoughtlessly'), but that does not make the action any less free: the conditions for a 'free society' are necessarily more elaborate than for a free action. But to be tolerant, in any possible sense, implies that I must at least claim to have some knowledge of what I am tolerating: if I cannot explain my disapproval, I must at least be able to acknowledge it and, having done that, give some kind of account of why I think I can (let alone should) forbear, partially accept or tolerate.

Racial tolerance

'Ethnic', of course, or cultural, is what we really mean, or what Dr King calls 'identity tolerance' and intolerance; but we are stuck with the terms 'racial' and 'race relations' in all official policies and even most scholarly writings, even though the word enshrines a fallacious concept. Here again the literature is vast, but much of the historical record is still to be written and many changes of attitude are yet to be explained. The treatment of strangers, foreigners and people who are perceived as ethnically different again involves some simple categorization, but once done can be treated both comparatively and through time in particular countries or areas. Mere description of the position of the stranger, foreigner or other race in, say, medieval England, let alone a mere documentation of expressed attitudes, is not likely to be very interesting as such: but whenever tolerance becomes extended, compared to some point in the past which seemed to contemporaries to be significant, or whenever intolerance similarly occurs, then light can be shed not merely on particular episodes and periods but some findings of more general application may emerge. Here I suspect the historian and the sociologist, perhaps the social psychologist too, have something to discuss and compare: contemporary results need checking in terms of historical material, and divergences need to be explained; and the historian may find that some factors are worth looking for in the past, in the light of contemporary research today, which might not otherwise appear significant. I suspect that there are, to use a dangerously old-fashioned phrase, some lessons to be learned in particular from Roman experience where the ability to create a civic culture which cut across ethnic perceptions was both a condition of Roman expansion, and, on occasion, a deliberate political instrument.

Two main points follow, one methodological and contemporary and the other moral.

Much contemporary sociological and social psychological research centres on the concept of prejudice. And many sociologists and social psychologists have developed various scales by which people can be ranked in order in response to questions put to them in various ways. Commonly the scales have 'Prejudice' at one pole and 'Tolerance' at the other, or sometimes 'Intolerance' and 'Tolerance'. Let me leave aside all technical questions of how to ask these questions: I personally, unlike some political philosophers and historians, am convinced that such procedures are valid in principle, so long as their limitations are understood and the findings are not misused. And leave aside also the more formidable objection that the jump from 'attitudes' to 'behaviour' is often assumed. There are scales whose inventors appear crudely to believe that attitudes entail behaviour, rather than that they are only some kind of useful clue to behaviour, but not necessarily causally connected, certainly not in that one direction only; for behaviour can also condition attitudes (e.g. get people marching or demonstrating and they will feel full of fraternity and solidarity, etc.). But more sophisticated work makes more limited claims.

The real general objection is that 'intolerance' is not the opposite of 'tolerance'. As we have already argued, the opposite of tolerance is indifference (when disapproval does not arise); and the opposite of intolerance is full acceptance or love (when the disapproval vanishes). Most survey research reduces these two-dimensions (disapproval-acceptance) to a crude single dimension. And this single dimension is then almost invariably treated as simply an attitude scale – from which no inferences for behaviour can possibly be drawn without making large assumptions about other factors.

Consider the findings of Mark Abrams's research in the justly famous *Colour and Citizenship: A Report on British Race Relations* volume, by E. J. B. Rose and associates (Oxford University Press, 1969). 10 per cent of the population are ranked as 'prejudiced'; 17 per cent as 'prejudice-inclined'; 38 per cent as 'tolerant-inclined'; and 35 per cent (our hats are waving in the air) as 'tolerant'. And the questions are sensible ones, professionally administered and analysed – as far as I know. But is the man of great prejudice necessarily devoid of tolerance? He may be so much aware of his race prejudice that, according to other principles, which are equally or more important to him, he leans over backwards in his behaviour towards coloured people – perhaps even seeks them out to be nice to them. And is the man certified as 'tolerant' necessarily devoid of prejudice? He may never meet coloured people, have all the right attitudes, but somehow, and in fact, never question that his office, his firm, his household never employs or entertains a coloured person. To call him tolerant on the basis of his attitudes is meaningless; he could be intolerant, or the problem could simply never have arisen in his experience, so that the forms in which hypothetical questions are posed to him mean nothing: of course he will let his daughter marry a black man, when he may never have encountered one socially and may not even have a daughter.

Even if one asks questions about actual behaviour, the matter may be no clearer. Bad guys who won't meet, eat or sleep with Blacks, Jews and Blue-Haired Folk come out at the moral bottom of the scale; and good guys who'll happily take it all – and more – happily float to the top. But two objections arise. The good guys who are 'tolerant' may in fact *like* Jews, Blacks and Blue-Haired Folk – toleration does not arise: society has passed beyond the need for 'mere tolerance', or if it has not, then the respondent simply earns himself a false reputation for being tolerant. And the bad guys who may be attitudinally prejudiced beyond doubt, may in fact behave more tolerantly than they think or say (according to the code of the work situation, for instance, if both union and employer are tough for multi-racial hiring). The interview may actually be the therapeutic confessional for consciously repressed desires (as the old Irish confessional story has it, 'What the men confess to me over a year simply doesn't square with the physical appearance of the young women').

'Intolerance' and 'tolerance' are thus not logical antitheses. And this also gives me some worry about translating studies of tolerance too readily, as might seem plausible, into studies of intolerance: intolerance is only a significant clue to the conditions of tolerance if it, in historical terms, negates a previous tolerance; but this in turn, I would then argue, always must be seen as the negation of a prior intolerance: thus one must work forward from intolerance to tolerance, not backwards from intolerance to tolerance. Certainly, 'mere tolerance' is only a minimal negation of intolerance – but it happens to be the most important one historically and the one with which, in fact, we are concerned. It should be possible to devise attitude scales which could attempt to measure not simple one-dimensional attitudes, but the relationship between measures of acceptance and measures of disapproval or rejection.[1] And this needs to be done.

Specifically for race relations, a moral point follows. Tom Paine and Marcuse's objections are here at their strongest: a danger that toleration itself as a concept helps to perpetuate, even to legitimize, prejudice. To be tolerant in race relations is to be tolerant of error and evil: for there are no such things as races in the sense that lead men to discriminate on such a basis. I would grant this danger. In religious and political toleration a justification of toleration turns upon our acceptance of strongly held and differing viewpoints as being

1. As Mr Geoffrey Green, formerly of Sheffield University, is trying to do in his thesis research. I have borrowed many ideas from him.

87

natural to man. But this argument would indeed be racialist itself if applied to race relations. Here it is clear that toleration is a second-order principle, or a procedural rather than a substantive argument. In religion and politics I would justify saying 'one should always be as tolerant as possible'. But in 'race relations' one can only say, but must say, *contra* both Black Power and the liberal assimilationist, 'one must be as tolerant as one has to be', that is before the conditions for full acceptance have arrived.

To be aware of the danger is to be armed against it. There is no need to throw out the good with the bad. The good is that there is hope, given time, knowledge and effort, that such problems can be resolved. Prejudice itself may never be eliminated, but the battle against prejudice, particularly when waged from the classroom, may be the pursuit of an evil chimera: it is hard to conceive of a world without pre-judgements. Prejudice may become irrelevant to behaviour and happiness and may, if social conditions are made right or become right, diminish into something that only depth-interviews and dreams reveal, rather than a threat to others and an irritant. But the *study* of racial prejudice seems to me to be quite as important as the study of religious and civil intolerance–tolerance. We want to know, however depressing both the question and the result may be, the degree of acceptance or rejection of people whose differences are in fact commonly perceived as racial – although all the while we keep on saying 'cultural'. Unless we have more accurate knowledge of the social relationships between disapproval and acceptance, much public policy is likely to be direction-less. And I have little doubt that at the moment in Britain both theory and practice must advance on a double front: to increase tolerance of differences as perceived, both real and unreal, but at the same time a critique or exposure of unreal differences must be pursued. Differences will remain – of colour, for instance, but pigmentation may one day not appear significant; and differences of culture may also re-main, but here we are engulfed, indeed, in the very open debate about the meaning of 'pluralism'.

Tolerance and plurality

Here is not the place to discuss justifications of toleration or of particular tolerances. I am more interested in trying to show that studies of the conditions for tolerance are meaningful. But one objection strikes at the whole enterprise, at any attempt to use the concept objectively, the criticism of 'repressive tolerance' – which is a serious one – of Marcuse and Wolff.

First, however, let me make clear that I have some scepticism about espousing toleration as a general principle. 'One should always be as tolerant as possible' – that is as far as I think it sensible to go. Toleration has to find its place among other principles. There is no magic formula for justice: several different principles can be relevant to a problem and have to be reasoned about in some mutually acceptable way. And in any society there are some things which cannot be tolerated without either breakdown or a change so drastic that it is no longer sensible to say that we are dealing with the same society. And for the individual there will always be some things which he cannot tolerate – even if hypothetically, if he had power not to do so.

So on one level Wolff, Marcuse and Moore in their *A Critique of Pure Tolerance* are not attacking toleration so much as a debased misunderstanding of it. It is a polemic against the excessive tolerance in American liberalism. They have every right to be angry at all sorts of failures to act decisively in contemporary America, but are they right to blame toleration? If so, then only in a sense of toleration which would equate toleration with sheer indifference or extreme permissiveness (which they seem against politically and economically, but oddly not sexually). 'Tolerance is an end in itself.' Thus speaks Marcuse – opening the door to a passionate attack on a man-of-straw: 'Tolerance is extended to policies, conditions and modes of behaviour which should not be tolerated because they are impeding, if not destroying the chances of creating an existence without fear or misery.'[1]

1. *A Critique of Pure Tolerance* (Beacon Press, 1969), p. 84.

89

Indeed such modes of behaviour should not be tolerated, but only if one believes that 'tolerance is an end in itself' does such intolerance necessarily imply repression. It may only imply argument and persuasion. If there are many people who in fact do not denounce social evils because they think it intolerant to denounce anything, then Marcuse is right – at least to ascribe to others a belief in tolerance as an end in itself. But this belief, as we have shown, is a false one. He attacks a worthy enemy, perhaps, but in a way that not merely throws out the baby with the bath water, but gratuitously strangles him first. 'The tolerance which enlarged the range and content of freedom was always partisan – intolerant towards the protagonists of the status quo.'[1] And he makes clear that reactionaries who tolerate the word but repress the deed have to be paid out in reverse coin (the 'negation of the negation', no less). The oddest thing, however, is that Marcuse seems aware that his 'pure tolerance' or 'end in itself' is meaningless. He certainly acknowledges degrees of tolerance, or degrees of disapproval-yet-acceptance, in comparing 'totalitarian democracy' with 'dictatorship'.[2] But when he sets out to justify sporadic violence, he does so by contrast to an inaction and unconcern for social justice, which he then claims arises *because* of tolerance. The whole book seems, in fact, most charitably read as a polemic not against tolerance but against liberalism. Liberalism certainly presupposes tolerance, but tolerance is not limited to liberalism. (Barrington Moore's essay has little to do with

1. ibid., p. 85.
2. 'The factual barriers which totalitarian democracy erects against the efficacy of qualitative dissent are weak and pleasant enough compared with the practices of a dictatorship which claims to educate the people in the truth. With all its limitations and distortions, democratic tolerance is under all circumstances more humane than an institutionalized intolerance which sacrifices the rights and liberties of the living generations for the sake of future generations. The question is whether this is the only alternative.' (ibid., p. 99). And the further question is whether his alternative allows further alternatives. His answer seems to be, 'Sorry, necessarily no', based, I honestly believe, on some mysticism about the number three or triadic progressions.

either Marcuse's or Wolff's and is far more coherent and subtle in the one remark it does make about tolerance. 'Science', he says, 'is tolerant of reason; relentlessly intolerant of unreason and sham.')

But there is another level, a more profound objection is made which links tolerance to 'pluralism'. Wolff argues

Finally, the virtue of the modern pluralist democracy which has emerged in contemporary America is TOLERANCE. Political tolerance is that state of mind and condition of society which enables a pluralist democracy to function well and to realize the ideal of pluralism. For that reason, if we wish to understand tolerance *as a political virtue* we must study it not through a psychological or moral investigation of prejudice, but by means of an analysis of the theory and practice of democratic pluralism.[1]

But he surely muddles – or deliberately obscures – a distinction between pluralism as a procedural ideal and as a substantive ideal. I think, personally, that it is likely that men will differ significantly in their ideals of interests even in a perfect society. But this is infinitely arguable. What is less arguable, however, is that even if in a perfect society in which pluralism of ideals will be exposed or 'unmasked' as the perpetuation of errors, the only possible road to such a society compatible with reason and freedom is through procedures which allow a plurality of viewpoints to be experienced. But a plurality of viewpoint does not imply any weird equality of all sincere opinions as truth – what Ernest Gellner has elsewhere called 'sloppy pluralism'.[2]

In Wolff's *The Poverty of Liberalism* he gives deadly examples of American political scientists who confuse a description of pluralism in society with a justification of all present differ-

1. ibid., p. 4.
2. See his 'Myth, Ideology and Revolution', pp. 212–13 in B. Crick and W. A. Robson, eds., *Protest and Discontent*, Pelican, 1970. But I am alarmed to find myself put in such company by him. My *In Defence of Politics* simply offered a minimal justification of political activity as conciliating groups. I did not ever suggest that this was more than the framework in which we debate – or shall debate – 'What should be done?', political justice.

91

ences – a confusion that Lionel Trilling exposed in an essay on the Kinsey Report over twenty years ago in his *The Liberal Imagination*. So he comes to argue that: 'To the champion of pluralism as an instrument of democracy, tolerance is the live-and-let-live moderation of the market place.'[1] This is undoubtedly the belief of some. But the alternative then posed by Wolff is a false one. More sensible formulations of both 'pluralism' and 'tolerance' are not therefore condemned. What if pluralism is simply *part* of a description of democracy? I may tolerate here and now 'the market place', to a degree, but I can also denounce it and work against it. And toleration is concerned with far more than the economic market place. Wolff's small difficulty is that he does not want anyone to be tolerated, for all political authority is oppressive or insultingly condescending; he wants everyone to be both free and right – therefore his *In Defence of Anarchism* (1970).

I would want both to value and to study the tolerance that comes not through caring for nothing (here I share some of Marcuse's and Wolff's worries), but through caring for many things (but they, I think, only care, or believe that they should care for one thing). In every actual circumstance, these things will create limitations on general tolerance; but it may be that there are some distinctive patterns in these circumstances which can be studied and compared philosophically, historically and sociologically. Easier, in a sentence, perhaps to think that we will be studying the limits of tolerance quite as much as the circumstances, material and moral, in which toleration becomes seen as a conscious principle or (*ceteris paribus*) an overriding maxim of statecraft.

Tolerance could then be a general way of looking at the properties of social systems, perhaps some way to deal with the value of 'freedom' empirically. To what extent do various societies allow the expression of ideas or behaviour of which they disapprove and which threaten them – admittedly threaten them – if carried too far? Take, to conclude, ever so

1. *The Poverty of Liberalism* (Beacon Press, 1968), p. 136.

briefly the dilemmas of race relations in Great Britain. 'Assimilation' used to be accepted as the object of public policy and the morally proper thing. As well as being a value judgement, it could also be studied, and still can, quite objectively: to what degree are immigrants assimilated (i.e. can the concept be rendered operational)? Now take the shift of thought and events towards some sort of value being attached to communal representation – or put it another way, the shift towards seeing 'integration' as a function of communities, not of individuals, and as a partial not a total process. Integration can also be an object of policy (help the immigrants to help themselves as immigrants) and be seen as the morally proper thing (how dare we presume that a West Indian wants to become fully or only an Englishman any more than a Jew does not walk, and is not accepted as walking, with feet in two worlds?). It can also be studied quantitatively: to what degree do the immigrants behave as if they are members of a community defined by its place of origin? Without coming down politically or morally on the side of either individual assimilation or integration as 'communal co-existence', both can be studied as processes – to see which are more typical of what sort of situations.

But if we were to follow the logic of the concept of 'toleration', it would be towards the latter, in some form, rather than the former that we would move, at least in the foreseeable future. 'Pluralism' may be an odd ideal, but it is at least a moral and sensible procedure. Certainly if there were complete assimilation, there would be no need for toleration; but this would be to work on a long-term time scale which would be largely irrelevant to the problems we in fact face in the short run of practice or the middle period of policy. Equally certain, even so, we would want to be firmer than most of us are in seeing the superior moral values of 'Englishness' to see this as a proper goal at all. Toleration, like liberty, springs partly from doubts; but doubts not about what we are, but about how far that justifies our actions towards others. However, never should we think that to be tolerant is to avoid open disapproval; it is simply to limit that dis-

93

approval. I may detest certain principles, but it does not follow that I try to prevent their expression. To be tolerant is never to accept fully; it is simply not to reject utterly. Such an attitude is never enough, but it is the only civilized beginning in the world as we face it. To say that a society was wholly tolerant would be to say little about whether it was a just society or not, certainly to say nothing about whether it was as just as could be. But to say that a society is intolerant is to imply that it is unjust. Toleration, then, is a necessary condition of a just society, but not a sufficient condition. Nothing is, however, compounded of a single element. Those who have some simple, single criterion of justice and are determined to get it next week, are doomed to cruel intolerance in their political behaviour, however libertarian their personal behaviour. It is odd and it is disreputable that some libertarians, or 'liberationists', should now wish to adopt the position of the Scottish Presbyterian Major-General whom Cromwell rebuked so heavily and sensibly for cashiering an Anabaptist: 'Admit he be, shall that render him incapable to serve the public? . . . Sir, the State in choosing men to serve them takes no notice of their opinions; if they be willing faithfully to serve them, that satisfies.'[1]

Some things, like religion, are too important to pretend that differences do not exist and should not be expressed. It is not the differences as such that lead to intolerance, but the manner in which they are expressed. Differences of political doctrine and of social culture are also too important to be suppressed or repressed, unless the behaviour associated with them is intolerant of accepted legal restraints.

Perhaps then it is not 'prejudice' as such which is pernicious, but the expressions of it and the rigidity it *may* create in behaviour patterns. It is hard to imagine, indeed, a world in which we could operate without prejudging things. What is bad, both morally and scientifically, is when we are not prepared to change our prejudices in the light of experience. We commonly do. If somehow people can be got to work to-

1. Quoted by Christopher Hill in his *God's Englishman: Oliver Cromwell and the English Revolution* (Weidenfeld & Nicolson, 1970), pp. 67–8.

gether, although full of racial or religious prejudice, we know that prejudice often diminishes: attitudes can follow behaviour, they do not always shape it. But just as people who are highly prejudiced on attitude scales may act tolerantly – indeed being aware of my prejudices I may consciously be very careful and very successful in acting tolerantly, so also people who may appear relatively unprejudiced on attitude scales can be intolerant in their behaviour: not out of 'prejudice' at all, but out of habit and simple conformity with the behaviour of – for instance – the other workers, the other men in the office. There is, in other words, a good deal of psychological evidence which suggests that intolerant behaviour is best remedied by, in quite old-fashioned terms, increased *knowledge* of the other group's culture, rather than by direct attacks on 'prejudice', still less by naive orations (especially to schoolchildren) that all men – and women? – are the same.

We should be intolerant of any who seek to explain cultural differences in terms of racial theory: we should be intellectually intolerant, because the theory has been refuted scientifically; and we should be politically intolerant, because it leads to treating men not according to their behaviour, but according to some unchangeable (and irrelevant) factor of race. But we should be socially tolerant, tolerant in our behaviour of wide cultural divergences because, for one reason among others, this appears to be what people want, and because it is the only way to behave until we can all persuade ourselves sublimely into a moral consensus which may be the mark of a heaven on earth, or may be the mark of the withering away of thought and character. To be tolerant is not to value everything equally, or to refrain from criticism, still worse to protect one's own group from criticism. The whole problem is how to create a society in which different communities can enjoy very different habits and beliefs, but in such a way that there are no unreasonable barriers to individuals moving out of 'their' group and moving into the majority culture, or occasionally some other group. We neither want a mass society, nor a segregated society, and nor is it likely that the only differences of values that divide men are a product of economic class. The concept of toleration, while not an end in itself, represents the only kind of social condition which allows for development of both equality in the large society and deep identification with the smaller societies. Justification of toleration has always to be advanced and examined critically, as do justifications of particular tolerances. But the desirable must be the possible even if it goes far beyond the actual; so the conditions of toleration in general and of important cases and episodes of tolerance need studying historically and empirically, and both within countries and comparatively. An old subject needs to be restored by modern scholarship – a scholarship not so much morally engaged as simply morally relevant.

I have not presumed in this paper to suggest to other scholars what are the significant problems of toleration and tolerance in their fields; all I have tried to do is to show that it is a real and important topic that needs empirical study of its origins and conditions, following only some broad philosophical criteria of relevance, as well as specifically philosophical refinement, critique and – certainly – justification.

4

The Elementary Types of Government[1]

The age is running mad after innovation; all the business of the
world is to be done in a new way; men are to be hanged in a new
way; Tyburn itself is not free from the fury of innovation.

DR JOHNSON

The Problem

IN trying to achieve the simplicity of, in some sense, scientific
statements one must either, in the counsels of the wise, be
very laboured or very brief. I want to be very brief and to use
an essay as an essay, an attempt to try something out or on
before a learned audience, or a timely speculation (that is, in
time to be stopped) about whether a possible future voyage is
worth undertaking, not an account of actual discovery.

Ever so many schemes of classification of 'types of government' exist, or slightly more tendentious talk and writing
about 'typologies' and 'political systems'. The framing and
criticism of such schemes has become almost an established
branch of the academic study of politics, and everyone
can supply to taste their own footnotes full of examples
of such work both empirical (that is typologies purporting to be theories or generalizations) and analytical (that
is true by definition or internal coherence, usually called
'model building'), and – perhaps more often than either
alone – philosophically bewildering mixtures of the two. Are
there any grounds on which we can rationally prefer one
scheme to another? Are there, to think of common faults,
empirical schemes which are not so concrete that they lose all
generality (i.e. that there are a thousand-and-one types of

1. First published in *Government or Opposition*, Winter 1968.

97

government), nor yet so general that they are only models of some reformed or deformed world (i.e. 'ideal types') but not of the actual.

What, after all, are we classifying for anyway? It is necessary to ask this if one is to find some middle path of mutual comprehension between being too systematic and not systematic enough (between, speaking broadly, both the Marxist and the American behavioural schools, on the one hand, and the British and the modern German schools on the other).

There are some radical nominalists who would think that every system of government is *sui generis* – and they are right, of course, in respect of certain questions. We are unlikely to glean many answers from comparisons or generalizations to questions about the fall of Walpole, the rise of the Pelhams, the formation of Aberdeen's last ministry or the resignation of Macmillan. But other sorts of questions (say about the growth of party bureaucracy or of central planning) can hardly be answered without generalization or comparison. The distinction is not a logical one, or one between 'persons', 'events' or 'social forces' (all different ways of looking at the same things), but simply one between degrees of importance or triviality. And here we can do nothing but recognize that while 'importance' and 'triviality' may be definable in terms of influence on events, they are also – thank God – completely subjective according to what scholars, inventors, scientists, statesmen and lovers (or in other words, anyone) happen to be interested in. I may simply happen to be interested in 'War Games' or the Common Seal of Canada for their own sweet sakes – unlikely but possible.

All I think we can and should take for granted is that classifications which deserve to be commonly used must answer important questions. 'Importance' is then some guarantee of some degree of generality. For otherwise it might sensibly be said – as so many textbooks appear to exhibit – that we simply classify for convenience. The number of instances of unique governments (the extreme nominalist position) are so many that we have to adopt some, or any, more or less arbitrary (and let us not pretend that they are anything but arbitrary etc.) scheme of classification. Again, this view is not to be dismissed out of hand. It is at least wise to treat classifications as extremely tentative, even if not as purely arbitrary. Yet this view has one great disadvantage. I think in each case it could be shown, a wearisome if pointed exercise, not to be true. For every different classification answers, consciously or unconsciously, implicitly or explicitly, different questions about different aspects of society. People classify for a purpose, and these purposes have to be ascertained. Some of these purposes are highly moralistic. For instance, most people, if the problem arises at all, operate with 'good' and 'bad', or with 'free government' and (a great variety of abusive words) 'the rest'. And, of course, such classifications have their uses. Other classifications strive to be ethically neutral, so that, for instance, whether countries have constitutions or not becomes significant – and an endless source of reverberating quibbles about what 'constitution' means. Many classifications, probably most, are inspired by some political doctrine attempting to blend the *is* and the *ought* (one cannot conceive of a political doctrine which did not offer grounds as to why what it held to be desirable was not also possible). For instance, to give only broad examples, the liberal tends to classify states by their type of electoral and representative institutions (by which there are then some naughty governments which are scarcely states at all); the conservative by the character of the ruling elite, and the socialist by the degree of working-class control of the economy (and if the criteria do not appear to fit, then so much the worse for these states – morally – or else they are deemed to be, always a much better bet, unstable – empirically).

So my first simple-minded point is that we are very unlikely to find any interesting or important classifications which do not contain both some moralistic element (i.e. one would like these distinctions to hold) *and* some empirical elements (i.e. that these distinctions have held). Every different classification answers, consciously or not, different questions about differing aspects of politics. There are institutional classifications, there are classifications by systems of authority and legitimacy; there are modern attempts to correlate either, or both, to types of social structure; and there are economic and even allegedly psychological classifications. Usually some kind of neo-Cartesian separation between 'ideas' and 'institutions' is assumed, and the bridges between them are then called 'processes' – and to some the world is nothing but 'process': there is neither fire nor pot, but only boiling; and there are no points of departure or final resting places, but only travelling (though they then have to identify many sorts of process all with strange patent names). And all of these new inventions stay together if put together, but there seem no compelling reasons why we should ever adopt one rather than another.

Every classification, then, serves some purpose, though usually very limited purposes either connected with some moral doctrine or with those aspects of society which any particular scholar happens to find interesting.

I take the simple view that it is most helpful to use words which embrace the largest numbers of different questions – questions perhaps initially of intellectual convenience only, but which must finally be shown to be of political relevance.

The questions and answers

So I set out initially just to identify the range of questions which have traditionally been asked about forms of government in political literature. 'Questions', but, of course, each of these following questions can, if thought to be the only significant question (as each of them has by some writers who have in fact done reasonably useful work), be treated as *the unique answer*. It should be obvious that there are no such single answers, even though people have believed that there are. But it is not so obvious, as I think I can show, that the questions deemed to be significant each yields a different answer in relation to possible or actual situations, and that all these answers fall into three broad clusters which are readily named. If the relations between them do not necessarily constitute a 'system', yet they are apparently systematic.

Ten subjects for questions appear to dominate both the traditional and the modern literature of politics. I do not claim that they are all either logically or pragmatically distinct, a different reading would define them differently and produce a different number. But I do claim that such a list as this is reasonably precise and exhaustive, and the answers to further significant questions would be unlikely to involve the discovery or definition of new types of government.

Questions have been asked which have assumed the dominant importance of each of these categories: (1) the role of the inhabitants; (2) the official doctrine; (3) the typical social structure; (4) the character and composition of the elite group; (5) the typical institution of government; (6) the type of economy; (7) the prevalent attitudes to law; (8) attitudes to knowledge; (9) attitudes to the diffusion of information and (10) attitudes to politics (or 'opposition', 'contestation' or 'public and legitimate conflict') itself.

What I want to suggest is that while the role and interaction of these categories of question and answer will vary uniquely for any particular society or system of government, yet they are all present in any known or seriously attempted form of government; and that these forms of government are basically, if reduced to their elements without contingent embellishments, three. I would name the three simply: Autocratic, Republican and Totalitarian government.

Premature definitions

'Autocratic' I take as either the government of an autocrat ('tyrant', 'despot', 'chieftain', 'king' or 'emperor' all being associated words of local and varying shades of meaning) or of an autocracy ('aristocracy', 'oligarchy', 'theocracy', 'bureaucracy', 'military caste', etc.). There is, at this level of generality, no significant difference of behaviour between regimes ruled by a few or by one. The oldest authorities agreed on this. Aristotle's 'Monarchy' is really an empty class, or a theoretical speculation – though admittedly one more real to the Greeks than to us: *if* there was a perfect man, then he should be made king, for a perfect man was clearly a god. (His distinction only helps us, even in modern times, to understand why some great autocrats have acted as if they were literally super-human.) Machiavelli's dramatized 'Prince' turns out in the *Discourses*, more soberly and yet even more powerfully, to be princely power (or absolute power), a function of government which Republics can even (or especially *should*) embrace who have not lost their *virtú* (political guts). And Hobbes also makes quite clear that the power of Leviathan can be found in one or in many. *Autocracy, to anticipate from what follows, is then the form of government which attempts to solve the basic problem of the adjustment of order to diversity by the authoritative enforcement of one of the diverse interests (whether seen as material or moral – almost always, in fact, both) as an officially sponsored and static ideology.*

'Republican' (or following Aristotle strictly, 'political governments' or 'polities', that is those who accept and even honour politics rather than trying either to suppress it, or to surpass it) is a far more comprehensive and accurate term than 'democratic'. There were republics long before the majority of inhabitants became enfranchised, and if 'democracy' is taken to mean something like government by the consent of the majority, then this is true for *any* modern state: the Soviets and the Chinese, unlike ancient and even early-modern (i.e. pre-industrial) autocrats, are as desperately dependent on the consent of the majority as are the Americans or the Swiss. That this consent may be due to force, chicane or lack of genuine choice is another matter (only confusing if one sees a necessary, rather than a desirable, but far from inevitable, connection between democracy and freedom). The point is that all industrial or industrializing regimes must (because of their dependence on the skilled factory worker) be democratic in a sense that autocracies facing vast peasantries had no need. And if the Americans, to speak broadly, have debased the word 'democracy' into almost total uselessness as a scientific term, the French tradition of 'republic', to speak with equal pedantry, has made us forget the Roman, the British Whig and the Dutch traditions in which 'republican virtues' and 'republican institutions' certainly did not imply 'no king', still less a dead one. So *Republican government*, to anticipate from what follows, *is then the attempt to solve the basic problem of the adjustment of order to diversity by conciliating differing interests by letting them share in the government or in the competitive choosing of the government.*

'Totalitarian' may appear to beg many questions, and is a term, for different reasons, almost impossible to use in some company, but if it is taken as a category of aspiration, not of performance, then I think events in this century have shown its persistent plausibility. Thus it rests on a different basis as a classifying term than 'autocratic' and 'republican', both of which, no one could deny, describe many actual present and past situations. But even if, which I accept, indeed claim (*pace* some passages in Hannah Arendt and most in Carl Friedrich), no modern government has in fact been able to exercise total power, yet it is necessary to recognize that the idea has arisen, that many conditions of the modern world make it plausible, that it has been tried and could well be tried again. If actual societies show no pattern of total governmental power, great events have occurred which can only be explained as consequences of the attempt to control totally or to keep alive such a hope. It is a peculiarity of the modern world (stemming from a belief in inevitable progress) that a category of aspiration, not subject to immediate empirical validation, becomes relevant as a classification. That some prophecies can now seek to be self-validating is now predictable enough. Arendt, Friedrich and others have argued the unique primacy of ideology in 'totalitarian states', which is true, but it does not make these states in fact total in their control of their inhabitants. Perhaps what should really emerge is a formulation even more abstract than 'ideology', but psychologically even more compelling: the uniqueness to the modern world of 'consciousness', as Marx and Hegel argued, that ideas and circumstances are both uniquely related to each other, are knowable and thus manipulable. Consciousness, breaking from habit and tradition, alone constitutes both the necessary condition of morality and the possibility of controlled social change (or predictable progress towards a definite and final social goal) – itself a distinctively modern concept. To come down to earth, were autocrats conscious of governing autocratically? I very much doubt it, except in pejorative moral senses. Did they see themselves as deliberately operating a specific system, or merely as simply governing? But the Nazis, the Soviets and the new Chinese have all, in very different ways, been stridently explicit about *trying* (whereas the Italians and the Spaniards merely pretended) to do something new and comprehensive. 'Politics' itself they denounced as selfish, as something not of or in the general interest; or they have defined it, correctly, as being concerned with partial interests and relative truths and not with 'the truth' and the total management of society and a general or mass welfare. To those who see the whole concept of totalitarianism (rather than its abuse) as simply a product of 'the cold war', I would say that we all should, indeed, have been railing against the impossibility of totalitarianism more than its iniquity; but that it is after all (as has happened in Russia and Germany, and may be happening in China) precisely the attempt to do the impossible which has killed men in millions where the autocrats killed in their tens of thousands. So *Totalitarian government*, to anticipate from what follows, *is the attempt to solve the basic problem of the adjustment of order to diversity by creating a completely new society such that conflict would no longer arise: it attempts to do this by means of the guidance and enforcement of a revolutionary ideology which claims to be scientific, thus comprehensive and necessary, both for knowledge and allegiance.*

I suggest that these definitions are premature in the sense that their validity depends not on their familiarity and customary usage, but because empirically each of them yields a different answer to the dominant questions set out above. Am I finding the categories to fit the concepts, or vice versa? What I think I have done is to ask the above questions of all types of government of which I have ever read, then to find that the answers fall into three clusters consistent with the above *a priori* or traditional (with the exception of 'totalitarian') concepts.

The pattern

So, very *briefly* and *schematically*, let me try to show the apparent pattern or clustering of particular answers to general questions (otherwise it is 800 pages, if it proves, after criticism, worth trying to show the sources and authorities – which would be all very traditional and conventional – for this rather obvious, but simple and useful, classification).

I THE ROLE OF THE INHABITANTS

AUTOCRATIC: *passive obedience and social deference* ('suffer the powers that be' and 'the rich man at his castle, the poor man at his gate . . .'); but then general mobilization for deliberate social change is impossible.

REPUBLICAN: *voluntary and individual participation* ('republican virtues' and 'active citizenship' are required, but hence a man is free to act as a citizen or not; so a discriminatory or a partial kind of loyalty: only in time of war can the state mobilize all its inhabitants, and in other times any individual can, but some must, move backwards and forwards between private and public life).

TOTALITARIAN: *mass participation and compulsory explicit enthusiasm* (passive obedience is rejected as inadequate or suspect. 'Who are those who are not the friends of the people but are the enemies of the people?').

2 THE OFFICIAL DOCTRINE

AUTOCRATIC: allegiance is *a religious duty and government is part of divine order* (when the basis of political legitimacy is made transcendental and beyond question: Gibbon's sneer, 'the usefulness of christianity to civil polity' deserves to be generalized).[1] None the less, only open disbelief is punished (inner reservations to the doctrine are tolerated if they remain private).

REPUBLICAN: allegiance is demanded and given *on utilitarian and secular grounds* (when practical benefits in the here-and-now must be demonstrated: if authority is not precisely a contract, yet a contractual language of 'rights and duties' is spoken). None the less, occasional conformity (though often trivial) is demanded to each particular formulation of the doctrine.

TOTALITARIAN: allegiance is *ideological* (when it is supposed to be all-embracing, exclusive and predetermined for necessary purposes, since all thought is a *product* of circumstance – whether material or racial – so that only when all social contradictions are completely removed, the task of the revolution, is a single truth possible). Inner reservations must be exposed and punished just as surely as open dissent.

3 TYPICAL SOCIAL STRUCTURE

AUTOCRATIC: *a highly stratified caste or class structure* usually involving some slavery or serfdom.

REPUBLICAN: a large *middle class or bourgeoisie* (on this all authorities, despite difficulties of definition, are agreed, from Aristotle, Machiavelli, Montesquieu, Harrington and Marx to modern political sociologists like Kornhauser or Lipset). But note that 'middle', in modern conditions, need not imply that other classes exist: the classless society, when it comes, will be bourgeois in its structure and values – not proletarian. 'Proletarian' is a category of oppression not of dominance:

1. And if this sounds like a piece of Enlightenment or Victorian rationalism, it is: I think they were right on this point – though the converse does not necessarily hold, that religion is dependent on autocracy. Now the only possible proof of this generalization, like all the generalizations I am recounting, is not any listing of authorities however vast, *but whether it is possible to think of a contrary instance*. (So this one footnote can serve for all.)

the 'dictatorship of the proletariat' inevitably becomes that of, at the best, a 'new class'.

TOTALITARIAN: *egalitarian* in aspiration, possibly the half-way fraud of 'national equality' (but in fact a social structure mainly determined by political function).

4 ELITE GROUP

AUTOCRATIC: *Self-perpetuating and exclusive* (almost always fortified by myths, biological or religious, of descent from gods or great men). Relatively small in numbers.

REPUBLICAN: *a stable political class enjoying social prestige*, but not exclusively, and readily penetrable by candidates from political and educational institutions designed to encourage mobility (then always the political and especially the democratic argument turns around, 'how much mobility?' – but always some). Relatively large in numbers.

TOTALITARIAN: in theory *a meritocracy based on perfect social mobility* ('to each according to his needs, from each according to his abilities'). In practice a relatively small 'inner party' with a relatively large 'outer party'.

5 TYPICAL INSTITUTION OF GOVERNMENT

AUTOCRATIC: *the Court or the Palace* (a visible, physically locatable, militarily defensible awe-inspiring but isolated and private society within a society: the place where either an inner aristocracy resides permanently, or where all the aristocracy has to reside occasionally. There may be rival courts in some types of autocracy, particularly the feudal, but it is always regarded as unnatural and temporary. 'Come ye not to Court? To whose Court, to the King's Court or to Hampton Court?').

REPUBLICAN: *a Parliament, Assembly or Congress* (sometimes by which, but more often through which, the country can only be governed).

TOTALITARIANISM: the *single party* (who function as both the elite group and as the ideologists who can foretell the future development of the ideology through changing circumstances). Note that a single party with a genuine ideology is a quite different institution from any single party, even the overwhelmingly dominant one, in states with public contestation between groups – which is the usual, but not the invariable, pattern of republics. (Surviving autocracies all claim to have parties, but this is very rarely true: African political parties, for instance, have often turned out to be personal followings, which could not outlive their leader, with – the vital point – no powers of self-perpetuation).

6 THE ECONOMY

AUTOCRATIC: *agrarian* (and if a relatively large country, almost invariably either following a theory of 'autarky' or involved in constant political and military attempts to dominate markets and sources of supplies). Certainly *pre-industrial*: industrialism either leads into one of the other categories, or results in a chronic instability for autocracies.

REPUBLICAN: originally a *market or capitalist economy, finally a 'mixed economy'* (that is self-consciously mixed, as a matter of public policy; fully and rationally planned economies do not exist, the aspiration towards them only arose from the experience of the First World War – even to Marx production was either a product of class interest or else, after the great qualitative changes, would be spontaneous; but to put an economy on a war-time footing of total planning usually demands war, whether internal or external).

TOTALITARIAN: *the war economy* or planned and *rapid* industrialization (the rejection of 'mere' economic criteria).

7 ATTITUDE TO LAW

AUTOCRATIC: *customary and god-given*: the law *is* the State, both indistinguishable and both (officially) unchangeable. (Autocracies, history was invented to tell us, are founded by gods, demi-gods or supermen who *give* the thus sacred laws. More mundanely, the actual law that is applied to individuals will be a product of their status, and the lower their status, the more arbitrary it will be in application, timing and outcome.)

REPUBLICAN: both *custom and statute* (parliaments as makers of *new* laws, but greatly limited by custom and convention, particularly in *how* they make law. So both 'the good old laws' and 'the will of the State'. Law between individuals is largely a matter of contract and its application is regular or general, but invariably slow even if reasonably predictable.)

TOTALITARIAN: *laws of history* (to be interpreted by party ideologists, who themselves have varying degrees of conviction, but all believe that some parts of the ideology constitute necessary laws of social development). Actual law is interpreted by its intention, not by what it says; and it is arbitrary and swift in application, but regular and general in outcome if applied.

8 ATTITUDES TO KNOWLEDGE

AUTOCRATIC: all knowledge is seen as one and as part of the hidden '*mystery of power*' or inexplicable '*reason of State*' (to be accepted on authority, if questioned at all then only among – and often for the entertainment of – the ruling elite, so within the palace walls); hence *censorship* as a general (but negative) institution (if there are universities or learned academies, they are part of the court circle). Knowledge is power and is to be guarded jealously.

REPUBLICAN: *knowledge is fragmented*, most moral truths become seen as relative (and distinguished from scientific truths), and all moral truths become open to some form of *public questioning*; further, there is official patronage of independent or semi-independent institutions of learning (there will be censorship, but of a residual, limited and negative kind). Knowledge has to be spread for this kind of society to work effectively.

TOTALITARIAN: all knowledge is seen as one and is *ideological*: the censorship is general (as in autocracy), but it is also positive: *propaganda becomes a State institution*. (Universities and academies are under complete party control, and science is seen only as technology.) Knowledge is graded according to recognized degrees of ideological awareness, and at the appropriate level its acquisition is compulsory.

9 ATTITUDES TO THE DIFFUSION OF INFORMATION

AUTOCRATIC: Proclamations, but no regular news, hence *rumour and gossip as institutions* (used and exploited by both rulers and ruled), hence both the spy as eavesdropper, who reports what people say, and the satirist or wise-buffoon also become institutionalized. (So mainly oral communication, but some private circulation of manuscripts about how things happen, or should happen. If these 'Books of Power' come to be printed, or otherwise made readily available, it is a sign that republican conditions are beginning to arise: the Prince himself is needing to know more accurately how people and forces beyond his immediate control will react, and authors think that there are useful allies outside the palace.) The truth cannot be told about how the regime works (hence only a covert or allegorical study of politics).

REPUBLICAN: *newspapers* and a growingly popular market for them, some at least not under the control of the state. (Printed materials outpace oral communication, whether rumours or speeches, both in quantity and accuracy as sources of political information and speculation.) The effective working of these regimes comes to depend on more and more people having access to accurate information about how the State is run and on the State being able to measure public opinion reasonably accurately; hence considerable neutrality and objectivity in official publications, polls and surveys in democratic republics and a thriving literature of politics – both in treatises and novels.

TOTALITARIAN: *mass communications* controlled completely

by the party and a compulsory market for them. (The encyclopaedia and the newspaper preferred to the book, and novels specifically, but all other art forms generally, are required to be propaganda. No objective studies of politics, and hence extreme unreliability of all kinds of official statistics – even for the party's own use – and no reliable knowledge of public opinion.)

10 ATTITUDES TO POLITICS

AUTOCRATIC: either *above politics*, or politics is *limited* to the secrecy of the palace or the court (conflict and opposition are always expected, and sometimes tolerated, so long as they do not become public or appeal to a public outside the ruling class). Politics is conspiracy.

REPUBLICAN: *politics is always tolerated*, sometimes encouraged, and opposition can be made public and is sometimes institutionalized. Politics is conciliation.

TOTALITARIAN: *politics and opposition are seen as subversive*, and not just personal intrigue or conspiracy, but a symptom of social contradictions yet to be eradicated. Politics is a bourgeois sham.

Some conclusions and difficulties

My contention is that this scheme is not just analytically clear and simple, but is empirically true: that types of regime studied historically (including contemporary history) reveal these broad characteristics; and also that these characteristics, if the questions they answer separately are put together, are in some way systematically related – as best expressed by the three main concepts. One should reach the same results whichever way one works. This is, of course, too neat by far. The characteristics are themselves generalizations of a considerable degree of abstraction, like any generalizations, so liable to particular exceptions and peculiar and famous hybrids at any given time and place. But the argument comes down to this (if advanced in full): to convince the historian that generalization is sensible and that any generalization involves simplification or abstraction; and to convince the political scientist that these apparent systematic relationships can be expressed thus simply – without any more elaborate conceptual framework or any special vocabulary of induced (i.e. quite unknown to the actors in political events) processes.

What I have not done, of course, is to *explain* these relationships – which is a huge and perhaps impossible task. How far, for instance are (1) and (4) or (3) and (10) related to each other? I would simply assume that there is *some* systematic relationship: to treat them all as independent variables would seem mildly crazy; but so would it be to claim that they are all necessarily dependent on each other (still more that one could ever express these relationships quantitatively, although perhaps symbolically, if that were helpful).

Perhaps what is worrying is what one may mean by 'systematic' and still more by 'system'. But if my attempt to summarize traditional knowledge is acceptable, if the generalizations appear to be broadly true, perhaps we need not worry too much about this. If we say that there is a political system or a social system, we are saying that every factor in it interacts with, conditions and is conditioned by everything else. (Hence to say either 'political' or 'social' will not matter very much *if* there is such a system: we are only singling out, rather improperly and tendentiously, what we think to be a particularly important factor, but not one in any sense autonomous.) Now I think this to be true of anything one can sensibly call a society. It sounds silly even to bother to say this, because it is really a truism. In societies everything does interact (albeit for many things quite trivially). But it is worth saying because often the concept of 'system' is a tautology: simply what we mean by society, or by societies as they appear when we study them. Economic theory, for instance, assumes that there is an economic system: but then economists are for ever complaining that political factors spoil the rationality of the assumed economic system (and this can be said by both liberals and Marxists, though by no one else). I think we can properly be more empirical than economists, even at the price of being less systematic. But this does not mean that we need be unsystematic.

If, then, 'system' is a truism or a tautology, no inferences can be drawn from any particular formulation. We must draw concepts of 'system' from what we observe, not vice versa. Suppose we ask, is it true in fact that everything important interacts, conditions or is conditioned by everything else in the political or social system? The answer is obviously, not. 'Importance' makes the difference. To vary factor 'X' within a social system may have effects on all the other factors, but many of them are almost certain to be trivial. And I do not see how much further one can go than this: some criteria of importance must be introduced into any systematic analysis of politics. Usually these criteria are themselves political. I do not see how this can be avoided, nor really why it should. I have tried to show in the first essay the close and inevitable connection between political theories and political doctrines. What is important for science is not that the motive is pure, but that the particular generalization is of such a kind that it can be confirmed or refuted.

If my generalizations are mainly true, some important systematic relationships appear – as I will soon briefly show. But a final double objection against wishing for too high a degree of abstraction, however internally consistent the theory then appears – the neo-Parsonian 'systems analysis' approach. Firstly, it is unnecessary, seeing how much one can draw together with simpler, traditional methods; and secondly, strictly speaking if there were a fully interdependent social system, there would be no politics. This was, indeed, famously the view of Marx and, on a methodological level, is that of Parsons too. Is politics just a derivative of all other social relations, as some sociologists argue; or is it that which alone holds, by will and reason, any society together – as Hobbes argued?

Such extreme views are probably not very helpful. Government arises because there is no spontaneously operating relationship between social groups such as to ensure their continuity and survival without political skill or invention. Social structure is never completely systematic (except in misleading models of society): it is government that, at the very least, picks up the loose ends, improvises connections for those that have broken, and hammers or oils others into easier motion. No amount of political skill can transform some situations, but none uniquely *determine* any form of government. All one could say is that the difficulties get progressively greater, practically overwhelming, if the prince or autocrat, fortunate in war, wishes to govern a state whose, say, (1), (3), (6) and and (8) are all more usually associated with, broadly speaking, republican government.

If political sociology were simply a reduction of politics to sociology it would be either (as it sometimes is) an unhelpfully abstract and over-systematic way of looking at things, or else empirically false. The real question, at this level of abstraction, is always a double one: 'How far are types of government determined by social structure?'; *and* 'How far is social structure determined by government?'

All this as postscript or interjection because I am so conscious of fighting on a double front: against those who see no use in any such systematic analysis as I have sketched out above, and against those who might say either that it is not systematic enough (that is not quantifiable), or (the objection that worries me more) too specific and concrete.

What, of importance, follows from such an analysis? If the ten different clusterings within three types are even broadly correct empirically, it argues considerable stability for any regime when they coincide. I did not set out to set down the conditions of political stability: this may be the master question, but then there are obviously many conditions common to any possible forms of government. (Hence the longer list of conditions for the stability of 'political regimes' or republics in the Appendix to the Pelican edition of my *In Defence of Politics*.) But it would seem that subsuming all other classifications which answer different questions, such as 'empire' (the rule of one culture over another which can occur in all three forms), or sub-categories of any one form, like oriental despotism and feudal government as distinct types of autocratic rule, that the tendency is for states to be somewhere firmly within these three clusterings, or else to be unstable.

This is why all the attempts to define what is so obvious a question in the modern world prove futile – the distinct form of government of the 'New Nations', the 'Emergent Territories', 'the Third World' and other names. They have no distinct form. It is either romantic of us or ultra-sociological to think, as so many think, that they necessarily must. Simply to take governments in former British, Belgian and French Africa, their most common characteristic is chronic instability. The social systems seem largely independent of the political. The governments would like to transform society, sometimes even they have a totalitarian impulse, but they have no possibility of succeeding in that way. They are mainly autocracies, but rendered unstable by aroused economic expectations both in their elites and in their general populations – expectations arising from completely external factors and which cannot possibly be met internally. This does argue, it is hard to avoid the conclusion, that the long term effects of the industrial and the French revolutions have been (as our liberal ancestors said) to render autocratic government less and less viable, though to make totalitarian government a tempting alternative aspiration, and in some circumstances almost as plausible as republican government would be.

There is some case for calling all these many different types of government, 'transitional government' or some such equivocal term; but this is only to lump together as a classification what is, in fact, a problem or a dilemma. It is indeed very hard to show what systematic relationships these new governments all have in common, especially when their problems mainly arise, taken one by one, from their lack as yet (or else utter collapse, which in some cases is possible) of sufficient coherence between political and social structure. Even David Apter's concept of 'modernizing autocracies' confuses, I think, a problem, a dilemma, an aspiration with genuinely systematic political relationships. The above analysis would suggest that a 'modernizing autocracy' is a contradiction in terms, or something which must be overcome (and then probably in the one direction or the other), if it is to have any hopes of permanence, of overcoming 'internal contractions'.

This is why 'democracy' is unhelpful as a classification of systems of government. It is a common condition of all industrial or industrializing governments (and has nothing necessarily to do with personal freedom). Modern republican government (that is post-industrial revolution) *and* totalitarian government both depend upon and need to mobilize the energies of the mass of their population in a way that autocracies cannot. And 'nationalism' as a doctrine has no more proved a sufficient condition for stability in new states than it has proved a necessary condition for stability in all old states. (To avoid misunderstanding let me underline one point: it seemed to me historically wrong to make a competitive party system a necessary condition for republican government; and it is also wrong in the modern world: Tanzania, for instance, must fall squarely under my republican criteria, and several of the People's Republics in Eastern Europe seem to be moving that way.) So my analysis makes me both pessimistic and optimistic. That some regimes which are at present autocratic systems will have to become more and more republican in form in order to industrialize or to apply industrial methods to agriculture; but also that others may try, with outside help, the path of total transformation. A rather obvious prophecy emerges: an increased polarization between 'Republican' and 'Totalitarian' systems of government, so long as one grants that persistent instability will be the lot, for many many years, of many governments in new nations.

The actual advantages of republics in survival and the tempting prospects of totalitarianism in permanence are plainly bound up with their superior capacity, compared to autocracies, to institutionalize change – whether by self-generating processes, by state planning or the far more ordinary mixtures of both. Stability, in other words, is not a static category. Renewal and adjustment to changing circumstances is the test of stable government, not simply longevity: consider, for example, the incredibly tenuous, but seventy-year life span, of the French Third Republic – simply, as Professor Cobban has put it, 'its failure to collapse'. And I think I am plagiarizing from an American student's seminar paper to say that 'political stability is a process of organizing change so as to ensure future self-sustaining change without serious institutional rupture'. Yes.

One last objection to my proposed classification, an historical thesis to my mind more telling than 'Third World' objections: Wittfogel's magisterial correction of, or polemic against, Marx, that there was, in 'Oriental Despotism', a preindustrial form of total power. If so, this would completely shatter the sharp distinction drawn between old autocracy and aspirant totalitarianism; and any systematic relationships between the ten categories would be in doubt. They would be in doubt if all that followed for government and society from the need for vast schemes of hydraulic engineering for irrigation was as Wittfogel asserts.

Certainly this kind of despotism or autocratic rule could be more arbitrary, and thus powerful and unpredictable, than modern totalitarianism. But misuse of individuals is not the sole test of totalitarianism: one can readily concede that cruelties in these ancient regimes are more horrible, because seemingly more pointless and arbitrary and done with less sublime excuse. Yet one must add that such arbitrary cruelties and enforced labour were probably even less efficient than in Hitler's Germany or Stalin's Russia where the enthusiasm of large parties was evident and effective.

Certainly the scale of public works and the organization of it by the state surpasses, in Wittfogel's regimes, anything else in the annals of autocracy. They are a very special sub-category. But a sub-category none the less, for Wittfogel is surely wrong in his key assertion. Total power is only a very relative thing if it does not involve, as it has even in republics under conditions of modern war, total mobilization of manpower. Hydraulic planning was vast and great planning, involving the conscription and forced labour of tens and even hundreds of thousands of peasants. But the key institution was what he himself calls, by analogy, the *corvée*. It was a conscription of individuals or a mobilization of society only for certain seasons of the year for the essential public works of irrigation. Actual production of food remained, if not private, at least communal at a village level. Hence a segmented society. Production was not controlled by the state as in modern regimes. If the armies of diggers and ditchers were kept away from the villages for even one whole year, famine for the entire society would have followed. Only in industrial society, only through the factory and through specialization, can workers be conscripted in such a way that the actual exercise of total power does not result in total disruption and general starvation. But even so, it is necessary to remind ourselves that the third category is a category of aspiration: it has yet to be proved, in Russia or China, that agriculture can be fully industrialized or communized and the peasantry transformed or got rid of utterly.

Lastly, I stress 'elementary': many sub-categories are possible, and many questions are important that cut across these three categories completely. But if 'elementary', elementary in the sense of basic, not of simple: of *grundlagen* not of abstract models – even 'elemental', for it seems plain that there are strong causal connections between many of these categories, so that the three types of government constitute 'fields of force' which tend to exclude other alternatives and, in the long run, draw marginal cases one way or another towards the centre of one of the three constellations. This does have obvious implications for political practice – as Machiavelli long ago saw: if one is concerned with survival, then one thing clearly or another: intermediate positions prove fatal.[1] Personally I doubt if one can go much further than this, for instance to say which of the ten categories are the more open to deliberate control. This will probably vary greatly, as will

1. See further the sections on 'The Value of Conflict' and 'The Conditions for Republican Rule' in my Introduction to Machiavelli, *The Discourses* (Penguin Books, 1970).

their mutual importance, according to different circumstances and culture-patterns. At this point answers become very specific. But it is something to have tried to go as far as I have tried to go in summarizing a conventional wisdom which is far more systematic than is now generally believed, for: 'Though nothing can be immortal, which mortals make, yet if man had the use of reason they pretend to, their Commonwealths might be secured at least from perishing by internal diseases' (Thomas Hobbes).

5

The World of Michael Oakeshott[1]

The predicament of Western morals . . . is first that our moral
life has come to be dominated by the pursuit of ideals, a dominance ruinous to a settled habit of behaviour; and, secondly, that
we have come to think of this dominance as a benefit for which
we should be grateful or an achievement of which we should be
proud. And the only purpose to be served by this investigation of
our predicament is to disclose the corrupt consciousness, the self-
deception which reconciles us to our misfortunes.

Rationalist politics, I have said, are the politics of the felt need,
the felt need not qualified by a genuine, concrete knowledge of
the permanent interests and direction of movement of a society,
but interpreted by 'reason' and satisfied according to the technique of an ideology: they are the politics of the book.

The morality of the Rationalist is the morality of the self-made
man and of the self-made society. . . .

MICHAEL OAKESHOTT

A spectre is haunting the London School of Economics and
(please don't forget) Political Science. For ten years the
sceptical, polemical, dandiacal, paradoxical, gay and bitter
spirit of Michael Oakeshott has been haunting, rather than
filling, the Chair of Political Science formerly held by Harold
Laski. It is fair to put it this way, for the question at issue is
the one that he himself has raised: whether 'his subject' (or
the job he put in for) deserves to live at all, still less to be
lively. When we first heard the incantatory rise and fall of his

1. This was a review of Michael Oakeshott's collected essays, *Rationalism
in Politics*, and was published in *Encounter*, June 1963. (What space that
magazine can give its chosen reviewers – alas that I had to subsequently
write to the editor that I would gladly write again for *Encounter*, when
both its policies and its editor were changed.)

voice proclaim that famous passage of his inaugural lecture, *Political Education*:

In political activity, then, men sail a boundless and bottomless sea; there is neither harbour for shelter nor floor for anchorage, neither starting place nor appointed destination. The enterprise is to keep afloat on an even keel. . . .

and when he commented that this was a 'depressing doctrine' only for those moved by false hopes, or for 'those who have lost their nerve', we thought we were faced with a familiar project of conservative philosophers, even though one seldom attempted, a linking of the ocean of Hegel to the inland sea of Burke. Indeed as a student I once wrote across the back of an unopened notebook:

> Long ago in London town
> Marx turned Hegel upside-down
> Revealing him as *sans-culotte*;
> OAKESHOTT saved him from that blot,
> Restoring quick his balance true,
> He dressed him up in Tory blue;
> This seemed to be for LSE,
> Dialectical Indecency.

And so we were not much impressed then, or now, by Richard Crossman's brand of instant polemic in the old *New Statesman*, that Oakeshott was a CONSERVATIVE! It seemed that Crossman had forgotten what a free university was. But we quickly came to realize that if the language was that of Hegel and Bradley, and *some* of the sentiments were those of Burke, yet the matter was not merely an attack on metaphysics, as radical as any from the heirs of Wittgenstein; it was also an attack on the possibility of any theoretical knowledge about politics and society, and sprang from a complete scepticism that any political doctrines can have any philosophical foundation. Here was something beyond the fringe of normal conservative experience.

His reputation has been esoteric: one big book of highly abstract, synthetic philosophy in the mode of Bradley, largely unread – *Experience and Its Modes* (1933); an anthology called

Contemporary Political Thought (with the most perfunctory of introductions); the *Guide to the Classics* (of horses, not books); an introduction to an edition of Hobbes' *Leviathan* (a classic case of an Introduction which should be taken afterwards); and a handful of biting polemical essays in the former *Cambridge Journal*. But now that he has published his major essays, with even a few new ones, it is puzzling to see how reviewers have missed the point. Mr David Marquand handled him gingerly and respectfully, in the new *New Statesman*, as a most intelligent type of modern Conservative; it was the turn of the *TLS* to turn loose a nameless Crossman-like animus (such brave anonymity!), predictable as ever, accusing him of being a Conservative; and Mr Henry Fairlie steadied the drifting *Spectator* to hail Oakeshott as the high priest of modern Conservatism.

But Oakeshott's scepticism far transcends anything that can be called, in any possible party sense, 'Conservative' – and he has never sought such a label. If labels there must be, for quick readers and sluggish thinkers, he is Tory not Conservative, and if Tory, then, as Orwell once called Swift, 'a Tory anarchist'. He calls into question, with a profundity that neither polemic nor praise has done justice to, not merely the arbitrariness of all reformist thought (of all attempts to demonstrate objective 'needs' which 'must be realized'), but also the basic character of the ideas of that modern, Western, reformist, revisionist-Christian, technological civilization which normal conservatives and normal socialists like to say 'we have in common'. Oakeshott's account of politics at least has nothing in common with all those who believe that 'we must believe in certain fundamentals' in order to survive at all.

Now it is not always easy to be clear exactly what Oakeshott is saying. Partly, this is his own fault. He is so sure that he will be misunderstood that he often seems to welcome it: so that he can always find more fools to mock (particularly would-be disciples). Partly, it is a matter of the famous style. It is so full of tricks and whimsy, breath-taking leaps from the baroque to the colloquial, swift symphonic changes of cadence, verbal paradox and unlikely metaphor, that it becomes an end in itself. His is not, to speak mildly, a 'propositional prose'; it is often unclear where the weight should lie in the many assertions and witty qualifications of the very long sentences. And he speaks in at least three different voices. Although attacking all modernity, he does *live* in the modern world (his address is in the phone book) and part of him tries to revive the grand manner of the Tory pamphleteers of the age of Wellington and Eldon. But then there is reflection about the silliness of seriousness in a world of, at times, delightful vanity – all this is in the tone of the Dandy, and the appeal is made (as in *The Voice of Poetry in the Conversation of Mankind*), in politics, morals and art, to the connoisseur against the expert. Oakeshott, like Proust's Swann, if directly challenged for an opinion will say something erudite, but tantalizingly less than half relevant. There is also a philosophical voice which asks for reasons for so many good things which so many people take for granted, and then insinuates, with a gentle sharpness, that there can be no reasons for acting in these ways save that other people have already done so. The heart of his formal philosophy, in *Experience and Its Modes* (a greatly underestimated book), was an attempt to deny that Cartesian distinction between subject and object, observer and observed, fact and value, and to show that there is only a total flow of experience, from which we make some arbitrary 'arrests' and call them modes of knowing, but must indeed know them to be arbitrary. If, then, the only distinctions that can be drawn are between levels of experience – the more abstract and general, or the more concrete and limited – then he certainly practises what he preachers. The philosopher Oakeshott, the dandy-aesthete and the Tory Blood all jostle and mingle with each other in everything he writes. They do not aim to contradict each other; they are simply – in his favourite metaphor of the human condition – holding a conversation together. Only fools and ill-bred people, he tells us, confuse conversation with argument (argument hopes, vainly, to reach conclusions).

He tells us in the Preface that his essays 'although they do not compose a settled doctrine, they disclose a consistent style of disposition of thought'. If we look for a doctrine, it certainly has not settled; and, in any case, for Oakeshott all doctrines are doctrinaire. But there were certain key concepts which might help us at least to understand better 'our predicament' and 'our misfortunes'. First, there was 'experience' itself, soon gaining the more precise and political modulation of 'tradition'; this in turn gave way to the 'character' of something, then simply to the 'appropriateness' of one thing to another, now just – to cover all – 'style or disposition'. It is hard to see how he can achieve any higher abstraction without ceasing to converse publicly at all. The first is not contradicted by the last; he never repudiates or wholly abandons any of the subsequent concepts; the later ones are simply more comprehensive. And the substance is as fluid if we look at his gallery of errors: Rationalism, Collectivism, Technique, Liberalism (and, recently, the Vocational) all succeed each other as the *Enemy*, subsuming each other Hegel-like without wholly superseding their predecessor.

Since all these published essays overlap in ascending spirals, or are variations on a theme, it matters little which we examine in detail. Perhaps we may be impertinent and look at the most political of the essays – to examine his reputation as a Conservative.

What is possibly the only simple factual assertion in the book is wrong. 'Of these essays', begins the Preface (dated 1962), 'composed during the last twelve years. . . .' The first essay, 'Rationalism in Politics' is dated 1947, and the second, 'The Political Economy of Freedom' 1949. This is important, for the years of the Labour Government exhibit the part of Oakeshott which is simply – with not much philosophical nonsense about it – a brilliant Tory pamphleteer in the tradition of the *Edinburgh Review*, a man to thunder, bemoan, and squib with the best of them, firing volleys of red-hot shot at rival extremists, right above the heads of the centre. In the 'Political Economy of Freedom' he calls himself a 'libertarian' and rolls out best Burkean bluster: 'With eyes focused upon distant horizons and minds clouded with foreign clap-trap, the impatient and sophisticated generation now in the saddle has dissolved its partnership with its past and is careful of everything except its liberty.' Did anyone's flesh really creep at the Jacobinism of Major Attlee? This is clearly not the philosophical Oakeshott who shows that no one *can* break from tradition, but it is a Tory Oakeshott who castigates people for succeeding in breaking Burke's 'great partnership'. And more: 'The government of a collectivist society can tolerate only a very limited opposition to its plans; indeed, that hard-won distinction, which is one of the elements of our liberty, between opposition and treason is rejected: what is not obedience is sabotage.' Fortunately the order for his arrest got lost in the post. It all hangs together, but as a description of some other society. When he defines 'collectivist' one sees how his style of Tory wrath gets in the way of scholarly discrimination: 'Collectivism in the modern world . . . stands for a managed society, and its other titles are communism, national socialism, socialism, economic democracy and central planning.' Here is a bizarre failure to draw distinctions, something on a level with Churchill's 'Gestapo' polemic against Attlee.

Perhaps the book he happened to be reviewing was the first book of pure liberal economics he had read. 'The third object of this economic policy is a stable currency, maintained by an application of fixed and known rules and not by day-to-day administrative tricks. And that this belongs to the political economy of freedom needs no argument: inflation is the mother of servitude.' There is no need to deny that the 'fixed-money-crank' is a type of conservative, but he is a rather embarrassing one. So too was his 'there is good reason for supposing that labour monopolies are more dangerous than any others' – all good blunt party stuff. But what was extraordinary – for a 'libertarian' – was a sudden swing at the conventional importance of 'freedom of speech', the 'extraordinary emphasis' upon which was simply the self-interest of a 'small vocal section' of society!

. . . under the influence of misguided journalists and cunning tyrants, we are too ready to believe that so long as our freedom to speak is not impaired we have lost nothing of importance – which is not so. However secure may be a man's right to speak his thoughts, he may find what is to him a much more important freedom curtailed when his house is sold over his head by a public authority, or when he is deprived of his leasehold because his land-lord has sold out to a development company, or when his member-ship of a trade union is compulsory and debars him from an employment he would otherwise take.

It sounds as if our philosopher was having trouble with his lease. People may certainly choose property-tenure before freedom of speech; but we know that in the long run they are always mistaken. Speech is liberty, and it is in fact so patent that no one could ever take away 'all else' and just leave us with our 'mere' freedom of speech. Oakeshott knows that. But his abhorrence of mere sincerity, unless it has a cranky colour to it, extends even to 'freedom'. Perhaps, if all this deserves to be remembered at all, it does not deserve to be taken very seriously, except as an illustration of the varying levels on which Oakeshott can write.

The essay which should frighten Conservatives most (and was probably intended to do so), is 'On Being Conservative' (1956). Here is a more calm and measured mocking at things than the angry, bitter tone of the essays in the late 1940s when Oakeshott saw the hand of tyranny already upon us. The basic theme is clear and convincing; it concerns the character of politics as an activity, not the appropriateness of any type of politics. The 'conservative' and the 'politician' are virtually identified: men who reject the pursuit of pre-meditated goals, and see politics as the wise management of affairs and tendencies already at hand or afoot.

Coming to be at home in this commonplace world qualifies us (as no knowledge of 'political science' can ever qualify us), if we are so inclined and have nothing better to think about, to engage in what the man of conservative disposition understands to be political activity.

This is what politics is – making a home of the common-place world. To make new worlds may be held to be desirable, but it is simply not politics; certainly the methods of utopians are rarely political. This is an admirable breath of human warmth in a subject – as Oakeshott often points out – whose very vocabulary of description is often rotten with moralistic rhetoric of aspiration. But why the jejune cynicism of 'nothing better to think about'? Plainly anything we can mean by 'being at home', or civilized, depends (for all his fear of sincerity and earnestness) upon some distinction between acting politically and acting ideologically. Politics, for this reason, is the 'master-science' still. But Oakeshott means what he says: politics is not very important.

But further, there are activities, not involving human relationships, that may be engaged in, not for a prize, but for the enjoyment they generate, and for which the only appropriate disposition is the disposition to be conservative. Consider fishing. If your project is merely to catch fish it would be foolish to be unduly conservative. You will seek out the best tackle, you will discard practices which prove unsuccessful, you will not be bound by unprofitable attachments to particular localities, pieties will be fleeting, loyalties evanescent; you may even be wise to try anything once in the hope of improvement. But fishing is an activity that may be engaged in, not for the profits of a catch, but for its own sake; and the fisherman may return home in the evening not less content for being empty handed. Where this is so, the activity has become ritual and a conservative disposition is appropriate. Why worry about the best gear if you do not care whether or not you make a catch? What matters is the enjoyment of exercising skill (or, perhaps, merely passing the time), and this is to be had with any tackle, so long as it is familiar and is not grotesquely inappropriate.

Has this anything specifically to do with politics? The metaphor seems to embrace all of human life. It may give some comfort to some, none to others; appear realistic to some, romantic to others. It is a pretty picture that we may take or leave as we choose. But Oakeshott thinks it does have a kind of relevance. There is a footnote on the same page (the first of several Chinese tales) about a Prince who makes just such a fisherman a minister; he fears criticism, but 'he could not bear to think of the people being deprived of his influence'. Oakeshott is not merely characterizing politics in general, he is saying that the best politics, broadly speaking, does nothing – or is it that it may do anything, except things 'grotesquely inappropriate'? A minimum criterion for political management is being insinuated, but no objective tests, standards, or conditions are even hinted at. The magic word 'appropriate' is simply conjured with (three times even in this short passage). One either knows what is appropriate, or one has no business fishing, playing politics, or anything else. This is the great half-truth. 'Being a conservative' is usually the most appropriate disposition in politics. Each human reader must judge for himself whether this is wisdom or banality. But doesn't theoretical knowledge, which Oakeshott rejects in politics, at least make some attempt to explain in which situation it is possible to govern politically, and in which not?

So to be a conservative is not to have a doctrine, but simply a disposition – which will not always be appropriate. Consider how his style of writing leads us to think that such a naked conclusion is in fact well dressed:

But, beside the not inconsiderable class of activities which we can engage in only in virtue of a disposition to be conservative, there are occasions in the conduct of other activities when this is the most appropriate disposition; indeed there are few activities which do not, at some point or other, make a call upon it. Whenever stability is more profitable than improvement, whenever certainty is more valuable than speculation, whenever familiarity is more desirable than perfection, whenever agreed error is superior to controversial truth, whenever the disease is more sufferable than the cure, whenever the satisfaction of expectations is more important than the 'justice' of the expectations themselves, whenever a rule of some sort is better than having no rule at all, a disposition to be conservative will be more appropriate than any other; and on any reading of human conduct these cover a not negligible range of circumstances.

Again, that gentlemanly, indolent word, 'appropriate'. Notice also the love of incantatory repetition, and then of antithetical abstractions, some profound, some playful, some banal, some intended simply to shock (and would shock moralistic conservatives most of all). All are capable of almost any interpretation; there is rarely if ever a concrete example, though the demand that things should be made 'concrete' is a favourite Oakeshottian edict. These antitheses do not contain genuine alternatives, they are all words. Is knowledge simply a matter of defining things cleverly (indeed, in such a way that no sane man would ever make such choices)? The formula is this: 'whenever so-and-so sensible is preferred to such-and-such silly, that is what I mean by being conservative'.

There is never any discussion of whether one thing is intrinsically preferable to another. There are no principles; it is all a matter of analogy from previous experience (and if you have no previous experience, bad luck Jack, try again in three generations' time). There is never any discussion of how we recognize an appropriate analogy, or of how we recognize that something has ceased to be its abstract self and has become an inappropriate abstract something-else. No, it is all a matter of just knowing, by the right sort of habits or by 'intimations from tradition', the right sort of analogy. Also look at the number of double-negatives in this passage: the 'not inconsiderable', 'few . . . which do not', and 'not negligible'. In themselves they are a rather comic fusion of the Hegelian 'negation of negation' with the academic or 'speech day' prose of the English upper class and their servants. More than that, a double-negative serves to create depth, mystery or disqualification where there is none; it puts the mask of modest tentative conversation over what is, in fact, the arrogance of unexplained assertion. May one not share his love of alliterative prose, without thinking that plain clarity of meaning need so often be sacrificed to the appropriately assonant adjective?

The two passages I have quoted at length do raise the suspicion of self-parody. Oakeshott's scepticism goes very deep. Perhaps all this was a deliberately strong whiff of Oakeshott to punish some young Tories for having asked him to be serious and partisan about politics. Was it the irony of humanism or of absolute negation? '*Ich bin der Geist, der stets verneint.*' Probably even the author does not know; he must delight in the ambiguities and unexpected utterances of his own pen. He writes of public affairs like a poet waiting to see what the Muses have sent him. The result is cold comfort for Conservatives. He is a Tory all right, but a too High Tory to touch mere politics.

Definitions of 'the Rationalist' abound. Oakeshott is as prodigal in defining his great fallacies as he is coy and chaste in defining those few concepts which might offer us some even pale and frail guides to conduct – Tradition, Character, Appropriateness, etc. 'The myth of rationalist politics' is the 'assimilation of politics to engineering. . . . The politics it inspires may be called the politics of the felt need. . . . They are the politics of perfection, and they are the politics of uniformity. . . .' Rationalism confuses practical knowledge with technical knowledge. 'Technical knowledge can be learned from a book; it can be learned in a correspondence course. . . . Now, I have suggested that the knowledge involved in every concrete activity is never solely technical knowledge.' But, one is tempted to ask, who has ever thought that the knowledge involved in every concrete activity is solely technical knowledge? Perhaps a few people with reputable credentials have, from Bacon (in some moments) to Harold Lasswell (in nearly all). In the main it has not been a scholarly view, but a plain man's speculation. This is not to say that Oakeshott's Rationalist is entirely made of straw. One of the odd, rather paradoxical, strengths in Oakeshott's writings is that, amid all his cultivated idiosyncrasies, there are flashes of a common touch, an appreciation of the importance of common modes of thought usually ignored by academics. People do think like his picture of the rationalist. The question is, do they ever act like it consistently? and can they ever act with his converse 'pure practicality'? Suppose we say, all right, the knowledge is *never* purely technical, but always part and part? What happens to the problem then? One sees what happens when he does come down from building analytical Aunt Sallies to give concrete examples:

The project of the so-called Re-union of the Christian Churches, of open diplomacy, of a single tax, of a civil service whose members 'have no qualifications other than their personal abilities', of a self-consciously planned society, the Beveridge Report, the Education Act of 1944, Federalism, Nationalism, Votes for Women, the Catering Wages Act, the destruction of the Austro-Hungarian Empire, the World State (of H. G. Wells or anyone else) and the revival of Gaelic as the official language of Eire, are alike the progeny of Rationalism.

The conclusion is inescapable that Rationalism is, at least, unavoidable. Some rationalism (and some traditionalism) will enter into any political judgement, into any appreciation of the activity of governing a complex State. If it is, then, a matter of degree, let us talk about 'when too much' and 'when too little' in concrete terms – and stop banging these absolutes about the hall (especially when one does not believe in them). Oakeshott, the sceptical Hegelian, insists, for some quirkish reason, on attacking metaphysics in its own vocabulary. He does not believe in such categories himself (his wise self); but he believes, with modest arrogance, that almost everyone else does. What is plainly needed is a discussion, not of 'reason,' but of what people think of as being a *reasonable* way of conducting various activities and of making decisions; and discussion not of 'reason in ethics' but of 'reasoning in ethics'. If a decision has to be made (though this is pressing a proper Oakeshottian very far), how can we say that there is a rational way of going about it? Are there not simple rational things to do, like reading the evidence, reading it again, warily consulting 'experts'? Time may not allow, but what when it does? If one presses some of Oakeshott's examples historically, the appropriateness of 'Rationalism' crumbles. Where is an example of 'Federalism' ever having been a preconceived plan? Who carts around Federalism as an *a priori* panacea? Federalism has always appeared in any actual situation as a response to an *existing* division of power within a territory that comes together, or is thrust together, as one state. This should be a good, if obvious, Oakeshottian point about tradition. How, then, can it be at the same time an example of Rationalism?

Tradition itself suffers in Oakeshott from a similar excess of generality. The concept that 'moral and political "principles" are abridgements of traditional manners of behaviour' (not external criteria of conduct) is a good corrective to the Rationalist who thinks that he is both right and novel. It is easy to show that he is rarely, if ever, novel (though there may be some circumstances, as Machiavelli argued, in which it is simply not possible to follow custom and the established laws). But the objection is obvious that, on a practical level, there may be several traditions in any one society. On a philosophical level, to speak of a tradition is either an arbitrary abridgement of all the activities within a society, or some assumption about 'minimum law and order' (High Toryism in anthropological dress). Or else 'tradition' means the 'total situation,' in which case his whole use of the concept founders between tautology and truism. Oakeshott has defended himself (in an addition to the original essay on 'Political Education') by saying that he is considering 'a legally organized society . . . the manner in which its legal structure (which in spite of its incoherencies cannot be supposed to have a competitor) is reformed and amended.' The sudden faith in law is odd enough. But he has already defined a 'single community' in terms of sharing a tradition: 'To suppose a collection of people without recognized traditions of behaviour . . . is to suppose a people incapable of politics.' Yet there are people seemingly incapable of politics. Certainly there are communities in which very few people are involved in public life. Are these, then, not really 'communities', is it not really 'politics', or can there be either without tradition? I have argued in a recent book, starting from precisely this confusion or dilemma in Oakeshott, that what holds some communities together is a rational appreciation of the advantages of doing things politically rather than, for instance, by pure force, by total plan, or by just trying to 'keep afloat'.

But whether tradition is one or many, the fundamental dilemma in Oakeshott's view of the world is now, with all his major essays before us, apparent. Whether or not tradition simply describes how communities hold together, or whether it asserts the best conservative way of doing so, on either view tradition must surely have some historical content. We may not be able to reduce it to a descriptive catalogue, but it must have a history. The agony is that this history is itself rationalistic. I used to think that the Americans were a sufficient stumbling-block to Oakeshott's concept of tradition – their thriving tradition of anti-traditionalism; it is now clear why he does not worry about such a trifling, concrete, contrary example: for he sees the whole of European history as exhibiting that rationalism which most European conservatives have seen in America. At heart Oakeshott is condemning, like a gentlemanly anti-Christ, the whole moralistic, reformist, activist tradition of Western thought. The most obvious characteristic of Western thought – the belief that conscious political action can lead to human progress – is to him detestable. Not merely poetry should be seen only as a subject for 'contemplation and delight', but life itself. No wonder the number of little quietistic Chinese anecdotes. For he affects a literary oriental conceit of culture in which everything is rejected unless it serves the pure end of contemplation.

The root of the trouble is, of course, *Christianity*:

> But, whatever was the impulse of the change, it appears that by the middle of the third century there existed a Christian morality in the familiar form of the self-conscious pursuit of moral ideals [bad thing] . . . . A Christian morality in the form of a way of life [good thing] did not, of course, perish, and it has never completely disappeared. But from this time in the history of Christendom a Christian habit of moral behaviour (which had sprung from the circumstances of Christian life) was swamped by a Christian moral ideology, and the perception of the poetic character of human conduct was lost.

When even Nietzsche is turned upside down – Christianity is condemned, not for being a 'slave morality', or for preaching weakness and humanity, but, on the contrary, for activism –

the reader will see why there is something special about Oakeshott. He records that:

Rationalism has ceased to be merely one style in politics and has become the stylistic criterion of all respectable politics [and that] the politics of Rationalism are the politics of the politically inexperienced, and that the outstanding characteristic of European politics in the last four centuries is that they have suffered the incursion of at least three types of political inexperience – that of the new ruler, of the new ruling class, and of the new political society.

Can there be any wonder at the tone of bitterness and despair? If so bad in Europe, how much worse elsewhere? (And how irrelevant are these categories elsewhere!) Tradition is the only possible guide for us, but its roots are hopelessly tainted . . . with faith, hope and charity. And perhaps this is why, after all these years, scattered essays are published, and not a great masterpiece on the character of European politics. For, clearly, if all 'illusions' and pursuits of the ideal and 'new men' were stripped away, there would be nothing left: a kind of suicide of the man, the book, the subject and the tradition. The anarchical Tory becomes a lonely nihilist. We cannot by giving thought add a cubit to our stature, but we can find reasons to defend and improve the moral, activist, reforming tradition of European politics.

Oakeshott is right that politics is not the grasping of an ideal; for there are many ideals among which true politics must mediate. But it is itself a moral activity which will have to invent and engineer when tradition fails. The advice to 'consult tradition' is too partial. When Oakeshott looks narrowly, he means conservative England (which is narrow enough); and when he looks widely, we need other help since he himself shows that our entire Western culture is rotten with rationalism, thank God. Are we so unfortunate? Should we be so reconciled to our misfortunes? Oakeshott's counsel wavers between conservatism and nihilism. He must prune his rhetoric before he deserves to be understood, but he must draw distinctions before he can hope to be understood. Perhaps he does not hope to be. If not, why write?

6

'Them and Us': Public Impotence and Government Power[1]

THE moral proposition 'It is no concern of mine' must be closely related to the empirical proposition 'There is nothing I can do about it'. I wish to analyse the way we talk about and the way we understand the plain and huge gap between 'You' and 'I', and the 'It', 'Them', 'The Thing' or 'The System'. And, as if the problem were not difficult enough, someone has to remind us that the distance between 'Them' and 'Us' is complicated by an inherent relativity of viewpoint. If I am tempted to thunder or to be sly about 'them up there', immediately establishing a happy community of mutual grievance between all of us here, someone must remember that we all here look very like them up there in the eyes of those down there.

This is, however, to plunge into the middle. Let me start from the fact that many of our fellow citizens in this advanced and democratic civilization etcetera are either desperately worried by feelings that the powers that be are unreachably remote, unaccountably inept and spasmodically interfering, or else they simply do not feel themselves to be, in any possible sense, citizens at all – just inhabitants: they have given up, or never even taken up, the opportunities of interest and influence in public affairs. Among ordinary people a dull or cynical 'could-not-carelessitude' wrestles with the quick-witted response, 'it's all a fix'; and among intellectuals a-politicism wrestles with anti-politicism. At the best the would-be citizen gazes at the 'state' (or what he is told is the state) much as a small boy may look at the remote stars in the sky,

1. This was the Gaitskell Memorial Lecture, given at Nottingham University, 19 January 1968 and published in *Public Law*, Spring 1968.

and become so torn between curiosity and terror that he takes refuge in an almost deliberate incomprehension and insensibility.

Some of these worries are wholly misplaced and unreal, are a product of a false and romantic theory of democracy[1] – which is held with a special intensity, one should note, by those self-styled 'practical men' who are the least likely to claim to hold any kind of doctrine whatever. Most attempts to cure these deep troubles and worries are themselves vitiated by the same misleading theory of democracy, diverting attention from the real weaknesses of our society. For we are obsessed with the idea of democracy as direct participation – as if we lived in the *polis* of Athens, the Rochdale Co-op, or the Carlton Club – or else with perfecting representative institutions as the next best thing in a world that has most unfortunately grown too large for direct participation. But we are only at the beginning of seeing democracy as communication – as the maximization of a free flow of information and the enhanced guidance of a far more positive feed-back of information and knowledge between rulers and ruled. Participation, in societies as large as ours, is only valuable if it leads to increased communication. It is perfectly possible for radical increases in participation to have no effect on flows of communication, or even to have a negative one: for now that all we apostles of pure truth are on the Board or Committee, our attitudes to publicity and openness may perhaps change more than slightly; and a Party in power may not always have quite the same views as a Party in opposition. No wonder some reformers would now make a shibboleth of radical degrees of decentralization, but with very little discussion of the great risks this involves for – morally – equitable rewards and – socially – effective communications.

The problem is, however, very apparent and at least somewhat real. Michael Young once entitled a pamphlet, actually published by the Labour Party, 'Small Man in a Big World', and he quoted Aneurin Bevan: 'Bigness is the enemy of man-

1. See chapter 3, 'A Defence of Politics Against Democracy' of my *In Defence of Politics* (Weidenfeld & Nicolson, 1962; Pelican, 1964).

kind.' Often the diagnosis of the great anxiety has followed the hypothesis of size, scale and numbers. The scale of modern states is blamed for the feeling that individuals are impotent against the State. Others adhere, with more and more difficulty and cleverness, to traditional Marxist theories of the concentration of economic power and class oppression. Others, more subtly, see a monopoly of central communications in the hands of a governing class who brainwash us all, except these few fortunately alienated critics. And to others alienation is not an artistic and scientific talent or blessing, but is the disease itself – a product of so many things, of 'our whole commercial civilization', for instance, or of the gap between the work of our hands and the products of the machine; fundamentally it is the poignant gap between (as existentialism and common sense agree) how we know we could lead our lives and how in fact we lead our lives.

The problem remains, even if put socially and not individually. Dr Nordlinger in his recent book, *The Working Class Tories*, shows evidence of strong alienation even among regular political supporters of the major Parties.[1] Only 14 per cent of his sample of 320 Conservative working-class voters thought that 'people like themselves' had 'a good deal' of influence on governmental decisions, 54 per cent thought 'a little' and 31 per cent thought 'none'. And Labour working-class respondents were markedly more pessimistic (and, of course, about twice as large in absolute numbers): 10 per cent thought they had 'a good deal' of influence, 37 per cent 'a little' and 50 per cent thought 'none'.

The interpretation depends, of course, on what kind of influence one thinks that it is possible and desirable for populations to have upon governments. Part of the acute anxiety syndrome may be old Jacobinical fantasies about 'sovereignty of the people' or democracy as 'the rule of the people' – standards which, if taken literally, or hungered after as symbolic ideals, are inevitably self-frustrating. We may need to reinterpret the relationship of populations to

1. Eric A. Norlinger, *The Working Class Tories. Authority: Deference and Stable Democracy* (MacGibbon & Kee, 1967), p. 98.

governing classes in the same way as we are just beginning to get some commonsense about the relationship of, for example, Parliament to Government. Most of us are not now worried to think that Parliament does not govern, nor that it never did. We can see that it, among other things, calls governments to account, forces them to explain themselves, to some degree at least; we can see many advantages of being governed *through* Parliament without having to believe either that we ought to be or, in some strained and refined sense are, governed *by* Parliament.

Similarly with democracy. The majority cannot govern. Only a few can govern. But the few can stand in an almost infinite number of different relationships with the many. They can be oppressors dying of the pox or, more likely nowadays, dedicated public servants ulcerating themselves to death. They may succeed in ignoring the majority, they may succeed for short periods in holding it down by fraud and force, they may succeed in pleasing it with bread and circuses, or they may succeed occasionally in channelling the great power of the people to constructive public purposes. Democracy as participation, in other words, cannot sensibly be seen as a general description of any system of government of the scale of modern industrial states. It may be a necessary condition for any just state, but it is not a sufficient condition. The classical Greek, Roman and European Republican writers understood it better than we: that democracy is only – but no less than – a necessary element in good government which is always, in turn, mixed government. It is not sensible to say that Great Britain is or is not a democracy, only that it is too democratic or – as I would strongly contend – not democratic enough.

We are, in other words, often in danger of stirring up trouble by promising the impossible. Let me remind you that it was only as late as the First World War that anyone called the British political system 'democratic' in a descriptive sense: the cynicism of Lloyd George and the floundering of the Asquithian Liberals searching for a principle higher than patriotism to mobilize the population faced with the losses in

Flanders. And then the obliterating cant of Woodrow Wilson on top of all, making every intolerant nation democratic even. This is why personally I think it an illuminating pedantry to call our kind of system 'republican' or simply 'political' rather than 'democratic'. Russia and China, indeed any industrial or industrializing State, depend on the powers of the majority, unlike old autocracies, just as much as a State which can mobilize these powers sufficiently in a free, open and choiceful manner.

Let me also recall to memory the great Machiavelli's description of the three essential *qualità* – characteristics – which must to his mind be blended in any viable republic: *la potestà regia*, power to act quickly and with a concentration of resources; *la potenza degli Ottimati*, the influence of those of outstanding position – say elite groups; and lastly *il governo popolare*, of which the primary meaning is surely the restraint of the people or popular power as in 'the governor' of an engine, but whose secondary meaning is, indeed, power in the sense of effective action – if influenced and controlled aright.[1] His whole teaching on the subject of political power and his whole justification of republican government as, where it is possible, undoubtedly the best form of government, turns upon the double proposition that a multitude is useless without a head, but that the power of a State that is popular is far greater than that of any other. To put it in modern terms, republics are in a better position to mobilize the energies of the majority than are autocracies, but they are none the less restrained or governed, particularly in new policies, by what the majority will put up with.

Perhaps this puts the matter over-pragmatically. In old Cicero's formulation there was a moral edge, lacking, at first sight at least, in modern Machiavelli: *auctoritas in Senatu, potestas in populum* was his formula for just and effective government – authority, we may interpret it, can only be exercised by elites, but these elites will not stay in power or prove powerful if they do not respond to popular demands and carry the populace with them.

1. See Machiavelli, *Discourses*, Book I, sections 1–10.

139

Does this distinction solve the problem? Obviously not, it only shifts the problem: but on to a less slippery slope. We may begin to grasp it firmly. The problem is now one of the degree of restraint that populations impose on governments, and also of the degree of influence that governments can exert on populations. But one formulation we must drop entirely, or else answer very rudely: can the individual have any influence on the State? Answer plainly 'No', unless you are a Head of State or his assassin – and even if his assassin, then the individual influence will only be at the actual moment of the deed; and only in rare circumstances is assassination likely to make any difference anyway. Individuality in politics and society can only express itself in relationship with others, or in group actions and reactions. If any one individual feels impotent facing the State, it is probably because he is asking for more than the State can give him – he is probably asking, as the Greeks and the Romans would have seen, for immortality. He is asking for some proof that an 'I' will remembered for doing great deeds publicly – which may have little to do with the public interest, and was the bane of all aristocratic politics: men with one eye on the public purse but the other, far more dangerously, on posterity.

If we consider the individual, however, as a member of groups, the question falls into place quite differently. For surely as often as we complain about the inability of our group to get anything done, we complain about other groups having too much influence. WE, of course, are always small and THEY are always big, but it is not always clear what their bigness consists in. Sometimes it seems to lie more in their social access to the powers-that-be than in their wealth or their numbers.

I promise eventually to come down to earth. But my whole underlying point is that we conceive what we are in fact doing in a fundamentally misleading manner. Most of us, indeed, are sophisticatedly innocent that we hold any conceptions or pre-conceptions at all. Think of the impotence of populations gazing through the mists at their governments.

But equally think of the impotence of governments gazing through the mists at their populations. 'Yes, of course they will respond to the declaration of intent and a voluntary incomes policy. You do not know what they think. You were not a trade unionist. I was. I know what they think, and they will follow once it is explained to them.' But they did not: the whole thing was a fiasco. Perhaps *they* did not bother to explain to *them*, they certainly did not bother to prepare public opinion, nor to inquire beforehand what was likely to happen behaviourally (the Government does, after all, own a very efficient Social Survey). Someone may justly feel himself to be more representative of the people than some others one could also not name, but representativeness in this fine old democratic sense does not guarantee, in changing societies, continued knowledge of the probable reactions of the people, nor – apparently – sufficient authority for leadership to be followed.

Just as great a problem, after all, as the seemingly great inability of the public to control governments is the inability of governments to lead populations. It is perhaps too simple to say, like the five wise typists of Surbiton, 'Work half-an-hour harder' – for you may be working at something that is a dead loss on the export-import account: central leadership, in the sense of selective guidance, may be needed – however odd the results. For instance, the patriotic mill girl in Nottingham, one gathers, should not feel frustrated in working away at nylon tights: for these sell like hot cakes in Japan and Sweden. But even if the Government says, 'Work harder on a, b, c, but get out of d, e, and for God's sake leave f to Singapore', will it be followed? Will it hell! Not very likely. Or is it that there has been a neglect of this, some would say, authoritarian side of the equation. Professor Samuel Beer has recently pointed to the neglect of parliament by governments as a device for 'mobilizing consent' – and he is a good American Democrat of impeccable credentials.[1] Suppose there had

1. Samuel H. Beer, 'The Legislature and the Problem of Mobilizing Consent', in *Essays on Reform, 1967*, edited by Bernard Crick (Oxford University Press, 1967).

been a 'preparedness campaign' before the prices and incomes policy was announced, by parliamentary debate and the repercussions of publicity it can still engender. It might have made no difference. But it should have been attempted anyway. For many of our problems are now of such a type that it is no use a government explaining their decisions after they have been made, but that governments should prepare the population for not just accepting the new law, but for the *positive changes in behaviour* which are needed if any amount of law-making is to work – of the kind of 'work harder', 'be more efficient', 'restrain thy prices and thy wages', or 'be prepared to move'. To amend Bagehot, one cannot make men work by act of Parliament.

Personally I am as amazed at the inability of our Government to mobilize the population in the economic crisis, as we could do for the wickedly clear purposes of war, as others are amazed, I recognize, at the seeming indifference of the Government to public opinion. Myself I suspect that modern British governments are often too fatalistic about and subservient to public opinion: that they have lost all belief that they can influence it in fundamental ways.[1] There is a sense in which they are too democratic. At the heart of the seeming strength and stability of the British system of Prime-Minister-in-Cabinet there is some awful inability to affect popular behaviour. Power is there all right, if power is unchallengeability; but weakness is there if power is – as Bertrand Russell once defined it – the production of intended effects.[2]

One more flight of conceptual exorcism before I come down to earth and onions. Is it really 'power' at all – or what do we mean by power? If we chase the magnetic needle through the corridors will we come up with anything at all? If power is simply the production of intended effects, what then

1. As I argued in my contribution to *Essays on Reform*, *1967*, ibid., following Beer.

2. Bertrand Russell, *Power: a new social analysis* (Unwin Books edition, 1962), p. 25.

is the power behind power or what are Mr Richard Crossman and even the gentler Mr David Marquand talking about when they thunder or 'grimly remind us' time and time again of a mere platitude or definition? That politics they say – and please never forget it – *is about power*! If they are not saying nothing – and I would not dare suggest that – they are thinking of the special type of power which is threat or command supported by the possibility of coercion. And they are, quite simply, wrong. For power, in that sense, is then either the last resort or the first mistake: the breakdown of ordinary politics, not the typical case, the thing normally to be avoided in politics at almost any price. To think otherwise is a piece of pseudo-realism, or lurid sensationalism. 'This is what life is really like', scream the editors of the *News of the World*. Again it is a proper pedantry to insist that politics is really, far more often, not about power as coercion but about power as rational patterns of authority: why and how the many obey the few without direct coercion or threat – if power, then power to gain effects which may only be possible by persuasion or political means, not by threat or the simple 'Fee, Fi, Fo, Fum' of 'In the name of the Queen', Harold Wilson, Aubrey Jones, the United Nations or anything else. Coercive power is part of government, beyond doubt: the ability of a government to defend itself and its population from external or internal threat, or the lingering fear that a population might, in some circumstances, either rise or sit on their hands massively. Power in a republic, properly speaking, is limited to times of emergency. In all other times power, as we loosely speak, is authority: power, nakedly and plainly asserted, is the breakdown of authority. Authority depends not on the ultimate existence of the public hangman, as Mr Duncan Sandys so sincerely believes, but on persuasion and on the acceptance of powers as being rationally related to some useful function.

Consider the case of Captain Catt in Dylan Thomas's *Under Milk Wood*. In his blind and senile reminiscence, he suddenly cries out in memory: 'I'll take the mulatto, by God, who's captain here?' And the scene changes with no answer. For obviously the answer was that no one was Captain here if here was a brothel and not a ship, or rather that the rational accept- ance of command relative to skill and function might indicate a different captain in a brothel than on a ship. I hope to be no more than unfair, not indelicate, to hint that the attempts of civil servants to influence both trade unionists, industrialists and scientists often fall into the same abyss of the non- transferability of authority from one circumstance to another.

What kinds of authority have we? The authority of tradi- tion which is plainly worn out: any cat now may look at a King. The authority of policy and of good intentions – that seems discredited: not just by the folly and deceit of political leaders in promising too much, I grant, but by their lack of luck in dealing with unpredictable and uncontrollable events. If you act as if you are responsible for good weather, people will hold you to account for bad weather. What remains? Perhaps a new pattern of authority may emerge based on communication and functional skills: that the intellectual need to explain could come close to the political need of governments to mobilize opinion and of populations to act as governors on governments. Suppose we put far less emphasis on participation as the essence of democracy, and far more on communication – back and forth, on comprehensibility and achievement. Could one imagine an effective system of political authority based not just on making the right deci- sions, but on the decisions appearing to be right because they have been publicly canvassed, alternatives and all, from the earliest stages of their inception? The idea of authority that already applies to the professional classes, that we accept what we can be rationally persuaded of, should be applied to the whole working and productive population. If we can- not do this, then we cannot in fact control the kind of society we in fact have: democracy is then, as is plainly Enoch Powell's proper nightmare, insatiable and unstoppable in- flationary demand.

Consider voting. So often the authority of governments is held to depend upon the fact that they have been elected in a democratic manner. But so often it is felt either that elections offer few genuine choices or that governments never follow up what are thought to be their electoral pledges. Or are elections just an auction between purchasers who then have to borrow the price back from the electorate? Elections give governments authority to govern; but governments must then explain how they govern. This seems platitudinous. But consider how often it is believed, as if in deference to 'democracy', that elections commit governments to do certain things, so that if circumstances change they must then spend most of their time explaining why they could *not* act. Why, in other words, woo so ardently and with so many promises on Sundays but then confine intimacy in the week only to excuses? Or put it this other way, if they wooed a little and a little more openly and patiently every weekday, would they need such vulgar excesses on electoral Sundays? We are told 'awful truths', it seems, only in General Elections; but in between times Westminster and Whitehall isolate themselves as much as possible. And yet they expect us to respect their authority?

Even voting can be of exaggerated importance. What use is a loyal majority of ninety in the House of Commons if you cannot even affect people's basic behaviour on the shop floor and in the board room? Voting is not so much a matter of rights, nor is it the conferment of a precise set of detailed authorities to act. Voting is fundamentally a communications system: it enables governments to obtain support and also to gain a rough but ready knowledge both of what people want and of what they will stand for. Perhaps, quite simply, governments need to explain more and to base their power-as-authority not on astonishingly rigid voting habits, bribes to the marginal and on spasmodic cries of 'England in danger!' but on continuous rational explanation and on an exemplary and educative openness of conduct, forethought and public canvassing of alternatives. . . .

Such a concept is no abstract mystery or new idealistic heresy. The British army, even, chastened by defeat in 1940, came round to explaining. Soldiers were actually told what they were doing and briefed, in some kind of manner, about the objects and tactics of local and even major actions. It was felt, on balance correctly, that this both increased morale and discipline and allowed initiative when Commanders were killed or communications broke down. In the First World War soldiers sang a song that largely died out after 'Battle Drill' and the new-modelling of the army after 1940: 'We're here because we're here because we're here because we're here' – a product of nobody's ever explaining a command. To-day only students in British universities sing that song. University teachers are poor souls to criticize Cabinet Ministers when we so often grumble that our authority is diminished and yet refuse resolutely to explain why the syllabus is as it is or how we mark. Often, one suspects, one refuses because if one did attempt to explain, then the syllabus could not stay quite as it is, nor the kind of exams be set that are set and marked in quite the way they are marked. There are occasions when to be asked to find reasons for things is to find oneself at a loss.

It is, one hears rumours, now orthodoxy and not hetero-doxy, in advanced company management that 'all levels' should know how the firm is organized, at least the formal machinery of how decisions are made, and what each person is doing in relation to the whole. This is being done, one gathers, not out of belief in democracy, but out of belief that some greater degree of 'openness' in internal communica-tions is conducive to efficiency. And one gathers that this is what the Treasury now believes should apply to others.

I am not suggesting, to leap an obvious stage in the argu-ment, that we can expect the working population, whether educated to fifteen or sixteen, to read Select Committee Reports or White Papers. But one does believe, though this has not even been studied (the social sciences are in such infancy) that something filters down. The press, for all its faults, the radio and television, for all its shortage of space for politics, does a damned sight better than nothing. Something filters down and up. But not enough thought is given to how this takes place, how selective it is, or how it could be done better. Some politicians but few civil servants have grasped the fact that in the vast problems of economic mobilization and changing social habits that face us, explanation is a way of leadership. Postures of firmness – which can often degenerate into pig-headed obstinacy – are no substitute for having to give the kind of explanation that forces one to consider public reaction to it. Few civil servants have realized that 'thinking out loud' from the earliest stages is a way of gaining support for policies which may prove completely ineffective if hidden from public view until the triumphant day of unveiling in the First Reading, firm, unalterable, erect, but often strangely impotent.

One may consult with 'all those likely to be affected' until one is old and grey, but one has no guarantee, if some publicity has not followed these consultations, that the representatives of interest groups are in fact representative. Great mistakes could be avoided, as well as the populace won round, by thinking out loud. Too often someone with a better alternative or a serious objection on grounds of practicality only hears about the new Bill or the new Order when the thing is already cut, dried and passed over to the Whips to push through. Among the mysteries of our secretive Whitehall is the curious way in which independent expert advisers are consulted, often pledged to a flattering secrecy as a condition of being flatteringly exploited: often the only independent expert is muzzled with trivial consequences.

Governments are fundamentally restrained by being forced to explain themselves, and by knowing that we know – which we so seldom do – the grounds on which they make their decisions.

The secrecy of British governments is not merely undemocratic; it is, opinion and evidence mounts, inefficient. Openness is itself an education both for the governors and the governed, and a vital link between them. Populations are apathetic, ignorant and unable to serve national purposes because they are treated like children and not told, or told in silly patronizing ways; and governments lack both sufficient independent criticism by experts, alerted in time that something is beginning to stir in their field, and also sufficient warning of popular reaction – or lack of reaction – to particular policies. Such restraints can strengthen. Fast cars need good brakes. Governments that want to do anything need to be sure that they will be followed, and that the power of the people – to follow the republican Machiavelli again – is firmly planted behind their skill and resolution.

But the habit of keeping secret nearly everything connected with the administrative process and decision-taking in government goes deep. Here is not the place to consider how this came to be (the deliberate intention of the class-conscious reforms of the 1860s and the prestige the Civil Service gained through our victories in two world wars, when secrecy was at a premium, etc.): enough only to consider the consequences. The views of the two most acute contemporary American observers of British society can be adduced: 'The secrets of the governing classes of Britain', writes Edward Shils, 'are kept within the governing class. . . . The British ruling class is unequalled in secretiveness and taciturnity. . . . What is spoken in privacy is expected to be retained in privacy and withheld from the populace. When journalists are confided in, it is with the expectation that the confidence will be respected.'[1] And Samuel Beer comments that 'No formal arrangements of committees or staffs could quite free the British Government of its dependence upon the common rooms and lunch tables of the clubs of Pall Mall.'[2]

Examples are legion. Consider the refusal of the Treasury to publish its economic forecasts on which Budgets are based until long after the parliamentary debates are over. Consider the long battle to get a Council on Tribunals established, and their long battle, perhaps a perpetual one, to ensure that a

1. Edward Shils, *The Torment of Secrecy* (Heinemann, 1956), pp. 49–50. One might add that journalists and others are often confided in in order that the truth will not come out, ordinary though these truths usually are; and the Civil Servant or the Minister is often not above muzzling the Don with trivial confidences.
2. Samuel H. Beer, *Treasury Control* (Clarendon Press, 1956), p. 106.

reasoned explanation be given for decisions, not simply the decisions announced and promulgated. And consider the new restiveness of some judges at the 'incredible claim that the public service should not function properly unless commonplace communications between one civil servant and another were privileged from production' (The *Grosvenor Hotel* case).[1] I will not labour this point, others have put it so clearly. David Williams reminded us in his fascinating book, *Not in the Public Interest*, of the vain trumpet call of the Royal Commission on the Press of 1949:

The democratic form of society demands of its members an active and intelligent participation in the affairs of their community, whether local or national. It assumes that they are sufficiently well informed about the issues of the day to be able to form the broad judgements required by an election, and to maintain between elections the vigilance necessary in those whose governors are their servants and not their masters. . . . Democratic society, therefore, needs a clear and truthful account of events, of their background and their causes; a forum for discussion and informed criticism; and a means whereby individuals and groups can express a point of view or advocate a cause.[2]

The unnecessary, dog-in-the-silver-manger quality of official secrecy has lately been brilliantly exposed by public lawyers like Professor J. D. B. Mitchell and Professor John Griffith.[3]

1. Lord Justice Salmon quoted by Andrew Shonfield in his *Modern Capitalism: the Changing Balance of Public and Private Power* (Oxford University Press, 1965), p. 412.
2. David Williams, *Not in the Public Interest* (Hutchinson, 1955), p. 93.
3. See J. D. B. Mitchell, 'The Causes and Effects of the Absence of a System of Public Law in the United Kingdom', *Public Law*, Summer 1965, also his 'Administrative Law and Parliamentary Control', *Political Quarterly*, October–December, 1967; and J. A. G. Griffith, 'On Telling People', *Essays in Reform, 1967*, op. cit. My two favourite typical and trivial examples (that is leaving out the whole of economic planning) are (1) the arrogant failures of the recent Speaker's Conference on Electoral Reform, though composed of MPs, to give any reasons or evidence at all for their silly recommendations that the publication of opinion polls and betting odds should be prohibited immediately before General Elections, and that the Party name should *not* appear on the ballot (presumably there *was* no evidence, *they* just reasoned about it privately); and (2) the

And Andrew Shonfield in his masterly *Modern Capitalism*, Michael Shanks in his *The Innovators* and Max Nicholson in his eccentric but biting book, *The System*, have gone beyond this to argue the positive case for the greater efficiency of a far more open system of government.[1] One can stop far short of the established Swedish drill of making nearly every administrative document available to any member of the public or the press and still imagine a Whitehall that had a positive function to communicate at large, not just within the inner circle, and would be the more effective for it.

Lord Windlesham in his most interesting *Communication and Political Power* quotes the former American Supreme Court Justice, Arthur Goldberg, when he was Secretary of Labor in 1961:

> The Department of Labor is a public Department, and the public is entitled to know what the Department is doing, what I am doing, what all of the officials of the Department are doing. I am going to try my best to see that this type of policy prevails and that all officials of the Department, myself included, maintain an open door policy towards the press consistent, of course, with time and considerations.[2]

One could make a democratic slogan of 'the right to know'. But I am more inclined to argue that 'the right to know' is an administrative need, and also that the spread of knowledge about how we are governed – and of the grounds on which decisions are made – is the most effective democratic power

refusal of the Lawrence Committee on Members' Salaries of 1964 to publish, even in statistical and tabular form, the evidence they claim to have taken from MPs about their expenses, conditions of work and associated earnings (really, who pays whom for what?).

1. Griffith, ibid.; Shonfield, *Modern Capitalism*, op. cit.; Max Nicholson, *The System: the Misgovernment of Modern Britain* (Hodder & Stoughton, 1967); Michael Shanks, *The Innovators* (Pelican, 1967); and William Rees-Mogg, ed. *The Role of Palinurus*, The Granada Northern Lectures for 1967. (Panther, 1968): '. . . no government can be better than the information system on which it depends'.

2. Lord Windlesham, *Communication and Political Power* (Cape. 1966), p. 185.

of and check upon government, ordinarily far more obtainable and effective than heightened degrees of representation.

The problem is now plain. The irritable matrimonial alienation between rulers and ruled does not lie in the system oı
representation so much as in the system of communication.
And it does not lie in the scale, size or complexity of government as such, but in its comprehensibility – in its lack of
publicity and popularization. It is important to state this,
otherwise we go running (like Professor Max Beloff) after
some plausible Liberal gimmicks which might, in fact, be
cures worse than the disease. I have in mind the sudden
enthusiasm for regional government. Personally I see no good
reason to be frightened of bigness and to hide in so many
provincial holes. There may well be a strong case for de-
centralizing Whitehall – I think there is; but it is a gross
confusion to think that this implies regional government on
an elective basis. If, as I deeply believe, provincial influence
should be greater both in England and Great Britain (it is
too great in the United Kingdom, if we think of Ulster), it is
then useless concentrating that influence and power locally:
it needs to be focused on Whitehall and Westminster –
otherwise, once again, 'divide and rule'. We may be fobbed
off with regionally elected councils or assemblies, as Scotland
may be fobbed off with a parliament and a Black Rod with a
sporran. But will they be powerful? Their power would still
depend on national decisions about the allocation of resources. The Scottish and the Welsh Nationalists are mad if
they think that poverty can be remedied by independence.
What is really needed in every case, or – I grant – needed as
well, is more publicity about the grounds on which decisions
are made by the central government, and an effective early-
warning system that decisions are being contemplated so that
regional representations and protests can be timely and not,
as so often, hopelessly belated.

Regional devolution of administration, by all means, and
perhaps some regional councils or assemblies with watchdog,
ombudsman-like functions, but of big decision-taking, no;

nor must they replace the watchdog functions of the central Parliament, but only supplement or duplicate them – why not duplicate, it surely does no harm? For surely what we really want is better communications, not just improved participation. The Maud Report on the Management of Local Government tells us that there are 44,586 councillors in England and Wales, from Rural District to County Borough Councillors. Suppose, a wild assumption, that ten regional assemblies had 600 somebodies each, which brings the total to about 50,000, then we have about one councillor, one elected representative to 1,000 inhabitants. 'Two cheers for democracy', indeed. Or, as the poet rather than the novelist said of his two lovers parting by the ditch to death: 'Have we come all the way for this?' I mean, what difference could it credibly make if one in a thousand of our fellow latent-citizens have some say-so, compared to one in eleven hundred – particularly as, if other far more relevant national habits and malpractices are not changed, the immediate reaction of the good middle-class one-of-us on being elected to office is far too often to change from being a fierce proponent of publicity into a discreet advocate of privacy. What enterprising journalist was it who phoned up the Town Clerk's Department of Birmingham and asked 'What is the population of your city?', to receive the foreseeable first reply 'Why do you want to know?' and the inevitable second move. 'It is not my business to tell you'?

Regionally elective assemblies could make matters worse by diffusing authority and responsibility, thus impairing the feed-back of a national communications system. We need better communications before, long before, I think, increased individual participation. High levels of individual participation are only valuable, in large scale societies, if they lead to increased publicity and communication. Frankly, I have my fears that the kind of people who would want to be on regional parliaments are the very kind of people who believe that they are willing to do anything for the public, except rub shoulders with the public and make things public to the public. (To give a trivial example, the Peak Park Planning Board is an appointed body, but it is dominated by the mentality of an aggressive minority, the Council for the Preservation of Rural England (from the Working Classes). I have a dreadful feeling that if it were elected, the same people would be on it, or even if different ones, they would still view their office as a public trust to be preserved against the public; they would still be unwilling to explain to us the remarkable line of reasoning that leads them frequently to denounce trippers in motor-cars, litter-louts and worse, but not to provide adequate car parks, litter-bins and lavatories.)

It is a far higher priority to 'open up' Whitehall than to get back to the Folkmoots of the Saxon Heptarchy. Folly it would be, indeed, to create regional parliaments before the national Parliament at Westminster is able to call to account, in detail, management and total effectiveness, the dedicated, experienced, but far too retiring Lords of Whitehall. My whole case can be put in two phrases: 'first things first', and 'let things that are related together be considered together' – not split up into vulgar fractions, but subjected to *haute vulgarisation*.

Another false solution, somewhat by analogy to the 're-gional parliament' well-meaning nonsense, is increased consultation in Whitehall. The truth, if there are general truths, may be that they in Whitehall consult too much, but without examining the credentials of the 'representatives' or officers of large organizations. Do the spokesmen of the AA and the RAC, for instance, represent the views of ordinary British motorists – or the motor trade? But it is so convenient to assume that a few responsible people one can speak to, be they ex-racing motorists or Trade Union Peers, represent their sad members – in the simple and vital sense that they can foretell their reactions. Can they, I am afraid one must say, hell! Consultation can be carried too far. If consultation with representatives of interests is held to imply 'fairness' or 'effectiveness', then it must also be fairly recognized in the interests of efficiency that it can spell deadly delay and stulti-fying compromise.

Better by far to make decisions more openly and quickly –

the openness, particularly about when one is beginning to consider something, should make up for the quickness, than to make decisions only after consulting (as Departments so patiently do) with every other Department conceivably interested and with the official representatives of every organized interest. Better to learn by mistakes than to avoid them at the price not so much of sloth, but of that over-conscientious and cautious slowness which has come near to strangling our national energy.

'How can we then be saved?' What lines of leverage are there against the secrecy, cautiousness, constraint and conceit of the Establishment – in the hands of whichever Party? In fact, change is in the air, if only people take it seriously. Powerful committees or commissions are examining the Civil Service, the Trade Unions, and Local Government; and even Parliament itself has taken a few steps forward. We are in a period of self-doubt about our basic institutions, but – the whole question is – do we seek to remodel them according to middle-class professional and elitist ideas of what is rational or effective, or in such a way that they will enhance radically communications with the whole population, civic body, or – could it ever be? – community of citizens? Certainly 'if "ifs" and "ands" were pots and pans' there'd be no need for academic tinkers. Consider Richard Crossman's pamphlet, *Socialism and the New Despotism* of 1956:

> *The modern State with its huge units of organization, is inherently totalitarian, and its natural tendency is towards despotism. These tendencies can only be held in check if we are determined to build the constitutional safeguards of freedom – and personal responsibility.*
>
> I am convinced that these constitutional safeguards of freedom against the new despotism can only be built by a Labour Government. But if it is to do the job, that Government must return to the first principles of Socialism and decide boldly to make all irresponsible power accountable to the community. And if that is to be our aim, we had better realize that the way we manage our democratic institutions – including the Labour Party and the trade unions – is at least as important as the way we manage the economy of the nation.

'Accountable', that is the very point: how can any body be made accountable without publicity? (If it came to a hard choice I would rather trust the restraint of the *Daily Express* not to endanger national security, than trust any British Prime Minister not to use 'national security' as a dirty smokescreen for political or administrative convenience.) All this new promise of institutional reform is to be commended, in good Benthamite terms, *if* it leads, as John Stuart Mill saw, after his break from his father's and Bentham's ideas of benevolent professional leadership, to increased public awareness and accountability, or in a word – to knowledge, to a greater mobility and openness of both men and ideas.

The most far-reaching reform of all would be to abolish the non-contributory civil service pension, indeed to create a common and interchangeable national pension scheme between the civil service, industry and the universities (as we opportunistic educational patricians have it among ourselves). Among all the odd things suggested in 'the matter of Britain' debate, I would want to make a slogan or rallying cry of 'Horizontal Mobility'. Increased communications will follow from a far greater interchange between all groups of the managing elites, whether commercial, manufacturing, administrative, educational or publicizing than has traditionally been the case.[1] Social knowledge flows not from asking an 'expert' in to a committee for an afternoon, but from able men moving from occupation to occupation, service to service, industry to industry. Rubbing shoulders in committees with people from a great diversity of professions and backgrounds at least accelerates feedbacks more rapidly than a dozen textbooks or a score of memoranda.

Institutional reform must lead to increased occupational mobility, but also a third dimension must seize our attention:

1. See my 'Parliament and the Matter of Britain', *Essays on Reform*, op. cit., and also Max Nicholson, *The System*, p. 481: 'This leads us on to the question of how to get away from the monastic isolation of the British Civil Service and to make it simply the chief of a family of public and semi-public services, with much closer contact and mutual interchange. . . .'

the professionals of communication themselves, the journalists.

Here I must dare to quote George Wigg, his former Ministerial self.[1] And to quote what he actually said, sensibly and soberly last year at the Annual Conference of the Guild of British Newspaper Editors, not the indignant and selective reportage of *The Times* and the *Daily Mirror*, for his having dared to criticize British Journalists! He did, after all, admit:

> First of all, let me say that this is not a one-sided affair. There is much that we in the Government and in the political establishment can do to improve our contribution to the Fourth Estate. I think there has been a tendency in recent years towards too much secrecy in the affairs of Government, especially when that secrecy involves matters which are not a question of national security but of political expediency.

But he also said, which drew down the wrath of Juggernaut upon him, that:

> Because a flow of accurate information is essential to the conduct of democratic affairs, the public cannot rightly decide how their country should be run if they do not, day by day, have a true picture of the issues facing those who govern. And as I have said earlier, giving that true picture involves a great deal of hard work – more work, I am bound to say, than many papers seem prepared to finance. Of late, in the special inquiries launched by some Sunday and some daily papers, a major effort has been made to put this extra dimension into news coverage. I would like to see this enterprise carried into the coverage of every story. That would be costly, I know, but it would be a cost which in a democracy should be accepted and indeed must be accepted. And if it means more jobs for journalists – well I would be all for that. Because I am all for journalists – provided they are really diggers after facts, really quarrymen working to get at the truth, not just tale-bearers – even if the source of their tales is a politician.

The press must not be too touchy: 'the lady doth protest too much'. For the press is not merely concerned with the ephe-

1. *What George Wigg Really Said on the Press*, A Sogat Pamphlet, 1967, pp. 14 and 6, reprinting in full his speech of 8 September 1967.

meral day-to-day news, but carries the main burden of popularizing knowledge and of maintaining communications between rulers and ruled (the press is involved in, whether it likes it or not, whether it does it well or not, a continuous process of further education). Thus the press, being so important, must expect to be criticized and must expect that the profession of journalism will come under the same kind of scrutiny to which the old amateurism of British business and the public service have been subject, and may have to reform itself in the same kind of ways.

What I am getting at is something that should offend nobody – for it is only a theory: that maximization of participation is a false hare to pursue in the name of democracy, compared to, for a prospect of real change, a maximization of communication and publicity. Governments are to be restrained from harming us not by loyal party cohorts, but by knowing that we all know or can guess – at some level and to some degree – *why* they act as they do.

We no longer, no longer even we intellectuals, live in the *polis* of Athens, the Congregation of the Elect of God, the Jacobin Club, the sixth form commonroom, the active trade unionist branch, the Arts Council itself, the 1922 Committee or even the Parliamentary Labour Party. Most of us are not members. If they are to carry US with THEM, they must tell us what is happening more precisely and frequently, and share their thoughts with us more often – if they have any.

Participation as the criterion of democracy, direct democracy, does, indeed, make a large-scale democratic society unworkable. No wonder Aristotle gravely pondered that the size of a just state could be no larger than that in which the character of every citizen was known to every other citizen, or that Rousseau rolled on the floor and wept with despair that democracy was impossible in large states. But surely James Wilson of Pennsylvania in 1787 was right – and put his finger on the essence of modern politics – when he argued that precisely because he wished (against the 'states' rights' men) 'to raise the Federal pyramid to a great height' therefore 'its roots must go deep': strong government depends upon a firm democractic base.

I do not wish to claim any originality, only perhaps to be a truculent moderate in a time of either conventional ineffectuality or of wild irrelevance, so I will end on quotations. The last paragraph of David Williams's book on (his subtitle) 'The Problem of Security in Democracy':

> In short, it is desirable that as far as possible the workings of the central government should either be subject to publicity or subject to some form of independent scrutiny. Sweeping assertions of executive secrecy ought not to be tolerated in a democratic country. The responsibility for ensuring that they should not be tolerated rests in varying degrees with Parliament, the courts of law, the press (and other media of communication) and the central government itself. The country as a whole needs to beware of accepting too easily the basic assumptions of executive secrecy. The public interest has many facets, and it would be deplorable if the assessment of the public interest were to become the exclusive province of the executive itself. Secrecy and security have to be balanced against the legitimate demands for an informed public opinion which is, when all is said and done the essential element in a country which claims to be democratic.[1]

And Professor John Griffith ends his contribution to *Essays on Reform, 1967* with the unnatural – because exasperated – peroration:

> We read the newspapers, we listen to and look at political commentators, we hear ministerial statements, and we are conscious of the existence of another world, the other side of the moon. So we become cynical to the point of switching off radio and television during general election broadcasts because, simply, we do not believe what is being said. The evasions, the half-truths, the falsities shine through the words and we are angered because we are treated like children. So politicians are laughed at and remain powerful. Can all this play-acting really be necessary for the management of 50,000,000 people? Only if politicians trust the people, can they expect to be trusted. If politicians wish to be trusted, they must take us more into their confidence.[2]

1. Williams, op. cit., p. 216.   2. Griffith, op. cit., p. 23.

'Yes, yes, but do not be hasty,' they will say, 'the Fulton Committee is going to report soon and organization of the civil service will be reformed' – once every hundred years; but no institutional reforms can possibly affect our basic problems if they do not alter the Whitehall *and* Westminster *attitudes* to secrecy and publicity: that it is enough to make decisions honestly and wisely, no need to tell us how they were made and on what grounds nor even to discover if they are likely to have the intended effect.[1]

Finally we can only return, to point rather desperately forward, to that arch-Demagogue who could carry the people with him, Pericles of Athens, from the pen of Thucydides:

Here each individual is interested not only in his own affairs but in the affairs of the state as well: even those who are mostly occupied with their own business are extremely well-informed on general politics – this is a peculiarity of ours: we do not say that a man who takes no interest in politics is a man who minds his own business; we say that he has no business here at all. We Athenians, in our own persons, take our decisions on policy or submit them to proper discussions: for we do not think that there is an incompatibility between words and deeds; the worst thing is to rush into action before the consequences have been properly debated.[2]

The Labour Party, by the way, said something rather like that in its 1964 Election Manifesto.[3] When Labour leaders

1. Secrecy precludes much study of these processes, but a London Ph.D. dissertation, 'The Rent Act (1957) as an Example of the Legislative Process', by Malcolm J. Barnett, brilliantly assembles enough evidence to show that the Ministry drafted the Rent Act with grossly insufficient statistics of housing and tenancies and with no attempt to predict the consequences of the proposed changes. (Now published as *The Politics of Legislation* (Weidenfeld, 8 Nicolson, 1969).

2. Thucydides, *The Peloponnesian War*, translated by Rex Warner (Pelican, 1954), pp. 118–19.

3. Labour Party Election Manifesto, 1964: Reproduced in *The Times, House of Commons 1964*, p. 270. 'We offer no easy solution to our national problems. Time and effort will be required before they can be mastered. But Labour has a philosophy and a practical programme which is relevant to our contemporary needs. The starting point is our belief that the community must equip itself to take charge of its own

thus encourage us to hope for more consultation, why should they appear so petulant at our incomprehension, anger or cynicism when the contrary is done. And we should not be satisfied with democratic sops, with small increases in ritualistic processes of individual participation – unless such participation increases the flow of communication. I am not joining the Advisory Committee unless I am free to publish, and I suspect fewer Advisory Committees would be needed if more people (both outside and inside the public service) were free to publish, even urged to publish as policy.

WE know that YOU up there are working for us and all those benighted OTHERS, but we want to know why and how, and we want more preparation and warning about great things; if you convince US, we will work as hard as cart-horses; if you do not convince us, we will drag our feet, and if you continue to insult us by refusing even to share your thoughts with us and to take sensible steps about how to listen to and evaluate ours, then the nastier among us will spit delinquently in your God-like eyes.

---

destiny and no longer be ruled by market forces beyond its control. We are working for an active democracy, in which men and women as responsible citizens consciously assist in shaping the surrounds in which they live, and take part in deciding how the community's wealth is to be shared among all its members.'

7

The Proper Limits of Student Influence[1]

The idea of a university

UNIVERSITIES are – this at least is not open to reasonable
doubt – very *peculiar institutions*. And yet, on immediate
second thoughts, there are now some who have seriously
argued that they should not be peculiar (even if they are), but
should be – somewhat as Lenin saw the Communist Party –
simply the vanguard and the speeders-up of an emerging
social consciousness. When this Reformation is over, the
universities will lose their 'splendid isolation', their 'selfish
freedom' or their 'ingrained exclusiveness'; the 'ivory tower'
will then collapse, and its stones be used to build compulsive
(that is both free and compulsory) educational nests or cells
for all. Moreover, these same enthusiasts would wish to subsume or overcome (in some murky Hegelian sense), rather
than simply destroy, all 'institutions'. This objective is, however, just intellectual muddle, for what is meant by 'institution' by any social scientist is no longer a fixed body of rules
or visible edifice of bricks and mortar (full of signs saying 'Do
Not Walk on the Grass' and 'No Writing on the Walls' –
hence almost by definition 'bureaucratic'), but is the working
of some associated set of concepts. Any university, in this
sense, must necessarily be an institution, so that all we can
intellectually ask of those who passionately want it to be some
new kind of institution, something less peculiar (presumably

1. This appeared in David Martin, ed., *Anarchy and Culture: The Problem
of the Contemporary University*, (Routledge & Kegan Paul, 1969); but some
paragraphs in the middle section were adapted from my editorial,
'Student Politics', *Political Quarterly*, July–September 1967.

more natural) than the present institution, is that they make themselves a little bit more clear than they have yet done about what it is precisely they want. 'The ethically desirable must be the sociologically possible.'

How precise one can be is, of course, a difficult question. But certainly it is no new thing for people to advocate very specific-sounding accounts of what 'the idea of a university' must be. For instance, it was once held that universities existed for the Glory of God. Then it was held that universities should exist for the creation of character – as by Matthew Arnold, in his way, or John Dewey in his. A view arose, not necessarily wholly in conflict with these two views, that universities select and mould the governing class – a view as much that of Bismarck and Stalin, in their different ways, as of Macaulay and Trevelyan, both of whom saw university reform as a necessary adjunct of civil service reform. Others at all times command universities to be useful – a view in which Sir Paul Chambers and Prime Minister Kosygin would plainly both concur (and which is probably at all times the view that deserves to create the greatest fear). And now some tell us that universities have a special mission to be the Godly Congregations of some temporary revolutionary orthodoxy. The toughest form of this latest 'idea' is that of the handful of tiny Revolutionary Socialist Societies – of whom it is a gross flattery to be in the least fearful. And the gentlest articulation, held by very many more, is that universities should be, no longer the mentors of youth, but the *expression of youth*.

It is perhaps surprising that from all these various claims or assaults could have emerged and be taken so much for granted: '. . . the concept of universities as centres of education, learning and research' which 'exist to transmit knowledge from one generation to the next and to seek new knowledge and a better understanding of nature, man and society'; and as institutions which '. . . can achieve these purposes only in a climate in which rational discussion is universally accepted'.[1] The Vice-Chancellors made a fairly

1. From a statement or press release issued by the Committee of Vice-Chancellors and Principals, 17 June 1968.

good shot at a definition. It is, of course, an ostensive definition – it describes what is the case, or what is hoped to be the
case; but it does avoid the fallacy involved in that rather
dreadful phrase, 'the idea of a university'.[1] It would be better to
say simply that universities are (or should be) concerned with
ideas, and the stress must be on the plural, just as we had
better claim to be many minds in pursuit of truths rather
than, the fault of all such general definitions mentioned
above, to be a community in possession of or in pursuit of the
Truth. It is even to be doubted, if this understanding is
secure, why the Vice-Chancellors should have wanted to
insist that 'rational discussion is [i.e. should be] universally
accepted'. For it plainly is not, and nor should it be, unless
they can convince us what we should mean by 'rational'. It is
apparent that all the above past and would-be future authoritarian views still have some role to play for some people and
do, in fact, have some influence in many, if not most, actual
universities.

Academic freedom is not the absence of authority but it is
the arena in which rival authorities compete for allegiance.
For this competition to be fair, the arena needs certain ground-
rules and working conventions, but these rules and conventions are not ends in themselves – as some liberals suggest.
This needs saying, even if it sounds banal, for one cannot
beat something with nothing. Some toleration can be damn-
ably condescending or utterly empty; and freedom needs
exercise and activity, not eternal and unmolested repose. If
authorities are untouchably secure in their own truths, their
tolerance is unlikely to be morally acceptable – any man of
spirit then wants to throw stones; but equally if they are
tolerant because they hold no views themselves whatever,
then their tolerance is likely to be rejected psychologically
and denounced ideologically. If authorities are challenged

1. I take this point from Peter Laslett in his essay, 'The University in
High Industrial Society', in *Essays on Reform, 1967: a centenary tribute*
(Oxford University Press, 1967); see also Lord Annan's excellent essay
in the same volume, 'Higher Education', on the whole question of
university reform.

by rival views, however wild or repulsive, and will not answer back then they are hardly likely to maintain their
authority. It is less important for 'the authorities' to nerve
themselves to deal with wild bulls in their china shops than it
is for them to argue strongly and openly with the sacred
cows, not just to pride themselves on their preservation. Press
and television give extremists publicity, but it is only in
the universities themselves that they can be argued back
against.

On such grounds as these I will argue that the communication network is more important than the participation network. Increasing student participation is important: but it is
less important than explaining much more often and much
more publicly how decisions are made. If university authorities do not understand this (which I think is elementary
social science) they will be puzzled when they discover that
the real steps many are now taking to increase student participation and to set up more and more staff-student committees,
will be denounced as 'bureaucratic' by the very people they
thought wanted them, and will not, of themselves, allay the
present stirrings and discontents. Perhaps they should not
hope for too much in any case, for many of the reasons for the
present stirrings and discontents are quite beyond the control
of the universities. Some of the causes are very general and
we should not forget in all this discussion that in churches,
trade unions, businesses, firms, banks, local government
authorities, and even in Parliament and Government Departments, people are beginning to demand greater consultation
before decisions are made in their name or to bind them. The
going will be rougher and less dignified for all these authorities, but, if they keep their nerve and play their hands
properly, they may end up with greater effective power (if
they can carry their constituents with them) rather than what
is often at present an almost pathetically nominal power, unchallengeable but ineffective (which depends on letting lie
sleeping dogs whose energies might, if things were done
another way, be harnessed for common purposes).

The causes of the present discontents

The causes of the present discontents in England (I go no further) must be considered before considering how student influence may change, grow or become more institutionalized. I see at least fourteen different factors, and there may be more or slightly fewer according to definitions. To see their variety and multiplicity is important, although this is not to say that they necessarily 'add up' or are in any way systematically related – some are and some are not; and still less that they take the same form everywhere.

(1.) The specific example of LSE in 1967: genuine concern and bitterness in a highly cosmopolitan environment about the Government's Rhodesian policy, leading to a spontaneous, idealistic, ignorant, ungenerous and almost completely irrelevant outburst against their new Director's alleged record in Rhodesia; but after the fighting had broken out and had become frustrated of real enemies, new and slightly more rational sounding war aims were discovered to do, crazily, with 'student power' (an almost derogatory parody of the grim majesty of 'Black Power') or, more soberly, with student representation and influence – a long overdue (however muddled and rough) student interest in academic policy, syllabus, teaching methods and the examination system.

(2.) A more general sharing in international currents of 'Youth Nationalism' (more easily seen as 'anti-colonialism'), again a generalized cause searching for a local object: to this extent the 'generational argument' is true, that the cues for direct action tend to come from the international headlines ('They Stopped Berkeley, We'll Stop LSE' or the ever memorable 'Paris Here') rather than from the exhaustion of local grievance procedures.

(3.) Local grievances, none the less, concerned with antiquated teaching methods, inexplicable syllabuses and, very often, overcrowding and neglect by teachers busy elsewhere on public business or just plain making money advising this or that or televizing (two factors very evident at LSE).

(4.) A generalized feeling that 'Youth' is, *a priori*, always

165

right and should, *a fortiori*, make itself heard on every great issue through what then becomes seen as their own institution, the university; and the university is then not a place of learning, but a stage on which one must develop one's distinctive and flamboyant personality – and if one hasn't got one, one has, none the less, money and leisure to dress the part and to learn, however painfully, some impressive and threatening imposture.[1]

(5.) Alongside this, a bit of straight, old-fashioned trade union economic protest too: British student grants are *good*, both in scale and number, by any world or generational comparisons, but at half the national average wage students may well, without condemning them for arrogance or selfishness compared to working men supporting families in miserable environments, understandably feel some constrained itchiness of the purse, some frustration of expectations or sense of 'relative deprivation' – particularly as their age-group is the target of among the most poisoned shafts of consumer advertising: the plain style of dress, for instance, of the Communist student leaders of the 1930s and 1940s has now given way to the extravagant exoticism of nearly all the new leaders, as dully fashionable and as restlessly trendy

1. The role of fantasy can hardly be exaggerated. Why do people dress like Castro or Guevara who have not the slightest intention of going to help in Cuba, or wear inconvenient and expensive Maoist jackets (made by capitalist clothiers and sold in boutiques) who never dream of going to fight in Vietnam? In the 1930s, there was an International Brigade; in the 1960s, a tortuous process of reasoning or sheer fantasy which identifies London Bobbies with Fascism, and which can chalk up nonsense like 'US plus Napalm equals Fascism' – equals something morally terrible, certainly, but this slogan shows a complete misunderstanding of what fascist systems actually were, how they worked, and hence how best they are combated or prevented. 'Role playing' is carried very far; one thinks of Hermann Rauschning's argument (a totally different substance, but a parallel social function) that many disturbed and rootless people marched in the Nazi processions and street demonstrations not because they already felt full of 'racial brotherhood' or 'party fraternity', but because they wanted to achieve such feelings (in his *The Revolution of Nihilism*, Ryerson Press; 1939). Strictly speaking much that is now called socialism in the early 1970s deserves to be better understood as 'expressionism': the rational element in socialism can be entirely lacking.

as any ad-man could wish (what old-fashioned fascists would have correctly called, I suppose, 'decadent').

(6.) Some degree of genuine alienation from normal conciliatory politics among political activists, a real and wholly proper dislike of Mr Wilson and Mr Heath's tandem bicycle of consensus-politics (even if they are foolish to think that consensus as to ends necessarily arises from consensus as to means, and even if some of the alienation is largely self-induced – the paradox of the lads who say 'We are all brainwashed by the Interests', meaning that they are all responsible for their personal virtues but not for their common vices).

(7.) Incitement and conspiracy by 'Trotskyite' and other Revolutionary Socialist agitators: absurd as a general explanation, but not to be discounted in explaining the timing of some particular happenings – but it is always far more important to explain why such a few neurotic fanatics (who have always been around in one form or another, waiting for Armageddon) can now, in the right conditions, get such a large if temporary following of people who certainly do *not* share their specific opinions or general objectives (*pace* those journalists who are for ever talking about *the* views of *the* students, meaning the utterances of a few solemn madmen which are then built-up and publicized, often because of sheer laziness by journalists faced with the time-consuming problem of identifying opinions more typical of actual students and the many student sub-cultures).[1]

(8.) Also outside agitators and 'professional students' joining in for the hell of it; but students themselves, except when

1. This may be pot calling kettle black, for very little academic research has been done in Great Britain into student attitudes or behaviour of any relevance to the present unrest – we have not, as social scientists, exploited our captive audiences or showed a scientific interest in them to anything like the extent of the Americans. An informal conference on 'Research into Student Unrest' in July 1968, arranged by the Social Science Research Council (in conjunction with the Department of Social Psychology at Brighton), concentrated wholly on plans for future research – since the subject is interesting; but there was little to report from the past.

things have already got out of hand, are usually extremely suspicious of outside intervention (even Tariq Ali begins to look a bit old and Soho).

(9.) Mismanagement by academic authorities out of touch with (and much too busy to notice) ordinary student opinion, a peculiar academic pride that we all know intuitively what the students are thinking (so have no need to inquire formally or to survey scientifically); inconsistent handling of different cases which, whether Vice-Chancellors like it or not, are compared nationally, not according to local precedents (the great example of inconsistency being the indulgence of the LSE authorities about responsibility for the porter's death, then their attempted inflexibility in dealing with the nominal leaders); and an overall lack of wise public relations (students are not told enough or quickly enough and the press is something to be kept out at almost any cost).

(10.) Universities are too paternalistic and interfere too much with the lives of their students (usually true for some, those in Halls or Colleges and for women generally, but not at all for others).

(11.) They are at the same time far too secretive and never explain what they are doing and why.

(12.) Random protest symptoms or mild delinquent behaviour as a result of either disappointed expectations about university life, or the complete lack in some of any kind of prior expectations at all (the ideal image is 'to play it cool' in such circumstances, but the actual strains are so great as to produce tantrums).

(13.) The recent tradition of demonstrations and protest marches as the tactic of an alienated politics (not specifically student at all, except that students have more time on their hands and no jobs to lose by mid-week happenings); the reading of books and pamphlets and the drafting of programmes, even, is no longer fashionable compared with the joys and stimulus of 'direct action'[1] (and all such mass demon-

1. One thing that needs to be researched, by political sociologists or political theorists using concepts from social anthropology and methods from empirical social surveys, is the character of the 'oral tradition' of

strations, whether of Left- or Right-wing extremes, tend to become ends in themselves, happy just to be mutually provocative and mutually isolating).

(14.) And, lastly, just plain, good old-fashioned student ambivalence to authority (LSE students have usually been so terribly earnest compared to, say, the carnivorous-carnival spirit of Scottish student elections); and something still persists in the new demonstrations of the jocular, facetious and animal spirits of the post-war and pre-war student 'rags'.

If all these discontents and conditions came to a head at once – which is about as likely as 'if all the Greeks were to form one *polis* they could conquer the world'. But equally nothing anyone can do, certainly not university statesmen, can cure or even very much allay some of these conditions. The beginning of wisdom in the practical implementation of some greater student presence or voice in university counsels is to realize that nothing can be done simply to avoid trouble; it had better be done to make universities better places anyway, and thus more able to sustain the periodic troubles and affronts which all major national institutions will now undergo, but of which universities will get a disproportionate share because of the unique force of 'youth ideology'.

The smoke and the flame

To realize that total breakdown is as unlikely as any return to a passive normal should strengthen resistance to some demands, which are either absurd or which threaten the freedom and the pluralistic nature of universities, but should make us accept the challenge in other directions of trying to make the students feel more of a community with the whole university. Such moves are not weakness if they attempt to

---

popular Marxism and Revolutionary Socialism. I suspect that it depends very little on real Marxist writings, or any other, but has something of the spontaneity that its holders would wish to find in action, not in thought (but it may well have, if investigated in this way, a greater coherence than is apparent simply from reading the fugitive materials of the movement (or movements?)).

restore, or perhaps to create for the first time, a sense of community which subsumes both the function of teaching and the function of learning.

What are the most common complaints? Many students see the staff as too remote (although this can vary wildly – some see too much of them). The university itself is then incomprehensible and uninteresting as an institution. The syllabuses appear old-fashioned or, more often, highly random and fortuitous: they are changed without explanation: university or college statutes, ordinances and regulations are commonly set out in Calendars in such a way as to be totally incomprehensible to all students and to most members of Faculties. The course itself is always either (for one hears both) 'useless for the real world' or else 'cluttered up with practical stuff one can learn better on the job'. Reading lists are always too long and usually too unselective, and libraries are almost always too small and poorly stocked with multiple copies of much-used books.

Many staff see the students as unintellectual at the best and anti-intellectual all too often (as in the widespread craze to put juke-boxes in students' union commonrooms so that 'shop talk' is impossible). They are also often seen as lazy, purely career-minded and yet distrustful of any kind of authority (up to the moment of employment): more interested in buying a new shirt each week than a new book, a genera-tion – it seems at times – who have had education thrust at them on a silver plate and lack seriousness. They pass resolutions about 'wanting more staff/student contact', but seven-tenths of them cut tutorials without warning, apology or explanation and teachers could 'keep office hours' for ever without most of the students even wanting to call to discuss their work. They demand 'student participation' but are not willing to trust their own elected officers and they demand that the university explains itself, but do not bother to read the statutes and regulations and the annual reports of Faculties.

These mutual complaints are a mixture of smoke and real flame: some of the wood is very damp – perennial complaints, part of an almost agreeable tradition of mutual grumbling. But some elements are more serious. They perhaps resolve into three factors. Let me neatly give great blame to each side for one of them, but see the third as a general folly of our whole educational system: that staffs explain too little about universities and take too little care to keep or remake the system comprehensible in realistic terms; that students expect too much to be done for them and too readily think of themselves as a community of age and not of function (hence leaders of the contemporary, fashionable but quite peculiar – historically speaking – 'youth cult', not fellow members of a republic of learning or a timeless universe of discourse); but that the laws and conventions of our society send people into higher studies either before they are old enough or in such a way that university seems to be only a peculiar and less well organized extension of school – British students, like those in the USA, are nearly all far too young and too inexperienced in looking after themselves in a real work situation.

Far more could be done to explain what a university is: places that perpetuate traditions of learning and try to discover new methods of discovery. We are primarily interested in education for its own sake, not in training for practical ends. We need no longer pretend to be ancient Greeks; we see nothing base in interest in *techne* rather than in *schole*; but we must see it as something different. Frustration and incomprehension arise when the two are confused. This is easy to say, but hard to insist upon, as a rule, without at every step appearing to insult worthy colleagues; but it is a risk to be run rather than disappoint those students (for there are still some) who want to study 'the nature of things'. The disappointed are more dangerous than the indifferent or the purely mercenary.

Neither the Robbins Report nor Mr Crosland's gloss on it help very much. Instead of there being a university reform movement, university teachers rallied behind their pay claim in 1963, behind the Robbins Report of 1964, against the cuts in 1967, all quantitative and financial things; we tacitly agreed to close the ranks and not to purge them. Real issues of university reform (such as the rights of junior staff) and educational reform (such as the universities' relation with the schools) were either forgotten or not publicly debated; the students wishing for 'reform' lacked their natural leaders – the university teachers themselves Robbins looked at as numbers and disclaimed any responsibility for what should be taught *and* studied and how; Crosland created or discovered a dual system of 'university' and 'technical' studies, but only for future members in search of a club: the existing confusion of functions is, if anything, made worse. More does not mean, as Kingsley Amis oddly argued, 'worse'; worse than that, it has meant 'the same'. 'Worse' would give some incentive for rationalizing the system drastically between genuine (and fewer) universities and more technical or multi-purpose institutions; but with 'the same' we can muddle on: with Accountancy, Social Work, Metallurgy, Business and Civil Engineering studies all casting their cultural influences throughout universities as well as technical colleges. And even amid the intellectual disciplines, why need nearly every university have a department in nearly everything however small and second-rate?

Perhaps this is baying at the moon. But even within the present department stores (and we all know what bookshops in department stores are like), simple reforms in the direction of comprehensibility could take place. How rarely are student editors encouraged to report and comment upon changes in building plans, the creation of chairs and alterations and innovations in courses: the stuff of modern universities. How rarely is the Annual Report written as something to educate the students in what they are doing and where they are, rather than as a ritual regurgitation by Vice-Chancellors and Deans of stuff too well known already back to their senior colleagues. And if the civic universities and London have achieved some remarkable reforms of syllabus, so that the old narrow single honours programme is almost everywhere under competition from dual honours or even wider programmes, they have seldom gone in for simplification and codification of regulations. Nor are the methods of marking, the way classes of degree are decided, or even, very often, individual marks disclosed. Does such secrecy strengthen or weaken systems of government? These things remain mysteries to the average student. If he is not helped to take an intelligent interest in what affects him as a studious person, no wonder he often wanders off into the shadow politics of demanding 'equal student representation on all major committees'. Something approaching this could be given readily in most cases, and make no difference to academic authority whatever: the student generation is too short compared to the staff generation, and in a learned institution authority will inevitably flow from the learned.

False expectations and uncertainty

The real and the legitimate student demand is to hear and be heard on matters that affect him as a student or young scholar: not just on marginal things – athletics, lodgings and union premises. The protests and demonstrations against the raising of fees for overseas students stemmed from the whole university community – students and teachers together. But the student diminishes his authority as student when he demands a 'student voice' on all kinds of matters which are not university at all, but part of common citizenship. Every time a students' union racks itself with resolutions and counter-resolutions on world politics, it both diverts its members from their interests as students, and weakens its authority. By all means let students be politically active – no educational authority has any business intervening here (as teachers' training colleges and others need firmly reminding), but active as members of the community in groups catering for all ages and interests – like, for instance, political parties. Perhaps when the voting age is reduced to eighteen, student politics may well divert itself to more concrete political issues.

One last point on expectations and comprehensibility: schools are much at fault in not preparing their potential university students more. Some do, most do not: students commonly come up with no idea at all what a university is like. They feel neglected if they are not lectured at: they are at a complete loss how to use a library and yet, breaking from home and school together, they want to assert independence even if many of these assertions, like beards, bizarre 'strong views' and public petting, are disappointingly superficial. But there is no sense in allocating blame: universities should 'spoon-feed', if that is what it is, by giving specific instruction on how to make notes, how to use books, how to use finding aids, how to prepare essays and reports. There is no longer a tradition about these things (if ever there was) and it does not 'rub off somehow'.

Students often expect too much because they do not know what to expect. It does go back to the school teachers. But it also goes back to tendencies in our modern industrial culture particularly disturbing to any social-democrat; we may not be getting nearer the take off point, but slipping backwards. The development of 'personality' is somehow deemed more important than the pursuit of objective standards of truth, beauty or justice. The philistine student will, indeed, not feel himself challenged in his values by a genuine university teacher: for he is armoured already to think of such people as 'characters', tolerable as such. And perhaps they make themselves 'characters' rather than appear to offer a direct challenge to the values of their students. Probably most student political activists chase false hares because their teachers disappoint them by their lack of dedication; but it might be nothing to the uproar if their teachers really did treat them as members of an intellectual community and refused to simplify, only to discuss and to dispute obsessionally. John Saville, Lord Halifax, wrote in *The Character of a Trimmer* that 'the struggle for knowledge hath a pleasure in it like that of wrestling with a fine woman'. The student should at least be encouraged, even by example, not to compartmentalize his life.

In this light it is interesting that those practitioners of student politics who claim to be Marxists commonly lack nearly all the energy in research and scholarship associated with Marx, but rather exhibit a romantic individualism, anarchism more than socialism or communism, which ultimately stems from Rousseau (the anti-scholar) and not Marx (the enemy of mere-scholarship).

One of the problems is plainly the rather lovely mixture of great expectations and little experience. Indeed 'experience' is almost a dirty word to many students; it means to them a cynical and middle-aged realism, 'wordly-wise' in the worst sense, the doctrine of civilization as it is, rather than of society as it ought to be. The political implications of this are obvious; but contemporary 'youth culture' and the 'cult of youth' add on even greater burdens diverting student from ever becoming scholar, or 'young man' from being man. It is widely and solemnly believed, for instance, that all pleasures of secular life, notably travel and love, must end by twenty-one or twenty-two – all have to be crammed into those long vacations and monstrously short terms.

On a more mundane level, the real youthfulness of students of seventeen and eighteen forces universities into a whole range of completely unacademic activities, the grossest of which is the paternalism and the waste of money of Halls of Residence. If students were older they could either shift for themselves, which would have had some interesting implications for the location of new universities (or better, for which of the civic to have expanded); or else the university, if it had to be a builder of residential accommodations, would limit its subsequent role to that of landlord and rent collector.

Any who remember the post-war generation of ex-servicemen and women or who regularly teach some 'adult' or 'mature' students would argue that intangible factors of maturity do emerge with those extra years; that students would get more out of their studies had they done anything else for a couple of years between school and university; that they would have established a real personal independence from home and from school habits (so be less likely to make aggressive and largely meaningless big gestures of independence); and that they would be more conscious of the privilege they enjoy and responsibilities they owe the community. Curiously, students think of such points as 'conservative'; I think of them as socialist. Some real experience of work in an industrial society would remove those, perhaps few, but shamefully evident, sections of universities which seem like indulgent and arrogant youth clubs in permanent session at public expense.

The remedy for the faults of the universities, which are faults of rigid and unexplained teaching, methods and organization – not of political reaction – lies in the students' own hands. They can force the pace and show great gains when they will concentrate on issues that peculiarly affect them as students: people studying something as part of a wider academic community, not as a self-contained community in themselves.

Students have rights, which should be asserted: not to govern or share in the government of learned institutions, but to be consulted, to be told 'why' as well as 'how', and to be provided with conditions in which they can work effectively and syllabuses broad enough in which to study freely. But they have duties, too: to pursue their studies, to repay the community by useful service for what it has given them (at the expense of money from others and which might have helped others), and the duty to include even themselves in their pleasing scepticism at established authority.

For 'Youth' is no more acceptable as authority than 'Age': it is either adolescent or senile to think otherwise. We are all one of another. Rights and duties are reciprocal and authority is neither good nor bad as such: it depends on the uses to which it is put. Students should respect authority, but that authority must make itself both more comprehensible and more worthy of respect. Authority is relative to function: if we master our subject, we should yield to none, State, student or colleagues, as to how we teach it. But all authority is limited (except, some say, the authority of God and of the Revolution – but then absolute truth cannot concern us as truth-seeking and truth-doubting universities for that very reason). If we will not assert and publicly justify our learned authority, we deserve to be humiliated, but if we use it to pontificate or to intervene in the personal lives and beliefs of our students, we weaken it and bring it into contempt. The university is a community, but it is not a total community as both the old Oxbridge College mentality (even or especially in its civic university form of departmental paternalism) and the new Revolutionary Socialist creeds would have us believe and act accordingly. But being a community, there are many matters of common concern, between university authorities, junior staff and students, which must be publicly discussed. Take, for instance, the small but deadly issue of those few who take flight from reality into forms of drug addiction. As teachers we should neither tolerate this on principle nor should we use disciplinary power to go beyond what the civil authorities can do; but we should stand up and argue, publicly and privately, what we may think, as much as they, is right. But we should do so because we think it right to do so as individuals, not in virtue of our office. The distinction is difficult in practice, of course, but it is clear in principle and should be stated.

Text and commentary

Now, to conclude, anti-climax. What changes are likely to take place and should take place? I know no better starting point than the astonishingly sensible and radical 'Joint Statement from the Committee of Vice-Chancellors and Principals and the National Union of Students' of 7 October 1968 – a document which must be brought to life and rescued, on both sides, from the instinctive but false feeling that it is likely to be (if anyone read it) but a string of vague compromises and platitudes.

Let me quote the four key sections and offer only a brief commentary on the text.

Student Participation in University Decision-Making
4. The National Union of Students seeks effective student presence on all relevant committees. Our discussions identified three broad areas of operation of such committees: (a) the whole field of

student welfare – for example health services, catering facilities and the provision of accommodation – where there should in our view be varying degrees of participation of students in the decision-making process. Apart from this, there is the area which covers for example the operation of student unions and the management of a wide range of extra-curricular activities, in which most university student organizations rightly have long had complete responsibility, (b) that relating for example to curriculum and courses, teaching methods, major organizational matters, and issues concerning the planning and development of the university – where the ultimate decision must be that of the statutorily responsible body. In this area, we would regard it as essential that students' views should be properly taken into account, and (c) that involving for example decisions on appointments, promotions and other matters affecting the personal position of members of staff, the admissions of individuals and their academic assessment – where student presence would be inappropriate. Students should, however, have opportunities to discuss the general principles involved in such decisions and have their views properly considered.

The three categories are sensible. The first, (a), is obvious, although many local battles are still to be won, and beyond the universities this will and should cause constant trouble between Local Government Authorities, colleges in their sector pursuing university-level work and their students. If the second, (b), is taken seriously, a great change in atmosphere will take place. It is astonishing how little this is done, and it needs some modicum of formal institutions, it cannot be left to chance, sherry parties or to 'informal good relations'. Students must be given definite occasions on which they can put, either by staff-student committees or by general meetings (as they must themselves choose), questions, objections and reasoned alternatives to their teachers. This will lead to considerable changes, for there are some purely traditional elements in many syllabuses or types of teaching method which, if ever challenged at all, will surely change. It is always good to be forced to justify what one thinks one is doing. This will not, of course, always or often lead to changes so immediate that they benefit the students who make them – regulations cannot be changed overnight. But it will educate everyone in responsibility for the future years as well as to the past. One of the best methods of discovering 'consumer reaction', for instance, is obviously to survey students who have just finished their degree work, or some definite section of it. But then the results of such surveys must be fed back to the present generation of students, not kept as some secret of state or *arcana imperii*. From (c), matters of appointments and promotions of staff, students should be excluded; but they should be reassured that representatives of junior staff are consulted (even if the facts have to be changed to make these assurances true). If universities are self-appointing oligarchies, they are at least oligarchies penetrable by merit. The issue of wider consultation and justice being seen to be done in appointments and promotion is a clear case for university reform, not just student reforms.

Course Content and Teaching Methods
7. Discussion in this area must necessarily be subject to the clear right of the individual teacher, in consultation with his colleagues who by their scholarship in the relevant field of study have proved their right to an opinion, to decide on the way in which he presents his subject. Once this right is infringed from whatever quarter, from public pressure, from university governing bodies or from students themselves, the way is open to censorship and interference of every kind. We believe that the great majority of students are fully aware of the need to preserve this most essential of all academic freedoms. But we think that without any interference with this principle, it is possible and indeed right that there should be opportunities for students to enter into discussion about the content and structure of courses, about teaching methods in general, and about the effectiveness of the particular teaching which they are receiving. In general, the larger the university administrative division concerned, the more necessary it becomes that such opportunities should be offered through official committees at the appropriate levels.

Most of the above comments also apply here. And staff should brace themselves and their students to come to realize that public consultation is no meaningless substitute for direct participation in deciding such matters, but is usually a more effective control and always a necessary condition of public participation. The wildmen are quite right, in principle, to suspect that a few student representatives on university or department committees run the risk of being either bamboozled or, quite simply, Uncle Toms muzzled with discretion and self-importance. But the problem is a general one throughout our society: do all kinds of voluntary bodies really speak in the names of their members? and how often does the apostle of publicity become the defender of secrecy once he is elected or appointed to the Board? The answer, however, can never be more and more direct representation. Modern society is too large to go back to the market-place of the Athenian *polis*. The more likely answer is to increase publicity and effective communication. Publicity is at least as important as electoral representation in the history of democracy. If some are rightly suspicious that there is emerging a new cant of participation which could well be mere 'public relations' by some Vice-Chancellors and Dons, or Mr Wilson's secret weapon for resurrection on the national level, they will have only themselves to blame if it so degenerates. The door has been, some will think, dangerously opened: it is now the obvious tactic of those genuinely interested in university reform, staff and student, to push hard for the nominal or official policy and to insist that open-government results from, and is not subtly frustrated by, formal institutions of participation and consultation.

Examinations
11. In the view of the National Union of Students, the traditional examination technique assesses only one aspect of academic worth. Different methods of assessment test different aspects of a student's ability and it is therefore to be expected that a mixed system of assessment would present a truer picture of total ability and achievement.
12. It was common ground in our discussions that more research and experiment on the subject of examinations are required. There was no question but that methods of assessment which recognize the very varied abilities of university students, and which are accepted by the public and employers generally, are an

essential student interest. On this common foundation, we believe that useful discussions with the student bodies, nationally and in each university, can be continued.

Again, much the same general commentary, but the specific point that the dangers to 'individual independence' of continuous assessment must be considered in detail by the student body, quite as much as the prospects of greater equity and some release from the tension and fear of the 'all the eggs in one basket' of the traditional examination system. Here the students will learn that you cannot beat something with nothing, and they will need skilled study and advice from their national and local unions, and will probably come to find natural allies in the junior staff – which will at least do much to break down the irrational belief in a natural conflict of the generations and to recreate talk of 'university reform', seen as a whole, not the inherently temporary victories of student power, necessarily based on the all too short three-year generation.

Freedom of Speech
22. Freedom of discussion is one of the foundations on which the universities have been built. All members of a university should be prepared to tolerate, and indeed protect, the expression of unpopular opinions. It is the responsibility of all to ensure that within universities there are appropriate opportunities for hearing all sides on matters of current controversy. The right to freedom of speech, however, must not be exercised in ways which infringe the rights and freedoms of others.

But freedom of speech, like all freedom, must actually take place on both sides and be exercised. If students want to challenge things, they must be answered. We as teachers must be prepared to carry the ball into their court, to challenge their assumptions, not simply to tolerate them liberally, particularly as so many of their own assumptions are the products of materialistic and consumption-dominated society – against which they are rightly protesting in general terms but are rarely pausing long enough to study it and think how to draw specific conclusions. All this, emerging from all these

splendid, silly and muddled mixtures of stirrings and discontents, is something with which universities can cope while
moving out of their present traditional framework into something far more genuinely a universe of intense discourse than
has been the somewhat sleepy and complacent pattern of the
past. The 'Joint Statement' deserves to become a historic
document in British universities if it is used as a framework
and starting-point for consequences yet to be made concrete.[1]

1. Rereading this five years later I feel both more sceptical and more
radical: sceptical that the 'Joint Statement' can in fact lead to more than
modest benefits; but more radical to see the solution to 'youth' as being
discontent with 'youth' itself. More and more students I have talked to
about these problems wish that they could come up later. They think of
a guaranteed place two years hence. But there is a much more radical
point, a growing doubt that we are wise to cram the entire life's experience of further education for so many, but still only relatively few,
into three years. Could we not think in terms of a contraction of universities into research institutions, but then a great expansion of adult
education, polytechnics, FE colleges and teachers' colleges, with the
emphasis on a flexible variety of short-courses and refresher-courses, at
all sorts of levels, throughout people's working lives? Perhaps the two-
year qualification in Further Education recommended for teachers by
the James Report should be made general. No students should go straight
from school into university: universities should have a dual function of
research and of training teachers for the higher reaches of higher/further
education; and circulation of teachers throughout the system should be
made obligatory by changing rules of tenure and creating a unified
'service'. The only 'undergraduate-level' teaching department of universities could be the extra-mural department, thus a massive diversion of
funds from 'higher' to 'further' and a complete change of time-scale.
Courses could be far more 'on demand' if they were spread over time,
those taking them thus gaining progressively more knowledge of what
they really want; then student or consumer power would be meaningful.
    A bit futuristic? But I grow more and more convinced that 'university
education for all able to benefit' is not merely breaking down but stands
in the way of universal further or continuous education. Certainly the
liberal education versus vocational training dispute would be far less
important, far less exclusive of each other, if higher/further education
were spread through more time, indeed all our active life, amid jobs,
careers and leisure.

8

The Introducing of Politics in Schools[1]

SINCE it cannot be avoided, it had better be faced. Since it should not be avoided, quite a lot of care and time should be given to it. And since it is an interesting subject, it should be taught in an interesting manner. Civilized life and organized society depend upon the existence of governments, and what governments should do and can do with their power and authority depends, in turn, on the political structure and beliefs of the subsidiary societies within the range of influence of these governments. To take a Greek or a Jacobin view of the matter may now appear to go too far: that a man is only properly a man when he can be a citizen and takes part in public life. But it remains true that a man is still regarded as less of a man than he can be if he has no 'public spirit', has no concern for and takes no part in all the jostlings of self-interest, group interests and ideals that constitute politics. Only a few would maintain that the good life consists in the avoidance of public concerns; but nearly all would recognize that our whole culture or style of life is less rich, that is less various and shapely, and is less strong, that is less adaptable to change and circumstances, if people of any age-group believe that they should not or cannot influence authority.

This may sound very abstract, but the implications for education are embarrassingly concrete. Any worthwhile educa-

1. First published as the introductory essay to D. B. Heater, ed, *The Teaching of Politics* (Methuen Educational, 1969). Mr Heater's initiative in launching this book led to the founding of a now very active Politics Association, to improve standards of politics teaching in secondary and further education.

tion must include some explanation and, if necessary, justification of the naturalness of politics: that men both do and should want different things that are only obtainable by means or by leave of the public power, and that they can both study and control, in varying degrees, the means by which they reconcile or manage conflicts of interests and ideals.

The point of departure is all-important. When we ask for directions, there are occasions on which we should receive the rustic reply, 'I would not start from here if I were you.' In practical life, we have to start from where we are: perhaps as an inhabitant of a state that conceives politics as either subversive and divisive, or as the implementation of a single and authoritative set of truths which are to be extolled, but not questioned. But in education in a reasonably free society (and education in its full sense can only exist in reasonably free societies), we are reasonably free, despite practical limitations of various kinds, to start from where we choose. So we should start with politics itself. If we start from some other point, and I will discuss some of these conventional and innocent-sounding points of departure – such as 'the constitution' or 'good citizenship', we may risk either heading off in the wrong direction entirely or creating a positive distaste for the most positive and natural part of the journey. Faced with the growing 'alienation of youth' or the 'conflict of the generations', public authorities are likely to insist that schools put more time and effort into Civics. But this could prove a Greek gift to teachers of politics, and it could easily make matters worse if constitutional platitudes of the 'our glorious Parliament' kind are thrust on an already sceptical youth, rather than something realistic, racy and down-to-earth which focuses on politics as a lively contest between differing ideals and interests – not as a conventional set of stuffed rules. If, indeed, one were to explore school studies intended to be preparatory to university, I would have to admit to some scepticism as to their value. Even if existing 'A'-level syllabuses in 'British Constitution' were better, I would still not be unhappy for universities to have to start from scratch in teaching all the social sciences – with the sole and not very comforting exception of geography. In my own experience as a persistent first-year teacher both at LSE and Sheffield, where one may properly point to entrance standards among the highest in the country, it is rarely any advantage for a student to have taken 'British Constitution' at school, often the contrary. And this is not simply because he thinks that he knows it already, but because (as I will argue later) his mind is often astonishingly full of irrelevant and picturesque detail about parliamentary procedure and 'constitutional institutions', so that he has none of that inquisitive turbulence about the manifold relationships of ideas to institutions and to circumstances that is surely of the essence of a political education. Better that he had done history, English and either mathematics or a foreign language, in our present ludicrously over-specialized sixth forms, or, in some reformed system, these and almost any other reputable subjects. An interest in politics might more naturally spring from an old friend 'current affairs', which should, in any case, be a prominent part of secondary education throughout. The tendency of the universities to try to get schools to do their work for them is deplorable. The social sciences should not enter into a competitive race with other subjects for compulsory prerequisite subjects: for one thing, this perverts the purposes of secondary education, and for another, it is quite unnecessary – the social sciences are popular enough already despite the absence of prerequisite requirements and of offerings in the schools on like scale to the older, established school subjects.

As a professor of political studies, I am interested in political education at the secondary level of education because it should be there both in its own right and in the public interest, not as a feeder to the university Moloch. At some stage all young people in all kinds of secondary schools and in industrial day-release courses should gain some awareness of what politics is about. It is more important that all teenagers should learn to read newspapers critically for their political content than that they should have heard of Aristotle or know – may heaven forgive us all – when the Speaker's Mace is or was over or under the table. So the right age for a conscious political education to begin is the age at which children begin to read the newspapers anyway – their political puberty. And it should continue into people's careers.

I do insist that we must all start from such a point, and argue on its merits the case for helping children to understand what political conflicts are all about and what purposes they serve, not take refuge in some politically denatured 'British Constitution' or 'Good Citizenship' (by whatever name that genteel god goes).

There are three objections at least against beginning with 'the constitution', and these objections also apply to beginning with 'good citizenship'. 1) There is no such thing which is not itself a matter of intense political dispute. 2) It is usually just a subterfuge to escape *nasty* politics and usually does the very thing it seeks to avoid: insinuates partisan biases, none the less real for being oblique. 3) It makes an interesting and lively subject dull, safe and factual.

Let us take the constitution first. Taught in a legalistic manner, a study of politics is hardly worth having (although, it is fair to add, it is hardly likely to have much effect either). The analogy between the difficulties of teaching about political and sexual behaviour are irresistible. Both are natural activities in which it is as proper for the child to be curious as it is for the school to take up the burden of teaching what is socially acceptable and what is conventional morality. Some teachers and some parents wish strongly to avoid both or either of these things, while others conceive it their duty to be dogmatic – whether directly or indirectly; so the usual compromise or line of least resistance is to teach these things in a purely structural, anatomical or 'constitutional' way. But in both spheres the proper role of education must be to create an awareness of why it is that some people regard these matters as either taboo or as dogma, and to offer some practical protection to the child by instilling not a knowledge of what is right or wrong (which is beyond most of us to presume to teach), but a knowledge of what his society and the sub-groups in which he may move regard as right or wrong. I think we often overestimate the difficulties of leaving some questions quite open and explicitly quite open, without either shattering personal faith, trust in the teacher, or encouraging a sort of educational hypocrisy. As a political theorist, I seem to spend half my teaching life attempting to create a sense of the plausibility and practical importance of ideas that I do not myself accept either morally or as universally true empirically.

When asked, 'But what are *your* opinions, Sir,' I take a proper and political care, firstly, to make a little sermon that this is no way to settle any question; secondly, to be a little ironical at why my personal opinions are interesting to the questioner, and to explain that my skill which gives me some authority consists mainly in exposing bad answers, but does not extend as far as being equally sure that I can give true ones; and, thirdly, to give nevertheless an honest and reasonably full answer – although its fullness will naturally depend on the occasion and the context. I both can and should speak more freely and fully on contentious matters to students in a commonroom, a corridor, a cafeteria or in a bar than from the podium – or else I am a very dull dog – but I am no teacher if I use my classroom authority to be a preacher ('a hedge-priest for some doubtful orthodoxy', as Michael Oakeshott once put it). For a teacher must explain why so many honest men worship the Devil, whereas a preacher is bound only to blacken him – even if with that condescending type of tolerance which is the sign of not taking another person's views or behaviour seriously. We should encourage the holding of opinions – strong and firm opinions – but in a way that is open to argument and exposed to refutation. To have some doubt about all things is not to believe in nothing; we are sceptics because ideas are important, otherwise we would be mere cynics.

To teach 'the constitution' is like teaching elementary anatomy or biology instead of the nature of sexuality. They may be necessary first steps, or collateral studies, but by themselves they would either be an evasion, or quite simply something else. Much 'British Constitution' teaching in schools seems to me to be of the same nature: either nervous of politics, or a curious dedication to a vocational training in local government law or, still more odd, in parliamentary procedure. There is no constitution in the sense the syllabuses usually assume (it is a concept invented to be taught to others), or rather there is only one in a highly abstract sense that is very difficult to grasp. We learn games best, after all, by playing them – rarely by reading the rules. We read about the rules or attempt to formulate them clearly only when we begin to play very much more often, or want to play better or to play in different company. The British Constitution is those rules, formal and informal, by which we can practise the kind of politics that we have wished to practise. The conventions of the constitution have no legal force and cannot be reduced to precise formulations without intense political dispute. And it is important to be able to explain why. Let me digress slightly to give a concrete example. Most textbooks state that it is a convention of the Constitution, arising from Baldwin's selection as Prime Minister, that the Prime Minister 'shall come from' the House of Commons. Then there came the metamorphosis of the Earl of Home into Sir Alec (so that for a few days the Prime Minister was in neither House). Thus, at first sight, the constitutional rule was either wrong or, more likely, misformulated. So new editions hastily say that the convention is that the Prime Minister 'should not be in' the Lords, not that he must come from the Commons. This would make sense as a legal rule. But then look what happened. Not only was Sir Alec defeated, as happened to Baldwin twice, but, unlike Baldwin, he quickly lost the leadership of his party – though a man personally popular and of great selflessness and sincerity. Why did he resign as leader? Fairly obviously, because he could not control his powerful colleagues in the House of Commons. Why could he not? Partly temperamental factors, perhaps, but all these factors were subsumed in his lack of experience of attempting to do so before or of seeing it done at all recently as a House of Commons man. In other words, the original formulation may still be best, if seen not as a quasi-legal rule, but as a maxim drawn from political experience: 'leaders coming from the sheltered atmosphere of the House of Lords are unlikely to have had the kind of experience which in modern conditions would fit them to be able to control their followers in the far more stormy House of Commons'.

I simply give this as an example of political thinking, a concrete example of what even Sir Ivor Jennings meant by saying that 'conventions are obeyed because of the political difficulties which follow if they are not'.[1] Is this really too difficult or too contentious a point to get across to fourteen- or fifteen-year-olds? I would think the question an impertinence to ask of school teachers, if I had not found it hard to get across to twenty-year-olds and even to fifty-year-olds – so fixed in some people's minds is the disjunction between 'the Constitution' (good and teachable) and politics (bad and amorphous).

Here is not the place to examine the reasons for dislike of politics – whether by the unpolitical Conservative who may wish himself to rise above it, the a-political Liberal who wishes to protect from it everything he believes in, or those anti-political or revolutionary Socialists who see politics as the mark of an imperfectly unified society. But such mistaken sentiments assume a peculiar importance in education. Small wonder that politicians and educationalists eye each other so warily, each feeling that the other should 'keep out of his business', and yet each wanting something from the other very much – resources, on the one hand, and respect on the other. Plainly, nearly all educational progress makes people able to contribute more to the aggregate of social wealth and skills, but it also makes them less easy to be led by the nose, less respectful of authority – whether in politics or in education – simply by invocation of its name. The danger in states

---

1. Quoted by Geoffrey Marshall and Graeme C. Moodie in their admirable *Some Problems of the Constitution*, 4th edn (Hutchinson, 1967), p. 34, from Jennings's *Law and the Constitution*. They add that 'conventions describe the way that certain legal powers are to be exercised if the powers are to be tolerated by those affected'.

like ours is now, indeed, not lack of ability on the part of the people to contribute, nor any great popular desire to hinder, obstruct or radically change, but is simply indifference, incomprehension, alienation, the feeling of a huge gap between what we are told and what we see, and above all between what we are told we can do (the 'influence of public opinion' and every little vote adding up, etc.) and what we can in fact do.

Teachers of politics must themselves develop and thus be able to convey to others an intense sense that, as the good children would say, there are 'faults on both sides'. This is as good a fiction or framework as any and, in this basic problem of the relation between politics and education, it might be thought unreasonable to deny that it happens to be true.

We need to be able to say at the same time, 'Look how they govern!' and 'But look at how we educate about the business of good government!' A growing disillusionment with the government tends to increase either resistance to teaching politics at all, or, where it is taught, the determination to keep it narrow and dull. But disillusionment with governments – and I take for granted that I am writing at a time when no sane man can find more than a qualified enthusiasm for his party's performance or prospects – is a general phenomenon and has three obvious aspects, none of which are to be ignored. People are disillusioned with actual governments and hence with politics, 1) because of what governments do; 2) because of the limitations in which governments operate; and 3) because they expect too much.

These factors are all far more important than being sure that people 'know the Constitution'. Someone has to point them out and explain them. The press does a good job on the record of governments, but can rarely create any awareness of the second or third factors (general factors are never topical on the crazy day-to-day basis which the press regards as essential to form 'news', and the frustration of unreal expectations is too abstract a point when 'news' also has to be 'hard' and 'personal' as well as instantaneously topical). Perhaps it is the behaviour of politicians and political journalists which makes the teaching of politics, one should candidly admit, as difficult as it is important. They should be the first to explain the limitations of resources, existing commitments and environment under which any government must suffer. And politicians should be the first to warn against hoping for too much. But they are usually the last to do this. I am convinced that politicians talk down to people and that ordinary people are capable of understanding the basic facts about the economy – if they are simplified intelligently. At that point the professions of politics and education should meet, but rarely do. The politician is at fault for neglecting to adapt to modern educational standards his – as even Bagehot called it – 'educative function': the disputes between the parties are commonly conducted by intelligent men in a deliberately stupid and stupefying manner; and the public, including adolescents, seem well aware of this, often seeing politicians as figures of fun, especially at election time. But teachers are at fault for not trying to raise the level from below: they commonly teach 'the Constitution', but one can search in vain the standard school books on the British Constitution for the simplest list of what have been the major policy disputes between the parties in recent years, or the simplest diagrams of national income and expenditure under different headings (which possibly suffer from the double handicap of being 'Economics').

If politicians will not be more candid, it is hard to blame teachers for being evasive, especially when they are thus starved of interesting, topical and realistic teaching materials. To this point we must return, but sufficient for the moment to suggest that sometimes dull and abstract books have to be used, which avoid the subject-matter of political disputes and expound and extol highly dubious constitutional and legal limitations on government, simply in default of others more realistic.[1] There is a dearth of simple, informative books of what one could call, by other names, 'contemporary history'

1. Professor F. F. Ridley had some interesting and trenchant things to say on textbooks in his review article, 'Introductions to British Government', *Parliamentary Affairs*, Spring 1968, pp. 178–81.

or 'current affairs' (and here, of course, the university level textbook is completely unhelpful, even for the teacher, with its methodological rather than substantive or practical preoccupations).

The nature of politics demands that we should always teach and show the two sides of things: what we want the state to do for us, and what we wish it to be prevented from doing to us; or, quite simply, aspirations and limitations. For the one without the other is as misleading as it is useless. So it is not 'finding excuses' to talk more seriously than politicians commonly do of the nature of limitations. Indeed, to do so may protect children from that one great cause of radical disillusionment or alienation from politics which is simply a product of starting with quite unrealistic expectations. This can take a socialist form, of course, but can equally well take a liberal form, or what would be called in America 'a League of Women Voters', or here (once upon a time, at least) a 'Hansard Society' mentality. Even or particularly the idealist must remember that Pilgrim had to walk through both Vanity Fair and the Slough of Despond before he could attain the slopes of Mount Zion.

To give one more example. Rarely do the actual policies of parties figure much in teaching or classroom discussion – although any good journalist *could* give a reasonably objective and clear account of them. If policy is tackled at all, then a kind of half-way house of realism is gratefully found by reading and considering the party programmes. But to take programmes at their face value is positively to create disillusion. For we then measure the success or 'sincerity' of governments in terms of whether or not they have 'carried out their programme' – a kind of political football pools; and some actually denounce any trimming of the sails to changed winds as going against prior instructions or 'the mandate' (whatever that may be), and, therefore, arbitrary and undemocratic. Certain things have to be said first about programmes and manifestoes in general before there can be any meaningful discussion of their relationship with the actual policies pursued by a government. They were, for instance, originally almost exclusively a part of radical and reformist politics in the twentieth century; they were unknown in the nineteenth century except as socialist pipe-dreams; and the famous 'Tamworth Manifesto' of Peel was simply an unusually elaborate 'election cry': it entirely lacked the comprehensive character of a programme, and, in any case, one lark does not make even a false dawn. The Liberals did not offer a programme until Lloyd George's unofficial 'Yellow Books' of 1932, and Conservatives resisted having a comprehensive programme until as late as 1950 because, quite sensibly, they held that it was impossible to foretell the future and unwise to commit oneself to do things when circumstances might change – indeed this follows from their general view of politics as concerned basically with the management of existing interests, rather than with deliberately fermented change. Programmes are essentially a reformist and democratic device; but then even democracy has its limitations: it is no verbal quibble but a profound truth that government itself cannot be democratic, it can only be restrained or even strengthened by democratic devices. Another point to be made is that, in any case, programmes commit parties but not governments. So the unmoralistic lesson is surely to show that if programmes are seen as promises, then it is odd, by analogy, to employ a man for a job solely on what he promises to do without also considering his record. If he appears to promise too much, one will not necessarily hold it against him; one may sagely take his words with a pinch of salt, but only if his record is good. General elections, in other words, are not likely to be decided and nor should they be decided on programmes and promises alone, nor – in rapidly changing societies – on record alone; the record must show that someone is capable of adaptation and change. Again I put these points forward simply as an example of political thinking, and as realistic points that can be got across objectively and which are far more important, both from the point of view of 'civic morality' and of conveying correct information, than knowing weird details of election law.

Again, is it too difficult to show that parties hold different views not just about what should be done, but about the facts of the case? In the above case, the radical believes that a general election decides a programme to be carried out, but the Conservative believes that a general election decides which group of men shall be trusted with the complex and shifting business of government. I do not think it a weak or evasive conclusion to state that it would be an odd and bad world in which either conclusion were pushed to extremes. For strong and definite words should then be spoken of the folly of applying the right theory in the wrong circumstances. There is no prejudice in trying to show, to fish for a carefully matched pair of examples, that it was as politically unrealistic for the Conservatives to offer no real programme in 1945 as it was for Mr Wilson to saddle himself with over-elaborate programmes in the economic circumstances of 1964 and 1966.

What I argue for is the need for a more realistic study of – whatever we call it, and I have no objection to a grand old name like 'The British Constitution' (God bless it and preserve it from all enemies!), so long as we tacitly translate this eighteenth-century, Whiggish phrase as 'The British Political System' or simply 'British Politics' (although the question does arise, to which I will return, why just British?). A political education should be realistic and should chasten the idealist. Ideas are too important to be embalmed, they must be wrestled with and confronted, but fairly and openly. There is no room for evasion: as teachers we must openly argue with that kind of liberal who thinks that children should be protected from knowledge of politics, just as the grand old Constitution tries to protect us from party politics; and should argue too with that sort of businessman who thinks that we could do without it, that 'political factors' spoil rational economic calculations, forgetting as he does that probably nine-tenths of the big decisions in industry are political in the sense that they arise from distributions of personal power and influence rather than the logic of cost-accountancy.

A political education, too, should inform the ignorant; but realistically. Politics is, after all, like sexual activity, undeniably fascinating. If we act as if it is not and offer instead largely irrelevant background or constitutional facts, then children either see through us or are suitably bored. But realism involves talking coolly about politics, not striking hot political attitudes. The teacher who goes on and on about the Mace, the stages of Public Bills and the difference between the powers of the House of Lords and of the House of Commons in the scrutiny of Statutory Instruments, is only slightly less of a menace than the few teachers (but their fame goes a long way) who treat 'British Constitution' as a chance to indoctrinate students in their view of THE TRUTH. If sinners are far fewer than Local Education Authority committees and school governors sometimes imagine, the varieties of sin are probably greater. I meet quite as many first-year students who cite school-masters for the authority that 'Mr Wilson has violated the Constitution' (to which I reply, 'first catch her'), as for the more famous view that 'THE WHOLE SYSTEM is grinding down the workers' ('especially', I allow myself the comment, 'the third of the working class who regularly vote Tory').

It is all too easy to exaggerate the difficulties of a reasonably objective teaching of politics, so that most institutional nervousnesses that studying politics means partisan debate are quite unnecessary (and here one suspects that secondary schools are far more immune from nervous interventions by LEA committees than are colleges of further education). I say 'reasonably objective', however, because part of political morality, or the morality that tolerates real conflicts of opinion rather than seeks to stamp them out, consists in appreciating how much all our views of what we see in society are affected by what we want to see. This is no dark secret and nor should it make teachers worry that Politics is not as objective – may one sometimes say, 'cut and dried' ? – as some other school subjects: the element of subjectivity in perception is the basis of literature and art as well as of politics. We do not insist that one way of doing things is true. On the contrary, rational argument in politics and therefore in the teaching of politics follows a method of trying to show that on such and such an issue different people, who ordinarily see things rather differently, are for once, in fact, agreed. The artful Communist quotes *The Times* to support him, and the shrewd Conservative the *Morning Star*.

The teacher's task is, at whatever level, primarily a conceptual one, not a matter of conveying an agreed corpus of factual information. He has, above all, to show the difference between talking about an opinion and holding it. And from this he can go on to show how and why political events are interpreted in different ways by equally honest people. Here, to speak without undue irony, British popular newspapers furnish excellent and readily available teaching materials. The teacher must then be able to convey imaginatively an understanding of the plausibility (or, as Laski used to say, 'the inwardness') of different political doctrines, even using unusual and unpopular ones as examples. He must illuminate differences, not seek to show that 'we are all really agreed about fundamentals' – for we are plainly not, unless we have lost the capacity or inclination for thought. He is then in a position at least to avoid – even in the teeth of most of the textbooks – the most crippling and common of all errors in considering politics, the belief that institutions and ideas can be considered apart from each other, sometimes expressed as the difference between theory and practice. The teacher should show that all institutions serve certain purposes and must be judged by how they fulfil them; and equally he should show that ideas which do not seek some institutional realization are not political ideas at all. It should be a part of the beginning of political education, not the end which few then reach, to accustom people to probe and to discover what are, in fact, the general ideas of people who claim to hold no abstract ideas and to be acting in a purely practical manner. Those who claim to 'have no time for theory' commonly hold the most interesting, sometimes arbitrary, often quite fantastic, general views on how things work and should work. Think of all those who wondered what would happen to 'sovereignty' if we went into Europe, just as Rousseau, Lord North and Walter Bagehot once all thought that

Federal solutions were *impossible*. 'What do they really believe in?' and 'what do they really think they are doing?' are two questions that ordinary people, 'the People', should be taught to carry into every aspect of their dealings with authorities.

The teacher himself should not advocate one doctrine or another, even our 'British Way and Purpose' that was the title of a famous Army Education Corps manual during the Second World War. He simply points out the kind of conditions which appear to go with certain ideas and the kind of consequences which appear to go with holding them. For children must surely be brought to see society, in however elementary a form, as a system or a pattern of relationships (so that the Conservative will typically say, 'Don't meddle – the unexpected repercussions will overwhelm you'; the revolutionary socialist will say, 'All or nothing, partial reform is impossible'; and many others in pursuing limited objectives will try to reassure themselves that the unintended repercussions of their particular policies are either trivial or, with proper forethought, avoidable).

Naturally the teacher must begin by teaching what the received political ideas of our own society are, and how they relate to other social institutions. But he must avoid implying any finality or superiority to our traditional but severely local arrangements; and it is hard to see how such an implication can be avoided if, even or particularly at the beginning, some other system or systems are not also looked at, however superficially. I am not convinced that schoolchildren need to know *anything* about the intricacies of parliamentary procedure; I am convinced that they should know *something*, however superficially, about how Russia, the United States, China and come countries of the 'Third World' and of Europe are governed. The point is not to establish any hierarchy of institutions, either in our favour or to chasten insular pride; but simply to show that there are different sorts of relationships and that in none of them can political ideas or institutions be considered apart from their social or national setting. And it is precisely this that 'the

197

Constitution over-all' approach denies – to make this point for the last time.

Perhaps, however, a qualification or explanation is needed before proceeding. I would not suggest that some study of abstract models (for such they necessarily are) of institutional structure and of formalized customary rules does not have a place. But its place must follow and not precede some knowledge of the issues and traditions of actual politics. If it is put first, either in emphasis or in order of teaching, it is likely to distort understanding of government and politics to a degree almost, I find, beyond repair. For, after all and again, customary rules arise from political activity and experience, not the other way round; and the machinery of government is made and remade by men to serve their purposes, it is not a natural impediment.

The best analogy may well be with modern methods of language teaching. Grammar is discarded as the way in, but it is then introduced at a later stage as a framework with which to consolidate and extend our existing knowledge. Few would now believe that 'the direct method' alone suffices; some structure, whether called grammar (the Constitution) or structural linguistics (categories of political behaviour), must *follow*. But at the moment there is little doubt that most horses find the cart firmly harnessed up in front of them, and one can hardly go too far in possible exaggeration to redress a balance already weighed down ponderously in precisely the wrong direction.

Another common disguise or perversion of a study of politics is 'good citizenship': the use of Civics or Liberal Studies classes to urge participation in this and that. Sometimes this may degenerate into a crude moralism, and a rather romantic and prissy one at that – of 'the people versus the politicians' or 'I wouldn't let my daughter marry a politician' kind. There is a type of Civics which is straight, early-nineteenth-century Liberalism, teaching or preaching that the individual should directly influence this and that and make up his own mind in proud and independent isolation (whether he is a humble citizen or elected representative); and that he should avoid like the plague parties, pressure groups, unions and all other 'organized interests' (as if disorganized ones were better). This is simply unrealistic, individualistic in a thoroughly anti-social and unsociological sense, and often highly partisan: one must insist that Liberals, whether of ancient or modern ilk, must be no more immune than Tories or Socialists from some scepticism that their own account of what politics is all about is, taken by itself, fully adequate.

The less obvious danger of the 'be good boys and girls and participate' kind of teaching is the more insidious: the assumption that participation is both a good thing in itself and the best possible thing. Since personal participation in any sense more meaningful than simply casting a vote is plainly impossible for most people in societies as large as we need to ensure the benefits we demand, it follows that the teaching of participation as an end in itself is only likely to create disillusionment in practice – if it does succeed in influencing attitudes at all and does not simply sound so much cold pie in the classroom.

The virtues of participation are an important half-truth, but a lame half-truth if advanced alone. The other and complementary half is quite as important: that people must know, however vaguely, what decisions are made by governments, how they are made and what is happening. Informed and wide-ranging communications are as important for democratic politics as is direct participation – which, in practice, only involves a few, usually the few who preach it. Governing authorities of all kinds are more apt to urge participation, because they know that in a widespread manner it is impractical, than they are to study how to make themselves govern more openly and less secretively. Governments are fundamentally restrained and directed in societies such as ours not by the participant-representatives (who are mainly the recruiting ground for members of the government), but by their knowledge that nearly everything they do may become a matter of public knowledge. Governments can ordinarily depend on their parliamentary support but only to a far smaller degree on their electoral support. And by the same token the people's representatives can pass economic legislation and orders until they are red or blue in the face, but putting them into practice almost wholly depends on governments or other authorities being able to explain them and to obtain some response from the working population.

Knowledge of what is happening and how things happen is quite as important as theoretical opportunities for participation. Therefore, both in the light of the subject itself and for its practical consequences, I am highly sceptical of the American-style 'teaching of democracy' by way of fabricating democratic situations in the classroom games, debates, mock parliaments and class elections, etcetera. These may be fun, may teach some political manners, may develop some expressive skills and provide some alleviation of routine, but they are no substitute for a realistic knowledge of how the real system works. Governments are more restrained by knowing that their acts are publicized than by participant devices themselves. The absence of political censorship and the presence of an independent press are quite as important as free elections, and this should be said. When Aristotle talked about political justice he invoked two basic criteria: that we should rule or be ruled in turn – participation; and that the state should be no larger than that we can know the character of the other citizens or, as he otherwise put it, no larger than that the voice of the Stentor or herald could be heard from one boundary to another. Modern political ideas and theory have almost exclusively stressed the first criterion – as if abandoning the second as unrealistic, paradoxically at the very moment of time when mass communications have rendered it readily applicable to huge states, not just to small communities. Participation of persons and communication of knowledge must, in other words, go together.

Content must not be sacrificed for process. Even to play 'United Nations' is surely difficult if all the little countries or role-players have not some prior knowledge, however simple, of how their characters behave, both in New York and back home. Peanuts, perhaps, had it all. 'Charlie Brown, Charlie

Brown, gee, you were dumn in school today.' 'I thought I did alright.' 'Nope, you were dumn, downright dumn. You got everything wrong.' 'Gee, I misunderstood. I thought one only had to be sincere.'

It is quite plain that we in Great Britain can no longer take for granted, if ever we could, that people either here or elsewhere know or care much about our political institutions and ideas. We were once famed for our political abilities and knowledge. We now worry that our own younger generation is becoming actively alienated or sullenly indifferent to our political institutions; and internationally we have grown noticeably more silent about being an Athens of example now that we are no longer a Rome of power. It is almost as if we now have to begin all over again, like the seventeenth-century Commonwealth men and the eighteenth- and nineteenth-century radicals, rediscovering our nature and rethinking our possibilities. This can hardly begin too early, and it will surely fail or prove irrelevant if it is not done in a manner both stimulating and realistic. And this depends almost entirely on the schools. To give children the 'low-down' on how political institutions work and what political conflicts are about, rather than the dry bones of parliamentary procedure or the elevated abstractions of 'the Constitution', will not be to feed disillusion or to encourage cynicism, quite the contrary: it will encourage ordinary young citizens (and I speak technically, not rhetorically, as the voting age moves closer to the classroom), their teachers and their politicians to think in terms of common problems to be solved, and to talk about them in a common language, not to build up protective walls of mutual incomprehension. Says the teenager, 'We are being got at again'; says the headmaster or chairman of the governors or of the examining body, 'This is dangerous ground, be *very* careful, stick to clear *facts*, cleave to the Constitution . . . politics is not a real subject in educational tradition' (at which the ghosts of Aristotle and our great English Hobbes, Locke, Burke and Mill should arise to haunt them nastily and rebuke them for their ignorance); and says the politician, 'People do not understand what we are trying to do for them in very difficult circumstances, and blame us for mirroring their own divisions, doubts and uncertainties.'

The task of re-establishing a popular tradition of political discourse both critical and aspirant must begin in the schools and with teachers. And it will plainly have to precede a suitable literature. It is not my task or competence to review the literature on politics for schools – if it can be called such, for it is mostly about the structure of government and the rules and conventions of the Constitution, the dull and heavy statues of Prometheus waiting for a divine touch of humanity. Nearly all such books that I have seen in common use lack the two essentials of a political education: realistic accounts of how governments and parties work and critical discussions of political ideas – the moral assumptions and preconceptions that people carry, necessarily but usually unrecognized, into practical activities.[1] For instance, if teachers follow the arguments of *Colour and Citizenship: A Report on Race Relations* (E. J. B. Rose and associates, Oxford University Press, 1969) and lay stress on a tolerant perception of social differences rather than an assimilationist stress on common moral factors, they may soon find that there are better and more down-to-earth books being produced about the minority groups than about the English majority. But supply, being partly at least and often pleasantly venal, will inevitably follow demand – if the demand comes first, as indeed there are many signs, like this present volume (although this is certainly not for the children), that it is beginning to do. We all should love our subjects, or else, like benevolent autocrats, we are misplaced or due to be replaced. But the teacher of Politics can have some justification and pride in claiming that his subject has a peculiar combination of difficulty, importance and fascination.

1. See further my 'On Bias' in *Teaching Politics*, Spring 1972.

9

A Failure of Liberal Perception[1]

HERE is a study of a tragedy of misunderstanding. What views did the most intelligent and well-informed newspapers in Britain have of the rising Nazi movement? And why didn't the British press take seriously even the self-portrait of the rising Nazi movement? But this is not a descriptive monograph about public opinion in all its aspects; it is a critical and analytical study of a few of the most important sources in Britain for the qualitative perception of a new concept and movement – Nazism. The study is focused on the events which were happening in Germany at the time, not on the general background of British politics and public opinion: its aim is more modest and limited. But this very limitation gives it a greater rigour and relevance than most studies of public opinion. This essay is poised at the very point where political theory and political practice meet: the difficulty of recognizing something which is radically new both in purpose and behaviour.

Dr Granzow has also made a direct contribution to a growing body of serious literature concerned with explaining the rise, the character and the appeal of Nazism in Germany – a literature which we in this country too seldom look at, or even hear about, compared to the sensational, often semi-pornographic, popular interest in the Nazis. For British newspaper opinion on the Nazis provides a mirror which, when it reflected correctly many of the essential features of the new

1. This appeared as an introduction to Brigitte Granzow, *A Mirror of Nazism: British Opinion and the Emergence of Hitler, 1929–1933* (Gollancz, 1964).

phenomenon, did so with a revealing clarity by being free from the often clouding details of German history and politics; and when it distorted or failed to reflect at all some equally important features, it none the less showed vividly not merely how successfully deluding was Nazi propaganda, but also how inherently hard it was for all those, in any country, who believed in and practised normal politics to take as seriously some features of Nazism as time was to show they deserved.

This close reading of the leading British papers of the day reveals, in particular, how much the anti-Semitism and the racialism of the Nazis were played down. This happened not because British opinion was either sympathetic to or un-informed of what the Nazis said, but because it was often literally incredulous that men could actually mean to put into action what seemed merely a wearisomely reiterated rhetoric (though it became less easy to avoid the incredible once it was seen that this 'rhetoric' was vote-catching, at least). For these things had been, perhaps still are, more generally prevalent and even accepted than we find it easy to admit. The late-Victorian English and American historians, for instance, nearly all accepted in some degree that the 'Anglo-Saxon race' had a unique capacity for, happily, free-dom and politics. Disraeli himself had once told the House of Commons that 'All is Race'. We have only to look at the American John Fiske's lecture before the Royal Institution of Great Britain in 1880, 'The Manifest Destiny of the Anglo-Saxon Race', or at the dust-covered volumes of the Regius Professor at Cambridge, Sir John Seeley's *The Expansion of England*, and his Oxford contemporary E. A. Freeman's *Norman Conquest*, or at the great Sir Henry Maine's quest for the Teutonic roots of all liberties, to remind ourselves of the orthodoxy of a former generation. Even Lord Bryce's Creighton Lecture of 1915, 'Race Sentiment as a Factor in History', now appears ambivalent as much as critical. But still all this was thought of by most people as pure theory; and anti-Semitism was not directly linked to all this, but was uncomfortably accepted – or indulged – as a simple social prejudice – part Christian, part bourgeois; it was not conceived as the theoretical basis for a vast plan of action to remake society utterly.

A more fundamental point, however, emerges from this study. There was a failure in Britain, as in Germany, to grasp the nature of *ideological* thinking and of *totalitarianism* as a concept. People, in the framework of a liberal universe of discourse, simply could not conceive that the governing party of a great and civilized country could think in terms of a philosophy which claimed *to explain everything* in terms of Race, Struggle and Leadership, and which then sought to make, not a few improvements here and there, but a veritable heaven (or hell) on earth from which all divisive, and thus subversive, elements would be eliminated. Liberals did not think that men behaved that way, anyway; socialists thought that they had a monopoly of revolutionary and utopian thinking; and British conservatives thought that one government would probably be much like any other government when actually in power. And our political theory, whether of the podium or the platform, has typically been sceptical not merely of the meaningfulness of general ideas in politics, but even that such ideas can have much practical effect. In many ways we have led a fortunately sheltered island life, both politically and philosophically, since the mid-seventeenth century. We have always avoided extremes and observed constitutional ethics – if one excludes the Irish question in British politics, which, of course, in the myth-making selectivity of historical memory, we always do. This relatively smooth working of our institutions is usually envied and is often emulated, but this very fortune has made our perspectives narrow and our imagination, even of our own range of possibilities, often sadly limited. It is high time that someone hinted of us what we have often said of the Americans: that a long tradition of freedom and a fortunate isolation has its price in terms of understanding the circumstances and dilemmas of others.

Perhaps the most fascinating deceptions, which the Nazis succeeded in planting even on the British press, were those concerned with the third great element – after race and struggle – in the Nazi ideology, the *Führerprinzip*, the leadership principle itself, and the essential ambiguity in the Leader's own tactic of appearing to act legally. It is fascinating and disturbing reading to follow how the personal abilities of Hitler and his power in the Nazi movement, indeed the very *Führerprinzip* itself, were persistently played down in the great English newspapers. And hardly less interesting is the account of how they persistently distinguished the man from the Party, particularly from the S A – the Brown-Shirts – so that every act of terrorism and violence before 1933 was blamed on the 'unruly' SA, and Hitler's legality was accepted at its face value – not simply as a tactic and a sublime piece of double-think. Again good Liberals found it hard to accept that the encouragement and provocation of violence by the Nazis-united-under-Hitler actually appealed to masses of ordinary people, and was a deliberate part of his policy, not the excesses of S A extremists whom, it was then held, he did not really control anyway.

There is today a contrary tendency in Britain to play up the role of Hitler in Nazism, just as in Germany it is now played down. In Britain to say that Hitler should be seen as the centre of the picture usually means that the ideology is not to be taken seriously, was never important, and that it 'was all' Hitler, his power and personality, sane or insane. Dr Granzow, indeed, found her views on Hitler and the Nazis changing as she looked at their reflection in the British press during these crucial years. She now concludes that it is indeed hard to exaggerate the importance of Hitler in Nazism, but that this very importance is because he so admirably fitted the role of absolute Leader which was an essential part of the ideology. Nazism was largely the creation of Hitler, but he built his 'greatness' on the materials of an ideology which seemed to fit Germany all too well and to offer Germans hope, revenge and a sense of purpose. Hitler emerges as the centre of the picture because of the ideology. If it was a 'vehicle' he created, then it was the only one that could get him where he wanted to go, but one that only progressed by so many others actively sharing his sense of direction.

Another point of substance which emerges from this essay should be singled out. There was evidence in British opinion of these years of a general guilt-complex, throughout all parties, about the harsh terms of the Versailles Treaties. This played a big role in making many English journalists and editors give the Nazis the benefit of the doubt when they seemed to threaten to go too far; it even made some commentators willing to excuse 'these things' as being 'inevitable' consequences of the Allied politics of revenge at what should have been the peace table, and thus, like many Germans, to confuse Nazism with ordinary German nationalism (a confusion the Nazis enjoyed). It is necessary at times to remind ourselves that it is not true that *tout comprendre c'est tout pardonner*. We continue, for instance, often to be somewhat sentimental about the other great totalitarian ideology, Communism – analogies which the author wisely, though not nervously, leaves aside. Just because we comprehend something of its seeming 'necessity', and certainly are aware, both prudentially and morally, that it cannot be stamped out, as the Nazis could have been, we therefore are embarrassed even to recognize simply that many things in it are evil. One could wish to repudiate or revise Versailles, as many did in England – and for many different reasons, without coming even near to many of the most important and specific policies of the Nazis. In any case, it is a simple truth, often desperately to be hung on to, that two wrongs do not make a right. The first wrong only gives an excuse, and some popular following, for policies whose roots lie altogether elsewhere.

The roots of these policies, the intellectual and social origins of totalitarianism, do not concern us here. But underlying the argument of the essay is a massive historical condition for the fruition of these policies and beliefs (indeed, of totalitarianism generally), the failure to recognize the consequences of which was possibly the most basic failure in the liberal imagination: the First World War. The senseless slaughter of the trenches and the rational mobilization of technical resources for such an end had already destroyed for many any belief in the rational basis of a liberal social order. Liberalism had simply failed to contain two great disasters, of which 'Versailles' could seem a symbol of both – taken with its reparation clauses: war and mass-unemployment. Other countries besides Germany were shaken deeply by the consequences of the war and the world economic crisis of 1929. But the Nazis seemed to offer something more positive than a retreat into pacifism and economic autarchy. They showed that the permanent mobilization of peacetime society on a wartime footing could solve the unemployment problem, create a sense of purpose again and give prospects of, if not revenge, at least restoration.

German problems, and reactions to them, were not, of course, entirely unique. These events occurred in a wider context which affected the importance that foreign observers might have attached to them in their own right. The German economic crisis of these years, preceded as it was by the unexplained military defeat and by the grim inflation earlier in the decade, was greater both in scale and in psychological effect than the depression in Great Britain, France and the United States. But it is as well to remember that these three countries too were deeply shaken; their foundations did not collapse, or – in the case of France – not immediately, but many expected them to fall. It is hard to think of a time outside war in which political events were so fluid as in the years 1929–32, so capable of surprising and arbitrary turns. The normal predictability of orderly, free government seemed in danger of breaking down. Men hung on the words of great leaders – who could now use the radio more than the white horse – or hoped for exceptional deeds, or events of unparalleled luck, to save the normal political and social institutions.

Events in Germany were seen in this context. It was by no means self-evident, for instance, that the 'National Government' in England was to be just a conventional Conservatism with a popular figure-head. And if – what now may seem from hindsight – the crazy fears of the extreme Left that this might be Fascism or crypto-Fascism (whatever 'Fascism' meant, which itself was not clear) were discounted, this discounting was then applied to German politics: there was a whole school of thought who saw Adolf Hitler as a Ramsay Mac who could be weaned away from his Party by railway shares, kindness and soft-soap – a view, to apply hindsight impartially, almost equally crazy. Certainly few radicals or socialists in England imagined that the established form and procedures of Parliament would survive the crisis. That a real socialist government with a majority would need to govern by emergency decrees was the view of nearly all the Labour leaders who survived the 1931 elections – and this efficient temptation or speculation was not unheard of, by any means, on the Tory benches. All this affected, as we shall see, British views of 'Constitutional Dictatorship' in Germany. And it is an odd thought, as Colin Cross has pointed out in his recent book, *The Fascists in Britain*, that Sir Oswald Mosley was easily the most able of the younger Labour leaders and would, had he remained in the Labour Party, have been high in the line of succession to Attlee.

Even in the United States the great depression 'triggered off' a small host of extremist movements, politically contemptible taken individually, but together – if they could ever have got together – a frightening and unpredictable factor. They often had some interesting things in common with Fascism and Nazism: 'populist' roots and sentiments, trust in a single crazy solution expounded by a venerated leader (as in the Townsend Plan and Father Coughlin's followers), and, above all, a conspiracy theory of history (in which the conspirators were commonly the Jews, particularly those in Wall Street and the Bank of England). It is hard to exaggerate the effect of the depression on very large numbers of Americans; if it did not shatter their values at least it opened them up. And if these values were reasserted and healed, not exploited for new departures, this was largely the fortunate genius of Roosevelt's strange mixture of radicalism and conservatism – but even then it is notable that it took *a* man, a leader. But other strange and more desperate things could have happened – one thinks of the Italian-style Fascist regime of Huey Long, the 'King-Fish' of Louisiana, stopped by a bullet, not by the ballots.

So if the author argues strongly that there was nothing inevitable about the rise of Nazism in Germany, I would add that there was nothing inevitable about the survival of free politics even in its most famous homelands. And in France the Republic seemed in danger – perhaps one can say that the Third Republic never really recovered from the strain of these years; it was certainly discredited among nearly all sections of French opinion for indecision and petty squabbling while the wolf, first of want, then of war, was at the door.

Brigitte Granzow may seem, at first sight, to be unduly limited in her use of sources: she draws almost exclusively on *The Times*, the *Observer*, the *Manchester Guardian*, the *Daily Telegraph* and the *Economist* – with only an occasional use of the *New Statesman*, for it did not regularly contain both reportage and comment. But this is not meant to be a study of general public opinion in Britain – from whatever many and varied sources such a study could be drawn. Nor does she even draw upon important parliamentary debates, or the tittle-tattle of the memoirs and autobiographies of the period, or the beginnings of the later stream of books about Germany and Nazism. This is all deliberate and, I think, proper and wise. For the study is concerned with, once again, the recognition of the nature and the novelty of Nazism – a qualitative question. It is enough to show whether it was recognized at all (and if so, how). And the reasons for what was, in fact, the distorted recognition became more clear by following consistently a limited group of important sources in depth, than by beating around selectively all over the bush – through opinions that were hardly even public and through a public who held hardly any real opinions on this strange and novel matter. Such a half-recognition most significantly grows out of the day-to-day comments and reports of responsible and intelligent journalists in the great opinion-making papers. These are the true primary sources for such a study: parliamentary papers and printed books may be of more political importance in Britain, but they will not show the discussion and the investigation actually in progress; and in Britain they will, in any case, normally closely resemble – whether as cause or effect does not matter here – the opinions of what we now call 'the quality press'.

The text is, in fact, properly and mercifully, not as theoretical as this Introduction may seem to suggest. I am skimming the cream from what is mainly a down-to-earth, sometimes day-to-day, description of what the best British papers reported as the events in Germany. Students of the press, as most of us are in this country whose most popular vice still seems to be the compulsive consumption of newsprint, will find that this disinterment of old reporting and editorial writing has a fascination in its own right.

To read these accounts is, I have found, to gain a tremendous respect for the descriptive clarity and the generalizations, even the theoretical insights, of most of the anonymous working journalists of these papers at this period. There was, with few exceptions, an ultimate failure to see through Hitler's duplicity and to seize the importance of the Nazi ideology. But this is plainly not due to any failure in practical reporting or to any great editorial intrusions – like later in the 1930s when the reports of *The Times'* correspondents in Berlin were nightly toned down or mutilated in Printing House Square. It is due to the general factors of British opinion we have already alluded to, ultimately to a weakness in English political education and speculation.

The *Manchester Guardian*, for instance, was not misrepresenting facts, but was mirroring typically liberal prejudices and theories of politics when it resolutely argued, after the 1930 elections, that the Nazis *should* be taken into a coalition Cabinet because they were the second largest party – a constitutional doctrine – and *because* the exercise of power inevitably makes men more responsible – a pleasant political theory. There were plenty of facts to support this theory since it described, with unwitting accuracy, the tactics of the Nazis and, hence, their apparent actions. *The Times*, similarly, was not being grossly speculative when it saw the Nazis as essentially normal – if somewhat rough and inexperienced – politicians, it simply accepted that everyone in actual public life acts politically rather than ideologically, follows Burkean prudence rather than rationalist plans, *therefore* the explicitly anti-political fervour of the Nazis was dismissed as mere rhetoric, once again. There were plenty of facts to support this theory since German nationalist and conservative leaders were attempting to treat the Nazis in just this way.

Journalists simply found it hard to describe in concrete terms what seemed incredible. The wonder is that they were on occasion so deeply perceptive about the systematic importance of racialism, anti-Semitism, the *Führerprinzip*, the skill of Hitler's 'tactic of legality', the real attraction of violence and terror, and his appeal to the hitherto un-political. But these insights usually occurred only within fluctuations of day-to-day speculation in which there was a real, puzzled and open debate about the character of the Nazis; they did not form the basis for a prolonged and consistent interpretation of events such as might have alerted public opinion to the dangers to come. Often a crisis would stimulate appreciation of the radical novelty and threat of the Nazi movement, which would then be lost when things became relatively normal again.

The story begins with the emergence of the Nazis as, for the first time, a serious force in German national politics in 1929. It concludes with their coming to power in 1933. One can at least say that this period has been neglected in studying Anglo-German relations – indeed in direct studies of Nazism itself. It is almost incredible that so much is written about the later period, especially about the War, and so little addressed to the fundamental problems of 'how did they ever come to power at all?' and 'why were their real aims not recognized earlier?' Less than a fifth, for instance, of William Shirer's thousand-page *Rise and Fall of the Third Reich* is devoted to the whole period before 1933.

But one can say more: that in this period were firmly forged the misconceptions about Nazism and Germany that

were to play such havoc once Hitler began in the mid-1930s
his campaign of external expansion – an expansion inherent
in Nazi ideology and in the history of the Nazi movement,
but unrecognized by most people in Britain even as late as
1938. In my opinion, the recent study by Martin Gilbert and
Richard Gott, *The Appeasers*, while an admirably researched
polemic in many respects (and a proper reply in kind to
Mr A. J. P. Taylor's revisionism), yet errs badly on this
point. They exaggerate the personal nature of Chamberlain's
view of Hitler. It may, indeed, be hard to exaggerate his
credulous and implacable ignorance in the field of foreign
affairs; it may even be right to call the character of his
actions 'criminally irresponsible'; but it is not right to make
him a kind of alibi or scapegoat for everyone else, including
liberals and the British Left in this period. His views of
Hitler mirrored those already long established in the minds of
many others. That Chamberlain misled an innocent and unwilling British public about Hitler is as great a political
absurdity as to think that Hitler alone misled an innocent and
unwilling German public about the Nazis. Everywhere
'normal politicians' were confused when popular support
seemed to turn to policies that threatened freedom. Liberals
had forgotten the sober message of J. S. Mill and Tocqueville
that the only viable form of modern autocracy would be
'democratic'. Dr Granzow's case seems to me overwhelming
that the years 1929–33 furnished abundant evidence in the
British press for recognizing the character of that 'blind
beast' that was about to be born – but that it was not recognized. Her study explains why the evidence was misunderstood, and it shows that the opinions which were then formed
were those which were to recur, again and again, throughout
the 1930s. Some, indeed, seem to have survived even the war,
even the discovery of the extermination camps: the belief that
Hitler was just another German nationalist, or – most bizarre
of all – an appeasable politician.

So I commend this essay because I think it gives us a rare
passionate dispassion in a subject so often inhabited by

pomposity, prejudice, hindsight, wilful ignorance and evasions. Here is no excuse for the complicity of all Germans in the rise of the Nazis. I may say that my country failed in its plain duty to stop at least the Nazis' external expansion at a time when they could easily have been stopped (had they been recognized for what they were). But Frau Granzow does not say this, nor even want to: there are no outside excuses for the coming to power of the Nazis and for the failure to resist them once they abused their power. My fears were, on the contrary, that it might be full of irrelevant hatred for the great haters of humanity, even self-hatred. I do not think that this has proved so – and the reader will judge for himself whether the book has gone to the other extreme of what would be a pedantic and, considering the subject matter, a quite inhumanly academic avoidance of all value-judgements. But either extreme would be irrelevant, for the subject matter is about the rise and recognition of totalitarianism: it is an essay in the recognition of a concept. This does not, however, make it 'abstract'. For we are as much governed in politics by the concepts by which we understand politics as by the institutions through which we move, or by the abstract moral ideas which we may think to pursue. We master our past and defend our present by understanding, not by posturing or denunciation – least of all, by forgetfulness.

Thus Brigitte Granzow has sought to show, through the mirror of English opinion, the general difficulties, for Germans and foreigners alike, of grasping the nature of such a paradoxical and unprecedented phenomenon as Nazism. The subject matter is not unimportant historically, for the initial failure to recognize the world-shaking and unappeasable ambitions of the Nazis is to be found in this period of their immediate rise to, and consolidation of, power. From this stemmed the whole atmosphere favourable to Chamberlain's specific policies of appeasement. And the subject matter is not unimportant theoretically, if by theories we seek to recognize the situation we are in, as well as to do something about it. For it is sobering to realize how difficult it is to grasp the nature of something beyond the limits of one's own previous experience – even the extended experience of history; and how tempting then to try to reduce it, so as to deal with it, to familiar and 'practical' terms. The British Left were to have similar difficulties, later in the 1930s, with Communism and Spain.

I draw the conclusion, though the author may be more kind, that the British failure to recognize the totalitarian nature of the Nazis, indeed to take the measure of the whole concept, was not merely because the thing itself was unprecedented, but also because there was, and still is, a kind of commonsense empiricism in Britain which is a blinkered empiricism, a philosophical and political narrowness of imagination about the passions that can move men in politics.

In fact all men are moved by general ideas in politics, and in two ways: we may sometimes pursue doctrines which aim, for better or worse, at partial or even total change; but we will always understand the political and social world in the perspective of theories, whose explanations do much to determine what courses of action we think are possible. The surface level of this book, then, shows how certain 'foreign' doctrines proved hard to understand or take seriously – particularly since partial doctrines had become full-blown ideologies. But there is another and more profound level to this book which seeks to expose the theoretical preconceptions of practical, ordinary men – such as, again, the liberals to whom it was mere commonsense to believe that to share power would make an extremist party more responsible. Such studies as this, of the political ideas of those who think they merely report the facts, or of the selectivity concealed behind the invocation of 'commonsense' by normal politicians, are, I think, the true and much neglected tasks of political theory in relation to history. This kind of theory is directly related to practice. Something could have been done had things been understood correctly. But, let me repeat, this study is primarily analytical and interpretive, not theoretical or historical: it describes and then analyses the day-to-day reactions of a thoughtful press to strange and terrible events in a foreign country at a time of crisis.

IO

The Peaceable Kingdom[1]

PAGANS see nothing comic about Machiavelli's remark that the man who would restore an old State, whose citizens had lost their *virtú* (or nerve and energy), or who would found a new one, should be both 'a lion and a fox'; nor about Homer giving Achilles, his ideal man, 'the do'er of deeds and the speaker of words', a centaur as tutor, half man and half beast. But somehow there is something comic about Russian, Chinese or American leaders talking about being prepared to defend their 'peace-loving aspirations' with weapons of 'mass-destruction'. Perhaps here the comic is a mask or a refuge rather than a sudden vision of improbable conjunctions. For the conjunctions are not really improbable. The real comedy is that language itself has become so debased that 'defence', a perfectly respectable word, has had to become 'fighting for peace', because we are embarrassed at the duality of politics (compromise *and* power) and the duality of man (creation *and* destruction).

There are grounds for thinking that we British should be more fair than we often are to the legitimate claims of violence. In politics there is a difference between times of emergency and times of peace; and in social life the idea of a society free of conflict, free even of violence, could only be

1. Published in *Twentieth Century*, Winter 1964–5, thus written before the American urban riots, the student unrest and the re-emergence of a 'bomb-anarchist' philosophy (sentiment?), it is concerned not to condemn irrational violence but to warn what could happen if all violence is condemned equally. My review of Hannah Arendt's *On Violence*, perhaps her best and clearest book, may add something to the argument (*Political Quarterly*, April 1971, pp. 229–32).

that of a society of men reduced to the passivity of domestic animals, whether by voluntary therapy or totalitarian control. May I just make clear that this is an essay, something exploratory and tentative? I am writing not as a social scientist but as a person perplexed about these things, and yet prepared to be a little reckless, to risk being misunderstood by prissy liberals, because of a desire to render plausible a passion that we too often claim not to know. Violence is occasionally useful to obtain understanding of something, to break up established preconceptions.

In a country where William Blake's 'Jerusalem' has become a favourite patriotic piece for Tory ladies, one almost despairs of giving violence its due. The pill could be sugared by recalling that we do not like to go too far in anything, so perhaps we should not go too far even in rejecting violence. Our tendency to play down or to reject violence worries me in two different ways. First, it worries me because it leads to false observations about historical causation. British historians, sociologists, journalists and novelists (poets and dramatists are oddly not so much to blame) notably underestimate the appeal of violence. If a man appears to gain ground by conjuring with images of violence, say Carson in 1913 or Hitler in 1931, he is usually not taken seriously in time; and subsequently the obvious attraction of violence is not explained, but is explained away in terms of something else – a national or an economic factor. Curiously we accept Communism as a 'proper', if mistaken, explanatory doctrine, but not racialism or Fascism – we say they are simply absolute evils, and then we go on to say that they are really something else. Second, it worries me because it leads to false observations about psychological causation. Violence and creativity are more closely allied than blinkered British empiricism and liberal bourgeois morality will like to admit. The experience and delight of violence is seldom avoided, so much as experienced in vicarious or surrogate forms. Too often we think of a struggle between violence and peaceableness, between being authoritarian and being democratic, even between being nasty and nice, rational and irrational, as if some clear victory could be won either way – rather than that, in the imagery of Euripides' *Bacchae*, Dionysus and Apollo must be honoured jointly.

But the point of this essay is not to make justificatory noises about the 'fact of violence', but simply to suggest how often we misunderstand the problems we face (even assuming the most liberal and pacific ethic), and hence produce futile responses, because we suppress, not just violence itself, but any knowledge of its appeal. We are politically prudish. The sexual analogy is deliberate. It is foolish to argue that we *should* be less prudish in personal actions, but it is relevant to suggest that we should not be encouraged to suppress the facts. When violence does occur, it is seen as something personal and psychotic, rather than as something social and perennial. Partly, of course, this is part of a general Anglo-Saxon scepticism about the effect of ideas on action at all; but the scepticism is particularly deep about 'bad ideas'.

Violence is physical restraint, compulsion or injury to either persons or property. Its presence is inevitable in any complex society; the threat of violence is even useful at times. In fact, in free societies no one dreams of making threats of violence illegal, only certain clear acts of violence. Every strike, demonstration, rally or crowd in all kinds of circumstances can be heard muttering 'Do not try us too hard, or else. . . .' Sociologists have often defined the State, following Max Weber, as the monopolist of violence; but one must more accurately say, as Weber sometimes did, 'of legitimate violence'. For it would be absurd to think that all violence could be stamped out – unless, as we have said, all human freedom was stamped out too. The problem of violence is not to stamp it out, but to divert it into socially acceptable channels. Admittedly many threats of violence are either sheer bluff, or else attention-begging cries of 'Wolf, Wolf!' Usually there is more bark than bite, but then barking, far from being taboo, is almost the clearest mark of a free political system. 'Don't try me too hard,' cried G. Marx, 'I may collapse'. But we also say that even a worm may turn.

We commonly believe that we have been 'mercifully free', etc., from violence in public life since the Civil War, unlike the French and Spaniards, etc. This is true only as a comparative generalization, if we are seeking to explain why some points of British history have been different from those of some other countries. It is only a relative truth. It does not mean that we have, in fact, avoided violence – indeed to nothing like the extent we would believe. 'The Glorious Revolution of 1688' is remembered, glorious because 'and Bloodless' – largely bloodless in England (one forgets Monmouth's poor Devon peasants, even if more were killed without trial than by the 'Bloody Assizes' of legend). But in Belfast an icon of King William crossing the Boyne is, to this day, provocatively scrawled on the doors and walls of Catholic churches, and the three odd daubs under the vertical lines of the horse's neck stand for the Catholic blood, splashed by the horse's hoofs, as the river ran with it. And we forget another consequence of 1688: the depopulation of the Highlands which followed the failure of the 1745 Rebellion.

Anti-Catholic riots were endemic to eighteenth-century London. Mob violence, sometimes spontaneous, sometimes stirred up by politicians, was responsible for the repeal or non-enforcement of several Acts of Parliament long before the famous Stamp Act riots in the colonies. The 'Mother Gin' riots of 1736, for instance, prevented a tax on gin and on licensed premises – and got mixed up with anti-Irish sentiment when Irishmen were taken on construction gangs at a half or two-thirds of the wages of dismissed Londoners. The cry of 'Down with the Irish' was then first heard on the London streets, to reach its final apotheosis in the most horrible gibe hurled at the West Indians in the Notting Hill riots, 'Black Irish' (the honest racial cockney had seen it all before). The 'Jew Act' of 1754 was repealed because of popular disorder, as was the Cider Tax of the Earl of Bute. John Wilkes and his followers became positive artists in 'playing the popular engines', by which he meant raising a mob and publicly fearing that he might lose control of it. The Americans learned from Wilkes and became past-masters at the game. John Adams, in his usual precise way, distinguished between good and bad mobs: 'These private mobs I do and will detest.' But he could approve them, he wrote to Abigail, 'when fundamentals are threatened, nor then, but for absolute necessity, and with great caution'.

Things could go too far, of course. 'They found, as I told some of them,' wrote Governor Francis Bernard of the Boston merchants, 'that they had raised the devil and could not lay him again.' A letter printed in *Hansard* to Mr Secretary Conway about the Stamp Act riots asserted: 'The Boston mob, raised first by the instigations of many of the principal inhabitants, allured by plunder, rose shortly after of their own accord. . . . People began to be terrified at the spirit they had raised . . . and there has been as much pains taken since, to prevent insurrections of the people, as before to excite them.'

The great case of mass violence, of course, in this age of measure and manners was the Gordon Riots – a curious compound of anti-Catholicism, pro-Americanism, social protest and a sheer orgy of delinquency. It occurred in the summer of 1780 at the most dangerous time of the American War, the army defeated in America and a French fleet unopposed in the Channel. For four nights 'King Mob' was master of London. Every prison but one was broken open or razed, every Catholic chapel in London destroyed, nineteen public houses or distilleries sacked or burned, and numerous private houses torn down, including those of the Archbishop of Canterbury and the Lord Chief Justice; at least five hundred lives were lost, one hundred and twenty six people stood trial and twenty-five were executed. One of the volumes in the late Sir Lewis Namier's series, *England in the Age of the American Revolution*, dismisses this episode in a short paragraph. Suppression of the fact of violence can hardly go further. The Gordon Riots, in fact, remained an uneasy and indecent memory deep on into the nineteenth century. Twice Dickens returned to the theme of the Gordon Riots, seen as the threat of anarchy (just like in France), always bubbling beneath the surface, only held down by the stern efforts of the middle classes, but even they might fail to keep the lid on the cauldron if the upper classes did not grant necessary measures of reform. The threat was real and the threat was made use of. Our fear that a centralized police force would be continental and despotic, indeed, for a long time, that any form of police would be so, led to the creation of forces under the control of local authorities – with the famous exception of a metropolitan force controlled by the Home Secretary. The streets of the capital itself were too important and too threatened to be left to the negligence of local government – particularly as the London politicians were invariably in Opposition.

Disraeli's *Coningsby* and *Sybil* show how deep was the fear of mass violence in the early and mid-nineteenth century. The Great Charter was put to rest but the fear of organized working-class disorder then grew. The organizers of the industrial unions of the 1880s and 1890s used weapons of local violence, but they had a far stronger card in the existing fears of mass violence, fears that attributed a degree of mass organization to 'enemies of society' which was in fact far beyond the capabilities or even the imaginations of the few Socialist conspiriators. It has recently been argued by Professor Joseph Hamburger of Yale in his *James Mill and the Art of Revolution* that many of the 'authentic reports' of impending violence and insurrection in 1832, which may have played a decisive role in keeping the Whigs in line and persuading the Tory peers to let the Reform Bill through, were invented by James Mill, Francis Place and their allies. But threats of imaginary violence, if they are so successful, only prove how deep were the fears that it might happen.

This fear of violent anarchy, more than of premeditated revolution, underlies respectable Victorian political and social thought, rarely though it is mentioned. Clearly there was a marked change in personal ethics about violence from the eighteenth century. The more plebeian blood sports were suppressed; boxers put gloves on after Heenan and the 'Bennica Boy' had fought themselves to a crippling and bloody standstill; and public duelling was at an end by the 1860s. Not that the change was always all that great: 'Regency' and 'Victorian' are states of mind more than precise temporal categories: Gladstone's political lieutenant, Dilke, after all, spent his mornings boxing, fencing, reading cabinet papers and fornicating – and he did not hesitate to admit to the 'un-Victorian' combination of the first three. Indeed the Victorian *suppression* of violence is much like that of sexuality, a determined attempt more than a secure achievement, something more apparent publicly than privately. *Reynolds News* throughout the period kept up the old Wilkite alliance of radicalism and pornography, to which the *Daily Mirror* is a direct and conscious heir. Readers were titillated with constant accounts, both fictional and allegedly factual, of – the favourite theme – Dukes (often astonishingly Royal) attempting to rape the daughters of Radicals. This gets the best of both worlds.

And always the suppression of Ireland – in the double sense: the thing we cannot bear to remember. The Great Famine, the Land War and then the final competition in atrocities between Sinn Fein and the Black and Tans. Even before that, the Curragh Mutiny and the gun-running into Ulster, connived at by the leaders of the Conservative Party – all in this land of decent politics where the threat of violence has been unknown since, etc., etc. And then how Lloyd George seemed to accept the fact that only redoubled bloodshed could bring enough people to the treaty table. Ireland was particularly unfortunate in being so near. From early times of Imperialism it had been recognized that colonies might relieve the homeland of her share of men of violence – Burke had railed at Warren Hastings that 'the breakers of the law in India' might well become 'the makers of the law' in Britain, if he didn't keep his eyes open for us. But Ireland was both suppressed militarily and the methods used were suppressed in the national memory of each generation; only with difficulty did we grant them the dignity of tough combatants: they were treated either as 'poor, silly Paddy' or 'brutal Mike'.

Because of our prudery about violence we have missed seeing certain things at all and have misunderstood others.

We have been blind to the obvious advantages that come from war. The pacifism of ex-service men in Britain, France and Germany in the 1920s and 1930s was a highly ambivalent thing at best. What was most real to each group of men and common to them all was the memory of a certain fraternity that had been forged in the trenches and was missing in civilian life. A younger generation actually felt that they had *missed* the war. This was a spirit lacking indeed in modern competitive commercial life – Tawney wrote of it vividly in his essays, *The Attack*. But it was dissipated. Only in Germany was it seized upon, and perverted in the *Stahlhelm* and the SA. No politician in Britain or France could find William James's 'moral equivalent for war' – only perhaps, for a short period, Franklin Roosevelt in America. And modern war is a great agent of social change, both technologically and socially. We can do without such harsh stimulants. But that is not the point. The point is that we failed to seize the opportunities it created, largely because war was thought of as such an unholy exception, that the idea was that things would return to normal after some legal termination of hostilities; any social history of those years apart from a purely military history would somehow seem tainted. Mr Correlli Barnett has something of an unrecognized genius for showing the social conditions for types of military action; but no one, to my knowledge, has attempted to show the military conditions for social action. I sense, for instance, a certain suspicion and resentment (either at the facts or me) when I tell students that the Second World War accounts for the massive victory of Labour in 1945.

From 1929 to 1933 British opinion overwhelmingly failed to take Hitler and the Nazi Party seriously because he seemed so purely negative, so contradictory, so destructive, so irrational, so merely violent. When he glorified the use of violence and threatened bloody vengeance on his enemies once he came legally to power, they dismissed what he said as rant; and, further, the more he said it, the more convinced they were that such utterances, together with the actual violence of his Brown Shirts on the streets, would discredit him. It took a long time for 'responsible opinion', for respectable people, to realize that in some circumstances such appeals to violence and even the use of violence are actually attractive.

Pacifism, particularly between the wars, could become a kind of substitute militarism, a violent fanaticism which had little to do with realistic ways of preventing future war. To attempt to renounce violence was about as sensible as the attempt of the true church to renounce sexuality: as a general rule either would prove somewhat self-destructive. The great phrase 'fight for peace' was first heard in the early 1930s – and why not? It was only pacifism which made it absurd. The pacifists made it still harder to be frank about the attraction of violence. Even Communists justified the 'unfortunate necessity' of the Stalinist terror; they seldom recognized that it was often an attractive extravagance. 'Violence', wrote Auden in 1939, 'shall synchronize your movements like a tune.'

The suppression of violence still further heightened the liberal belief that freedom is a purely negative thing, rather than the positive activity of politics and active citizenship; and that politics itself, contaminated by power, is a philistine activity, certainly something that only a pervert would admit actually *enjoying*. The fierce masculine joy of striving for possession according to some more-or-less acknowledged rules of a game, this became a very much inferior activity to almost anything else – including the signing of almost infinite petitions or protests (to God?) on the many matters of pacific first principle which daily arise.

There grew up a taste for a style of leader who was supposed to look as if he was not leading, not becoming anything, but just being there: Stanley Baldwin, and Neville Chamberlain, Clement Attlee (even though in these latter two looks were belied by what they did), Eden, Macmillan and Douglas-Home. Even the language of violence was avoided in politics: a Bevan or a Hogg became the exception rather than the rule for leaders. Even the pose of creative fury was discredited. Polemic put on Sunday clothes. Perhaps they are at this moment being taken off, which is all to the good. 'Open rebuke', wrote Solomon, 'is better than private love.' But imagine any contemporary saying, as Disraeli said of Gladstone: '. . . an extraordinary mixture of envy, vindictiveness, hypocrisy and superstition'. Nowadays we are supposed not to hurt anyone's feelings. I don't know what else it is proper to hurt. Certainly politicians' feelings grow very fat and flabby if not exposed to constant punishment. Modern 'decent restraint' is not entirely to the good. All violence is not physical. Men of violent passions do get things done and are no harm if they can be restrained to political means; and politicians, like dramatists, sometimes need violent images if they are to break through the cake of custom and do their task at all – if circumstances change and people go on thinking in outmoded categories. Boredom is the only legitimate child of conformity and physical violence becomes its inevitable bastard. When public issues seem important, some personal violence can surely be sublimated.

The problem of civilization is not, as Plato saw, to try to kill those 'wild horses which ride through our minds at night', but to harness them to reason. There are many contexts in which violent impulses are morally completely neutral, it depends to what cause they are harnessed; but if they are kept stabled up, then they may indeed be beyond control when they break out. The public world of politics is an arena of legitimate conflict. Politics is action, against others, even if subject to some restraints. It may even be helpful to recognize this from a purely therapeutic point of view. But more obviously we can say that it is simply dangerous to deny this. If, to give a simple but highly important example, we teach children that politics is all about doing good to people, we both create cynicism about actual politics when they meet it and remove from them a potential arena of expression. Politics is an activity, not a set of aspirations or principles: at some end of the syndrome of politics is compromise, at the other is physical violence. The account is not truthful without the inclusion of both.

Liberals tend to be as prudish and often prurient about violence as they were once about sexuality. We English are not quite happy even about politics. It does not affect our own happiness very much perhaps, but it does limit our understanding of others. Tolerance is not enough. One simply cannot tolerate everybody. Action is often needed. And the intellectual basis of that action should be the attempt to comprehend the plausibility of as many human motivations as possible. And violence is among them. W. B. Yeats wrote:

> Know that when all words are said
> And a man is fighting mad,
> Something drops from eyes long blind,
> He completes his partial mind,
> For an instant stands at ease,
> Laughs aloud, his heart at peace.
> Even the wisest man grows tense
> With some sort of violence
> Before he can accomplish fate,
> Know his work or choose his mate.[1]

To some this will represent a part of knowledge. To others, perhaps, a vicarious experience. Many, after all, find their violence in literature or sport. And in both it is as sensible to claim that they are, generally speaking, therapeutic, as it is to claim that they are, generally speaking, provocative. Both the 'theatre of cruelty' (if that exists) and competitive professional boxing do really exist for themselves, innocent of such extrinsic aims as consciously doing good or evil.

What does seem fairly clear, however, is that there is some kind of connection between the decline of violence in public life in Britain and the great interest in it of both the literature of high culture and the popular press. And this is not because we have a very high crime rate – we in fact have a very low one by any historical or sociological standard. It is surely because – to be dangerously simple – violence is interesting and is a normal part of the human condition and therefore of public life. But this is not admitted, both the plausibility and the memory of actual violence is too often suppressed, or made

1. From *Under Ben Bulben*, reproduced by permission of Mrs Yeats.

the subject of furtive literature, fantasy literature or hypocritical literature which always ends, most unsatisfyingly,
with the arrest of any possible further violence – until the
next episode. We need to recognize that it is part of man in
the public world. Nothing so basic can be suppressed but, as
Goethe, Freud and Mann have all shown, 'only' harmonized
or synthesized. Genesis 49 xxv speaks of 'Blessings of heaven
above, blessings of the deep that lieth under'. Both are as real.

I I

A Reflection on Tyrannicide[1]

As John Wilkes Booth leaped to the stage, after having shot Lincoln in the theatre box, he shouted what he thought to be an appropriate Latin tag: '*Sic semper tyrannis*' – 'That's the way with tyrants', or, more literally, 'Ever thus to tyrants'. The phrase was associated with the greatest of tyrannicides, Marcus Brutus and was also – its relevance to Booth – the state motto of Virginia, framed in the days of resistance to the British.

Now, the fact that Lincoln was not a tyrant doesn't change the speculation that he could have been, or that there have been, perhaps even are, or might be again, tyrants in relation to whom Booth's mad and wicked deed could have been a just and exemplary act. The ancient authors of Greece and Rome invariably agreed that *tyrannicide* was a good thing and *assassination* was a bad thing, even though both were equally acts of violence. A tyrant deserved to die and it was the positive duty of freemen to do the deed.

Can, however, the personal violence of the killing of a great political leader ever be justified in the light of either Christian or of humanist ethics? With the lingering horror of Robert Kennedy's death upon us, so closely following that of Martin Luther King and of John Kennedy before, this might seem a morbid and irrelevant question to raise.

But I'm not sure. It is at least the sort of question that political philosophers used to consider. Much of our thinking in Western culture about the relationship of ethics to politics

1. A broadcast talk on the B.B.C. Third Programme, recorded 3 January 1969.

was shaped by long or half-forgotten disputes about the justification of killing despots or tyrants – 'tyrannicide' – disputes and discussions now more apt to be found in the theatre than in the books and articles of philosophers.

There was and is at least this ultimate deterrent of assassination over the abuses of personal power. So it is important to try to be precise about the quality of our horror at the death, for instance, of a Kennedy. Surely it is found in the apparent meaninglessness of the act, or in its irrelevance to the effects intended, not in the act itself, if seen simply as a political murder.

Some people object to any kind of 'murder' or killing. Absolute pacifists object both to capital punishment and to war on much the same grounds: that they take human life, and these good folk would also, presumably, forsake self-defence. But I take it that most people are prepared to admit that sometimes the taking of life is both unavoidable and justifiable. The killer running amok must be brought down, the blind man must be run over, even, if that is the only way to avoid a head-on collision between two crowded cars. And are not doctors in the heart-transplant controversy really being a little cowardly? They've let the argument become an almost meaningless one about the *moment* of death of the donor, instead of rationally discussing when it can be said that death is irreversibly near.

The question does arise, after all, why should we all appear to be more shocked – to stay with the Kennedys – by the successive deaths of two rich young men lusting for political power than in the death each day of hundreds in Vietnam?

The answer is perhaps a psychological one. We accept the deaths in Vietnam as a predictable part of the war. However deeply we may detest and oppose the war, the horror of the deaths simply does not – except to a few saints or hysterics – reimpose itself each day with the vividness of the dying of a close friend. And nor could it: we could not live with it if it did. And nor should it: for we are not responsible for Vietnam or even for road deaths in quite the direct way that robbed Macbeth of sleep.

But political assassination is not something that we any longer expect to happen. It was the primal horror of the completely unexpected and unaccountable. And yet one wonders why? It was not always so. Has it declined because of changing morality or because of its growing ineffectiveness to achieve the results once intended?

Should we be as shocked at the assassination of a tyrant as at the murder by a sexual pervert of an innocent and ordinary young girl? Suppose some patriotic German or ingenious allied agent had killed Hitler. Of course we would not be equally shocked. To be honest, I doubt if most of us would have been shocked at all. If a Dictator of Haiti or even the infinitely more civilized General – we'd better not name any names – were to fall to an assassin's bullet, I would myself find it hard to repress an ancient Roman cheer amid a liberal sigh of deprecation.

For the Romans would, there is no doubt, have praised such acts. They honoured the memory of tyrannicides, particularly that of Brutus, who killed the last King, the ancestor of the Brutus who killed the first Caesar. Even in Elizabethan London, with plots against the Queen's life current, a censor could allow and an audience could appreciate the incredibly balanced argument of Shakespeare's dramatic monograph on the ethics of assassination. Shakespeare leaves it unclear as to whether Julius Caesar was killed for the right motives. The real tragedy is the deception of Brutus by Cassius, who is moved by jealousy of Caesar more than by proper hatred of tyranny and injustice. But it is quite clear that Brutus could have killed Caesar justly and for the right reasons, and the fact that retribution followed did not make his action any the less praiseworthy: indeed, in a sense, his own death was simply the fair price to be paid. Must not all this have seemed, upon the Elizabethan stage, faintly seditious and apparently rather un-Christian stuff?

Fifty years later, Thomas Hobbes, in *The Leviathan*, railed against the whole classical tradition that it was from 'the reading of the books of Policy . . . of the ancient Greeks and

Romans' that young men were led into rebellion against their monarch. Hobbes went on to say:

> From the reading, I say, of such books men
> have undertaken to their kings, because
> the Greek and Latin writers, in their books
> and discourses of policy, make it lawful and
> laudable to do so; provided before he do it,
> he call him a tyrant. For they say not regicide,
> that is, killing of a king, but tyrannicide,
> that is, killing of a tyrant is lawful.

'What's in a name?' indeed; apparently to Hobbes, quite a lot. But Hobbes was not just ranting against the ancient Romans; as usual he was getting at the Church. For tyrannicide was, in fact, a part of received Christian orthodoxy – as Shakespeare well knew. St Thomas Aquinas had quoted favourably Cicero's very words that tyrannicide was praiseworthy – on certain conditions.

Thomas's explicit conditions for tyrannicide were three and his whole argument presumes a fourth – all of which, personally, I still find amazingly relevant.

Firstly, that the man to be killed had usurped power violently.

Secondly, that he had broken the divine and the natural law and was a threat to the lives and the morality of his subjects.

Thirdly, that there was no other remedy.

Fourthly, that his death would lead to some better state of affairs – it was not to be done just as 'an example', or for punishment or vengeance, these matters are for God alone; it must lead to some clear earthly and human remedy and betterment.

Let us apply Thomas's criteria to some real or imagined cases. To take one extreme example, why, after all, does not anyone sensibly think of shooting our present Prime Minister, Mr Harold Wilson? This would fail on all four tests. He came to power legitimately, he has not (as far as I know) broken the divine or the natural law, there will be some other remedy to remove him, and even if you think we cannot afford to wait a couple of years, then there is ample room for doubt that things might improve a little in the meantime.

Take, at the other extreme, the case of Adolf Hitler. He would, at first glance, have fitted the case on all four counts. He used violence to create his 'New Order'; he had broken the natural law or any possible understanding of it; he destroyed all opposition and thus ruled out alternative remedies to Germany's very real problems; and all this depended on his own life and personality. Or did he? Between 1936 and 1942, that is after the Nazis had completely taken over the State-machine and before the military defeats began, it is highly unlikely in fact that his own death would have made much difference. One could even argue that the leadership might have fallen into hands more realistic, efficient and effective than his. Nazi power at that time did not depend on Hitler alone, even though it may have done – or far more so – in both the early years and in the last years. In those years the case for tyrannicide was strong.

In the case of Stalin, it is almost ridiculous to think that his death would have made much difference to 'Stalinism' in the 1930s and 1940s. Even the Nazis and still more the Communists had what no ancient tyranny had, a disciplined political party with an ideology – something that could and would outlive their creators.

It is not impossible, but very hard, indeed, to find examples in the modern world where oppression depends upon the person of one leader alone, though one is surprised that more people do not think so, however wrong they may be empirically, and act accordingly. It is particularly surprising that in the Second World War, the national leaders did not make continual and determined attempts to kill their rivals and enemies. Perhaps they were not restrained by moral considerations so much as by a very practical fear that the example would spread and the righteous arrow prove a crooked boomerang.

A more complicated set of cases were assassinations of Colonial Governors-General, Viceroys and Archdukes, etc., as the Fenians once shot down a Viceroy of Ireland. But these are almost deliberately not tyrannicide: they do not aim at the Head of State or the guilty one himself, but seek to shock or terrorize him into changes of policy, or simply to demonstrate their own sufferings abroad. Such acts are obnoxious because they strike the wrong man and usually lead to an intensification of tyranny rather than to its abatement. In such situations assassinations cannot be a 'relatively humane' substitute for civil war or rebellion. The whole point of terrorism, for such it is, is that it is aimed indiscriminately, whereas tyrannicide, even where mistaken, is reasonably precise.

Thus in the modern world there are both few and ever fewer societies whose fundamental condition depends on the character of one man. Perhaps France depends heavily on de Gaulle, but this is not by itself a sufficient reason to regard him as and to treat him as a tyrant. The Romans would have seen such men as, at the worst, candidates for exile rather than for the assassin's knife or for judicial murder – just as the Holy Alliance in 1815 was pleased to send Napoleon into exile rather than to the guillotine. So, in an age of bureaucrats, tyrannicide is plainly less useful than terror; tyrannicide belongs to an age of heroes, or to situations where the safety or the character of the state depends on the personality of one man. The fact that there was felt to be no need to catch and kill Nkrumah, but to depose him in his absence, is a measure both of how little the basic life of the country actually depended on him, and of how little it has changed. Contrast the deposition of Nkrumah with the insistence of the German generals in 1944 that Hitler must be stone cold dead before the slightest move could be made. Perhaps some rulers and societies in Africa and South America would still fit most of the Thomist bill, but their's are all too obviously highly unstable societies anyway. Time may bring, if not remedies, at least new opportunities, so the Thomist condition that there must be no other remedy would fail.

Certainly neither Communist China nor the United States could possibly be changed in its basic policies by the death of any one man. We grow rightly frightened that the public processes and procedures of free politics can be disrupted by the arbitrary and paranoic killings of radical political leaders; but we should still keep some hope that in some lands and at some times the worst abuses of power are limitable by fear of personal retribution.

Now these dark thoughts were plainly prompted by the death of Robert Kennedy, but I do not intend them to have more than an indirect relevance to it. His death was part of a long-established American tradition of political and personal violence – a tradition at least as old as the frontier and then vastly fortified by the political passions of the American Civil War and the creation then of huge citizen armies: the most able, self-trained, indisciplined and individualistic armies of modern history. The American homicide rates have for long proved record-breaking per head of population among all other civilized powers. They have internal variations so great that in Southern cities there are about six times as many murders in proportion to population as on the Pacific coast, and eighteen times as many as in New England.

The Presidential Commission which has been summoned to inquire into the reasons for violence has either got to learn a lot of history, if it is under the illusion that this is a new problem, or it will have to bring in proposals designed to reform American society from top to bottom – if it is really to grasp the nettle. The grim joke has long been that if the Welfare State ever comes to the United States, it would be to deal with the problems of unemployment created by peace and disarmament. And to this hard-headed witticism might now be added the thought that *if* the basic problems of racial tension, urban decay and rural poverty are to be tackled, it will be because the paranoic's fixation with murder spread from sidewalks and taverns to the national political platforms and killed yet another young Caesar, and threatened the new President.

One cannot help but take a very practical view of the mournful death of that man who might well have become President of the United States had he lived. It is incredible

234

that he did not have, with all the wealth he had, unlike the urban poor, better and many bodyguards. There was no other immediate solution; it did not mark the beginning in America of either good government or of revolution. But it might mark the beginning of a more open and healthy discussion of political violence. To say that all violence is bad is only to suppress violence to the depths at which it becomes soured and obscene. Even in political murders we still need to redraw old and fine distinctions. The victory of the rational over the irrational is not to be won by refusing to mention certain things. Hobbes was right that all regicides or killers of kings claim to be tyrannicides or killers of tyrants. But he was wrong to deny that some of them are truly so. Tyrannicide, properly conceived, is a vindication of freedom and of reason, not its ultimate denial. Tyrants should be defined closely and then killed.

12

Powell and Patriotism[1]

THAT old Tory Dr Johnson did not mean what we now often think he meant when he said: 'Patriotism, Sir, is the last refuge of a scoundrel.' He was not attacking nationalists, for he was one himself – witness his English scorn for the Scots. He was attacking the 'Patriot faction' as they were called on both sides of the Atlantic: the radicals. He meant those presumptuous fellows who thought that the land, the *patria*, was their land just because they lived in it and gave their labour to it, even if they did not own it and even if they did not have the innate aristocratic ability to govern others.

This was the Roman manner. A patriot was a citizen either because he participated in and loved his native institutions, or because he had wholeheartedly adopted them. But he could adopt them. This was the Roman political greatness: they did not bar men from citizenship on ethnic grounds. And this was why the American Colonists in dispute with Westminster called themselves 'Patriots' and why their English radical friends did likewise. It is our country because we work in it and 'they' depend upon our work.

The decline of conscious patriotism in English radical thought is a strange and complex history. Consider how the very word 'patriot' comes to be scorned by intellectuals and stolen from the common people by a certain kind of Tory: and think, for example, how the greatest and most violent revolutionary hymn in the language, Blake's 'Jerusalem', has come to be sung with fervour by Tory ladies in blue hats.

1. This was an article in the *Observer*, 16 February 1969, with some small and routine cuts restored and with a new final paragraph added.

George Orwell was about the last Left-winger to be consciously patriotic.

For what offends me at heart about the calculated outbursts of this half-Welsh demogogue, Powell, perhaps trying in part to prove his Englishness, is how un-English and unpatriotic his behaviour has become. Students of Fascism and of racialist mass movements have often commented how the leaders tend themselves to be socially or nationally marginal and insecure. Most West Indian immigrants are more traditionally English than he in their habits and beliefs.

For some centuries, certainly since the Civil War, we have been at most times a remarkably tolerant people. We have been so tolerant that some of us liberals can get quite disproportionately worked up about quite minor intolerances. Certainly our governors have been, by any comparative standard, remarkably tolerant – sometimes even enforcing toleration on violently hostile minorities.

But toleration does not imply complete acceptance. For instance, the public power can stop anti-Irish and anti-Jewish rioting, which was once endemic; but it cannot (fortunately, I think) force us to love one another: that is either going too far, or is unnecessary. Toleration does not promise or threaten complete acceptance. We are not, for instance, tolerant towards our friends as friends. A friend is a friend: which is the uttermost limit of acceptance (save love) of another person. We may have to be tolerant of the foibles of our friends, but these blemishes or annoyances will be minor. What we see as a friend is someone taken as a whole – warts, waywardness and all.

We have, then, been a tolerant people (relatively, by and large, comparatively, with exceptions, but none the less) towards strangers – not particularly friendly, indeed cold and reserved compared with American, or many Latin and African peoples; not given to changing ourselves to suit their ways, but equally far from insistent that they should change their ways to suit us.

Toleration of immigrants does not imply assimilation – quite the contrary. It implies simply limited acceptance –

just as all our personal relationships of any kind 'short of actual love' imply a limited acceptance. There is, after all, a certain hypocrisy or promiscuity in treating everyone equally – indeed an ultimate impossibility. We liberals, in our attacks on the original Bill limiting Commonwealth immigration, and in our preaching of the moral duty not to discriminate and not to be intolerant, may well have oversold and thus frightened people – particularly with talk of the possibility of assimilation.

It may be necessary to say publicly in a quiet but clear tone of voice that while there is no absolute moral or genetic objection to a West Indian marrying your daughter, it is not very likely to happen; nor are there any biological grounds for thinking that miscegenation is better or worse than in-breeding; it does rather depend, as most marriages do, on circumstances and on two individuals with two peculiar psychologies. Complete assimilation is neither a possible nor an especially desirable object of public policy. Mutual toleration is far more important and realizable.

We should simply accept that most coloured immigrants are tolerated (even merely tolerated). There is not much hope, or possibly even need for more than that; and I doubt, for instance, if most West Indians, Indians, Sikhs and Pakistanis in Great Britian want to be more than tolerated. If they were fully accepted or assimilated they would lose their communal individuality. And such is the very thing, ironically, for which we original Britishers (there is no national name for us) now seem to be striving: Welsh and Scottish national feeling newly heightened, the new provincial consciousness in culture and the arts, and the political attempts to find or to create authentic regions.[1]

1. Subsequently I had a small survey undertaken of syllabuses in schools which deal with 'race relations'. (It was a preliminary stage in an ambitious scheme to try to study the effect of such teaching—for which no support could be found.) We discovered that roughly a third of the syllabuses or teaching programmes had clear 'assimilationist' aims (i.e. everyone should be and could be like everyone else); another third assumed the rightness of and aimed at 'integration' (i.e. a plurality of groups but with no arbitrary bars to mobility between them); and about

I *think* I can honestly say that I do not have to try to tolerate the new immigrants, I simply accept their presence, even vaguely welcome it (wishing to see *more* variety and pluralism in British life, not less). But I do have to try rather hard and painfully to tolerate Powellites. It is hard to tolerate the intolerant. People who seek to force their opinions on others, or to remove others, should not be tolerated if their threats threaten to become real. But things have not yet gone that far, so I am sad when Mr Powell cannot get a hearing at a university society meeting; but I am surprised as to why any decent Englishmen should give him a platform on these matters.

What is repugnant about Powell is his deliberate attempt to stir up intolerance. In this he is not being patriotic, nor even nationalistic (for we are, anyway, three nations – or three and a half, counting Ulster – not one), but racialist. By any test of patriotism or even of nationalism, the new immigrants who have settled are as much British as the Irish immigrants, the Jewish and the Polish and other political immigrants of the 1930s and 40s.

None the less, it is not Powell but his following that is worrying. And here preachment is not likely to cut much ice. But some analysis of concepts (at which we empirical British are so bad) may help us to understand, sympathetically and tolerantly, why so many decent working-men, particularly, sympathize with his provocative and cowardly utterances.

First and obviously, the fear of economic competition – a traditional fear, as shown when in Notting Hill in 1956 the cockneys hurled the ultimate obscenity, 'Black Irish', at the astonished West Indians. This should be allayed by the ending of mass immigration, and by people answering back when Powell uses figures based on wild assumptions as to fertility and numbers of dependants. But somehow we don't want to

---

a third appeared to have no clear object at all! See Bernard Crick and Sally Jenkinson, 'Good Intentions and Muddled Thinking', *The Times Educational Supplement*, 6 November 1970.

answer him back. We liberals don't want to 'triumphantly prove' that the threat of numbers is exaggerated – we prefer to leave that dirty work to Mr Callaghan. If some of Mr Powell's supporters act as if any level of immigration is a threat, we must take care not to act as if we believe that no level of immigration is a threat – for no one will believe that either.

I think we have all come round to seeing that some ending of mass immigration was necessary, to preserve our own welfare and other institutions in times of economic crisis. And, after all, the restrictions are imposed not just against coloured people but against the whole poor world – Greeks and Italians are equally limited to actual jobs available. Are we ashamed of these simple, practical arguments? We tried to disagree on principle, but then accepted in practice. Something must be a little wrong with the principles.

Secondly, to repeat the vital point, 'we', all right, the liberal establishment the BBC, the press, Parliament and all, have been furtively reluctant to state clearly the obvious fact that toleration of those with us already and of the few to come does not imply assimilation. One cannot love everyone equally and at once. We have our peculiar institutions and there is no need not to be proud of many or most of them. I would argue – and I sense that this argument is growing – that we need a more dynamic Britain, drawing strength from the variety and rivalry of many different groups, not an advance towards a sterile uniformity and a politics ever more concerned with seeking consensus. We need to distinguish intellectually between consensus as to *means*, procedures and machinery – our great political virtue, and consensus as to *ends*, ways of life, goals and values – the growing national vice, shared by both the Powellites and liberals.

If people would speak out on these two themes, those who are worried would not feel that their leadership had deserted them. 'It is all right for *them*, they don't have to live with them.' But nor does anyone. We live side by side, not on top of each other. And to the extent that the poor overseas immigrant and the poor British internal immigrant do live

240

on top of each other in the twilight world of cheap houses and lodgings, the practical problem is a housing problem and a general problem of industrial mobility. If we had a national housing policy with *some* national allocation of housing, instead of the long local authority waiting lists, we could solve overnight all the harsher aspects of the external immigration problem and many of the internal economic problems which spring from the immobility of labour: we spend so much to take industry and housing to depressed areas, rather than to make it easier for people to leave for those areas if they choose.

This is not to deny, of course, that a grave economic crisis would not unleash terrible floods of racial antagonism. Fear of a recession should be a factor giving urgency to attempts to allay some of the fears of those who now look to Powell. But I do argue that, as of this moment, the economic factors are not the direct *cause* of prejudice, although some relatively simple new economic policies – primarily in the field of housing – could mitigate the more intolerable forms of this prejudice.

It is perfectly proper and right for any country to seek to preserve its native characteristics. There are usually some purely economic and practical limitations on the extent of immigration – we are not nineteenth-century America (though it is a pity that we do not know more accurately what these limitations are). But if anyone then wishes to join that country and to give it his allegiance, why should he not? And if anyone, whether native or immigrant, should wish *freely* to leave, why should he not? Patriotism is love of one's country – that country, ordinarily, in which one is born, but it can be, throughout the history of civilization, a country that one adopts.

Birth is, after all, somewhat fortuitous. One smiles at the immigrant who is 'more English than the English', but the compliment is obvious. If we are sneering at this, we are saying that it is *impossible*, not just *difficult*, to adopt a country and to be a patriot. Why is it *impossible*? The answer can only be in terms of racial characteristics. When Mr Powell argues for repatriation on grounds that even communal integration, let alone individual assimilation, is impossible, he reveals himself as a racial theorist. I think quite seriously that here Mr Powell's Welshness is significant. The pseudo-intellectual rabble-rouser is so often a socially and nationally marginal man. But I do not think that it is impossible for him to become an Englishman, if that is what he wants – for that is a cultural matter, not a racial matter; it is only, apparently, rather difficult in his case.

Nationalism is not the issue. A nationalist is a man who believes that whatever a nation is (and all perceptions of nationality are subjective and arbitrary), the only just unit of government is that which is co-terminous with a nation. There have been remarkably few genuine English nationalists since the Act of Union with Scotland. Nationalism is an element within the political unit of the United Kingdom – but there is no United Kingdom nationalism. There are Scottish and Welsh nationalisms and there might be an Ulster or an English nationalism. But the United Kingdom exists as a conscious *political* agreement of justice and utility, not as a nation. However, there is a United Kingdom or British *patriotism*. And many of us feel that the union of the three or four nations constitute the whole of our country or *patria* and are rather proud of such diversity-in-unity.

Patriotism is no bad thing (as among the English Left, only George Orwell was bold enough to argue). Nationalism can be a dangerous thing with its substantial elements of irrationality. But racialism is always a bad and dangerous thing. Racial interpretations of human conduct are plausible (and we should not underestimate the plausibility of them nor seek to explain them away in purely economic terms). But they are either false or superficial; and active *racialism* always implies taking action against 'inferior races'. Perhaps many commonsense people are falling prey to Powellite racialism because they have forgotten the inclusiveness of our real patriotism. I do not think that Beaverbrook was wrong to be a patriot; but I think his brand of patriotism was a parody of actual British history.

Enoch Powell's views are an obnoxious irrelevance except

that we should give him a kind of ironic thanks for exposing much hypocrisy and for forcing on us a debate about the fundamental nature of 'the national community', or, since it is in fact nationally divided, simply 'our country'. The main question, however, is why he can appear to have such a large following – even though we should not exaggerate the degree to which these prejudices are as yet threatening traditional social allegiances, such as, for instance, and most important, political party allegiance.

We have time, if we will use it wisely and firmly. Liberals should now conspire to give something to people – and to ourselves – to be proud about in England or – is it? – Great Britain. Have we not been suckers for everyone else's nationalism – accepting all their excuses for intolerance, persecution, unnecessary violence and mad conceit – while neglecting our own tolerant and multi-national patriotism?

Whether Powell believes his provocative racialist talk or not is a complete irrelevance; sincerity is no excuse for folly and still less when it results in the stirring up of communal prejudices. But, equally, sincerity by itself will not help good liberals to convince ordinary people that they are not threatened and that toleration does not imply mutual assimilation. We must learn that one cannot beat something as deep and deranged as racialism with nothing. We should study the real causes of the trouble and then start behaving as people who have a patriotic pride – in our toleration, in our diversity and in our political realism.

When Roy Jenkins was Home Secretary he gave a famous speech on the objects of public policy in race relations. He said that the main object was 'integration' which he defined thus: 'not as a flattening process of assimilation but equal opportunity, accompanied by cultural diversity, in an atmosphere of mutual tolerance'. A splendid definition. But it will be a hard and a long task to work out what it can mean in practice. Can there be equal opportunity while there are class barriers as well as cultural barriers, especially when the one fortifies the other? What kind of diversities are tolerable?

Polygamy? A serious question. The public authorities intervene more into the lives of some sub-cultures than of others to protect the equal opportunity of women and children particularly. And so they should – to a degree. What degree? Or rather, what moral criteria do we use in such debate?

The objective of Roy Jenkins *is* brilliantly defined – I am *not* mocking. It is only odd that we appear to lack or to have lost a traditional vocabulary of political and ethical theory which would enable us to talk rationally about what kind of inequalities and what kind of diversities do we think justifiable. Send for the statisticians and the social workers as much as is useful, but the problems both begin and end on different perceptions of social justice and of how men can argue reasonably and justly in public. We end as we began on the unity of theory and practice, the wretchedness of the belief that there can be practice without theory, and the need for more exercise of the old, Western, civilizing, speculative, unsettling, unfashionable but inescapably all these things at once tradition of political thought.